Do You Feel Like I Do?

Do You Feel Like I Do?

A Memoir

Peter Frampton

with

Alan Light

hachette
BOOKS
New York

Hachette Books
Hachette Book Group
1290 Avenue of the Americas
New York, NY 10104
HachetteBooks.com
Twitter.com/HachetteBooks
Instagram.com/HachetteBooks

First Edition: October 2020

Published by Hachette Books, an imprint of Perseus Books, LLC, a subsidiary of Hachette Book Group, Inc. The Hachette Books name and logo is a trademark of the Hachette Book Group.

The Hachette Speakers Bureau provides a wide range of authors for speaking events.

To find out more, go to www.hachettespeakersbureau.com or call (866) 376-6591.

The publisher is not responsible for websites (or their content) that are not owned by the publisher.

Print book interior design by Trish Wilkinson.

Library of Congress Cataloging-in-Publication Data

Names: Frampton, Peter, author. | Light, Alan, author.
Title: Do you feel like I do?: a memoir / Peter Frampton with Alan Light.
Description: First edition. | New York: Hachette Books, 2020.
Identifiers: LCCN 2020017752 | ISBN 9780316425315 (hardcover) | ISBN 9780306923753 (hardcover) | ISBN 9780306923760 (hardcover) | ISBN 9780316425339 (ebook)
Subjects: LCSH: Frampton, Peter. | Rock musicians—England—Biography. | Guitarists—England—Biography. | LCGFT: Autobiographies.
Classification: LCC ML420.F76 A3 2020 | DDC 782.42166092 [B]—dc23
LC record available at https://lccn.loc.gov/2020017752

ISBNs: 978-0-316-42531-5 (hardcover), 978-0-316-42533-9 (ebook), 978-0-306-92375-3 (B&N signed edition), 978-0-306-92376-0 (signed edition)

Printed in the United States of America

LSC-C

10 9 8 7 6 5 4 3 2 1

In loving memory of Owen and Peggy Frampton

*For my children, Jade, Julian, and Mia Frampton,
and my stepdaughter, Tiffany Wiest*

GRAND FESTIVAL
APPEAL FUND DANCE

★ DENNY MITCHELL SOUNDSATIONS
DECCA

★ THE HERD

★ THE OTHER TWO DECCA

★ THE KONRADS

★ THE TRUBEATS

★ THE PSYKONS

★ THE BURNETTES

★ CHRIS CONWAY

BRIAN SHOWELL

FREE COMPETITION
YOUR LUCKY NO IS R 115

Admission 5/-

FRIDAY 21st AUGUST
ASSEMBLY HALLS

Gates Green Road, Coney Hall
West Wickham

Which band wasn't I in?!

Do You Feel Like I Do?

"Let me tell you one thing—if Peter Frampton does not play, first I kill you, and then I kill Peter Frampton."

We were in a motel in Panama City, Panama, and I could overhear the local promoter threatening my road manager. We were supposed to play a sold-out stadium show that night, but the previous day, the cargo plane carrying our gear had crashed on the runway leaving Caracas, Venezuela, exploding and destroying all of our equipment on board—including my main guitar, a black 1954 Gibson Les Paul, the one I first played on Humble Pie's breakthrough album, *Performance: Rockin' the Fillmore*, the one on the cover of *Frampton Comes Alive!*

In Panama, I had sent the crew out to try to borrow some guitars, go to music shops, see if there was a PA company with enough sound equipment to fill a stadium. About five o'clock that evening, the crew came to my suite. I opened the door and they threw in some wires; for the talk box tube, they had gone to, like, Sears and got one of those black hoses for a washing machine. I put my mouth on it and my whole mouth turned black. I said, "That ain't gonna work!" They had nothing.

Rodney Eckerman, my road manager, called the promoter and said that it wasn't going to happen—and the promoter obviously told his buddy Manuel Noriega that we weren't going to play. Rodney said, "Everybody get into Peter's room so I've got you all together. I think we might have to escape this country."

This was Election Day 1980, when Reagan got in, and we were listening to the results coming in on the BBC World Service. The motel was built around the pool, so we could see Rodney at a table by the pool, talking to the promoter. We opened the window and we're listening, and Rodney's going, "I hate to tell you this, but we can't play and we're going to have to reschedule," and that's when we heard these death threats.

Rodney ran up and said, "Get yourself to Pan Am; I've already called, they know what's going on and they're prepared. They're keeping the plane for us, and they've told all the other passengers what's going on. I'll meet you there, I have to go with the promoter to sort this out." But there were all these armed police around the hotel, so we couldn't leave. We started talking to the guards and giving them beers and stuff, and we discovered they didn't know why they were there. I don't think they had any idea. So one by one, we snuck out of the hotel, walked away slowly, and got cabs to the airport.

We all made it there, but we've got no passports, because in Europe and South America, the promoter would keep your passports so that you had to do the gig. I don't know whether they still do this, but they did it then. We're going, "English, American—we've got one South African, the keyboard player, Arthur Stead; they'll never let him back into America!"

We got to the gate and Pan Am said, "Give us your boarding passes." They got immigration to stamp our boarding passes instead of our passports. It was bizarre. We got on the plane, they quickly shut the door, and the entire plane erupted in applause.

We still had to go to Puerto Rico to play a stadium there, so the road crew arranged for a complete set of gear to be flown down. I was playing guitars I'd never even heard of. But we made it back to America after Puerto Rico, and then my guitar tech, Jon "JD" Dworkow, went back down to Caracas to see the damage and what, if anything, was left. But there was nothing; it had been a fireball crash. The plane's tail had broken off; it was still all there, pretty much in one piece. The rest, there was nothing. And surely there was no way my beloved guitar had survived.

Chapter One

Growing up, my parents lived a couple of streets apart and would always see each other, and then in their early teens, they got together. Then they broke up but kept on seeing each other—it was one of those stories. And then finally they hooked up.

My dad would've been in his late teens, early twenties when the war broke out. He was born in 1919. He did only a year or two in college, and then he signed up for the war and went to Sandhurst for officer training. He was a lieutenant, or "leftenant," as we say in the UK.

During the war, he became an acting captain. He was in charge of 25-pounder guns, loads of them, and a whole team. At night, with his batman and radio operator, he'd go behind enemy lines to get the position they wanted to hit. You couldn't do it with gadgets then. It was guesswork—"I think it's two hundred yards," you know. He would come back and they'd load up all the stuff and he'd tell them, "This is where it's got to go."

After Europe was won, my dad stayed there another year because he was in charge of a displaced persons camp, sending White Russians back to Russia. The White Russians had fought on the side of the Germans, like the Vichy French. The deal

that Churchill, Stalin, and Roosevelt made at the Yalta confer-
ence in 1945 was that all prisoners of war would be repatriated
without choice. This sealed the fate of many Russian Cossacks,
or White Russians.

My dad sent the first train full of Cossacks back to Russia
as ordered. When the train returned, he could tell they had all
been shot and dragged off. When the second train came back
there were no windows left. They'd broken the windows and
used pieces of glass to commit family suicide, knowing what
horror awaited them. Every train car interior was red with
blood. And he said, "I can't do this." It was a big secret for a
long time; not until the 1970s did that story come out. My dad
was interviewed on the radio about it, and after witnessing the
second train return he signed his batman's de-mob papers and
vice versa, then they both headed home in shock. "This is mur-
der, I'm condemning them to death."

Not that I would blame him, but I think my father was a
drinker during the war. You and I would both be drinkers, too,
like soldiers in Vietnam with drugs—whatever floats your boat
and gets you through the day, I guess. After he came back, Mum
and Dad went out on the town a couple of times and tied it on,
and then he decided, "Now we're going back to college, gonna
do this . . . gonna do that . . ." Every Christmas my dad had one
nip of whiskey and that's all he had. I never asked him, because
I didn't want to embarrass him, but I think he decided that he
shouldn't drink. They say alcoholism is genetic and that's where
I got it from; I can't really say whether that's true or not. I don't
want to put my dad down, but I'm not really putting him down
because it's a disease.

I was born five years after the war, so I didn't live through the
bombing, and my parents and their friends weren't about to talk

about it with me, so I didn't really realize until a little later what they'd just gone through. When there was an air raid, going to the shelter was such a pain that my mum just got fed up and used to stand out on the balcony and watch the bombs come down—an "If I'm gonna go, I'm gonna go" kind of thing. All these other women would hand her their babies and go downstairs. So she'd be out there holding someone's baby. I don't know why they didn't take them—it's just what I've heard.

I think my parents were just so thrilled to have got through the war, with my mother being in the Blitz and my father being on the other end of the Blitz—in every major battle, in Europe, in Africa. He was at Monte Casino in Italy, he was in the desert against Rommel. He didn't see my mum for five or six years, and I think when he got back they just realized that they were so lucky to be alive. All I felt from my parents was incredible encouragement for me to do whatever I wanted to do, especially with music.

Victorianism went out the window in one fell swoop. My parents were children of the last tinges of Victorianism. When you're faced with nearly certain death every day for six years, and you survive, I think you would have to loosen up a little. It was a major change in outlook, especially in Europe, because we went down to nothing—there was very little in the shops, especially any fresh produce. What we did get was a lot of canned stuff from America, so thank you, America, for sending us Spam. And I got food poisoning from a tin of Spam! *"Spam, Spam, Spam, Spam, wonderful Spam!"*

Dad would tell us his G-rated war stories, but he would never tell us about the horrors he'd seen because we were kids. There was one surprise raid he spoke about, when he had to dive under the jeep while his batman was having a dump in the woods and being chased by a dud bouncing bomb. When the raid was over, my dad felt something sharp in his chest; to his shock he realized he was lying on hand grenades, and worse still, he had accidentally pulled the pin of one. I became extremely interested in World War II and have already learned so much, because I wanted to find out what Dad went through.

During WWII, Mum, Peggy Grace Frampton, was employed by the American Army. She wore a US Army uniform and worked for a US general. She also worked in a pool of secretaries for Churchill, based in the bunker below Selfridges. She wrote down everything that was said, in shorthand, during conferences between Churchill and Eisenhower. This also involved trips down to the now famous code-breaking center, Bletchley Park. The German Enigma code was broken there by Alan Turing and the incredible team of codebreakers referenced in the film *The Imitation Game*. Mum also worked with the team organizing D-Day for the year leading up to D-Day. When the Allies liberated Paris, Mum was flown out to work in the communications center on top of the Arc de Triomphe, as she spoke fluent French.

When Dad came back after the war, he got a job as an assistant teacher, and at night he went to college to get his degree, and then he became a full-fledged art teacher. History of architecture, printing, photography, pottery, still life—he did it all, and technical drawing, as well. It was a huge, brand-new school in South London and it must've been four huge rooms, plus a printing room, and a photography dark room. This is when the government was actually still funding the schools.

We were living at that time in the apartment in South London where my mother lived during the entire war, a high rise, if you can call it that in England. Sometime between my birth and about two or three years old, we moved in with my grandparents while our house was being built, also in South London. That's when I got to know my grandparents. And I got to know them almost as well as my parents, who were at work while I was at home. There was no day school for me; I was too young.

My grandparents—my father's parents, this is—were great. Except they had birds, budgerigars, which I wasn't a fan of because my grandparents would let them out of the cage and they would always come and land on my head and it scared the shit out of me. When we got our own house, and we were to go over to visit, I would ask, "Do we have to go?" Because I knew that just as we would sit down to eat, they'd let the budgies out and those things would always end up on my head.

My grandmother, Nanna, was a huge vaudeville fan; she had an upright piano in the living room. In those days, there was no TV, barely any radio, so friends would come by and play her piano for entertainment. Jack Kelly was a longtime friend of Nanna's, Uncle Jack to us. He was a vaudeville performer who later managed the Duke of York Theatre in London.

The new house we moved into was on Woodlea Drive, Bromley, Kent, and that's when I got to know the kids next door and it was a great street to grow up on. My father designed part of the house, and he designed the back and front gardens, and it looked like Kew Gardens. It was amazing. English people tend to do that, you know? It was unbelievable, what they did. He found a pond when he was digging to put turf down; he's digging away and he digs out this beautiful old pond.

This whole development was on the grounds of a big mansion that was up at the end of the road, which they turned into a club, like a lawn bowling club. There were tennis courts at the club, and it became a place where people would go on the weekends. So our garden had one of the many ponds in the development. It was beautiful. We had goldfish in it, and my dad would go out there and tap the side and they'd all come up and he'd feed them. You could touch them, and they liked it. We were very much into animals, and my dad was a very caring person. And God knows what he'd seen in the war.

Now he's got his wife, beautiful house—not a huge place, three bedrooms, but lovely—and a back garden. He was in his element. And then he got this great job as head of the art department at this brand-new school, Bromley Technical High School, which was literally just being built, and he had a say in how the art rooms were built.

When he first came back from the war, there was still some food rationing. I remember going down to the local government building in Bromley with Mum. Each child was supposed to have so much orange juice, and we'd go there with a ration card.

The end of the road, where eventually we had this parade of shops, I thought was a great place to play. When they started building those shops, my parents would let me walk up there and hang out with the workmen. Unfortunately, I picked up their vernacular. I came home one day and apparently said something along the lines of "Mum, how about a nice cup of fucking char?" I'd never heard that word before; I didn't understand that char meant tea. Mum just said, "That's the end of you going up to the end of the road with those laborers."

I was five when my brother, Clive, was born. Dad and I went to the Bromley Hospital in a cab to pick up Mum and baby number two. Mum's sitting on the jump seat looking at me in the back and says, "Oh, Peter, would you like to hold Clive?" And to be honest, he was the last thing I wanted to hold, because life had been pretty good up to this point—I remember thinking maybe I could just throw him out of this open window, otherwise this is the end of me being a very spoiled only child.

Being five years apart, we were into different things growing up. As we grew older, when age starts to matter less, we became very close and started to play music together.

Clive followed the second child syndrome. The first child gets all the attention, because first-time parents are trying to do everything in the book to do the right thing. Unfortunately, there is no one book that can be used as a baby manual. Because I arrived first, I got the first child treatment. It's probably why I ended up so needy! Clive was left to fend for himself a bit more, as the second child theory seems to bear out.

Clive has a gentle soul and is super patient. I'm more like a bull in a china shop. If someone gave me a new toy, I would rip the box open, throw the box . . . "Right, there it is. Oh no, it's broken." Clive would open the box very carefully, save it, and put the toy back in the box when he finished playing with it. We had quite a few Dinky and Matchbox toy cars, and he kept them all in pristine condition. Much later, my parents found those cars one day and my dad took pictures of them to show a collector. It turned out that Clive had thousands of pounds' worth of these old toys—so thank goodness he kept those boxes.

He took after dad and went into the art field. Clive is a freelance model maker for graphic design companies in London. If a company wants to see a new jewelry or perfume box for a new campaign, he works with the design department and then makes an original for them to see. After high school, Clive went to Ravensbourne College of Art, where he got his degree. He's also a great photographer, and a great guitar and flute player. He started the flute because I don't think he wanted to compete with me on the guitar. That was the same as me not wanting to compete with my father in the art field. He was so good I felt I needed to find something else. When I gave Clive a guitar, he started playing and then we started playing music together; we've written songs together and recorded them. We've always had a great relationship; I just wish we weren't living three thousand miles apart.

As a kid, I was hearing stuff on the radio that I liked, even though we were deprived of a lot of good new music—it was mostly the old BBC Symphony Orchestra and then an occasional Elvis song. And then I'd hear Cliff Richard and the Shadows, Billy Fury, and Adam Faith. But mainly I liked the Shadows. I wanted to be their guitarist, Hank Marvin. I even have a picture of me while I was in the Trubeats, my first band, when I was eleven or twelve, imitating his look. Because Hank Marvin wore the Buddy Holly horn-rimmed glasses, I went to Woolworths, found some horn-rimmed sunglasses, and knocked the glass out. I've got pictures of me playing with the band—I'm in the middle, and shorter than all of them— and we're mid–Shadows' walk, because they would do this sequenced walk as they played their instrumentals. And there I am with the horn-rimmed glasses on.

When I was seven, we were getting the suitcases down for vacation, and I went up into the attic with my dad and I found this little case. I said, "What's that?" And he said, "Oh, Nanna gave me this—it's an old vaudeville banjolele." One of her vaudeville friends had given her this banjolele and Nanna had said, "Maybe Peter would like to play this one day, you never know."

I said, "Well, let's get it down." So we did, and Dad tuned it up and played a little bit. He played me "Michael Row the Boat Ashore," "Tom Dooley," and "She'll Be Coming 'Round the Mountain When She Comes." All are two- or three-chord numbers, and I learned them very quickly. My dad and mum were looking at each other like, "What's going on here?" So after a few months, I said, "This is great, and it's great for my hands, 'cause I'm little and everything, but I need six strings."

There were all these other guitar sounds that I was hearing, all electric. I was eight when Dad bought me the first generic, no-name acoustic for Christmas, which was okay but I wanted an electric. I remember Dad was still playing Father Christmas. Because my brother was five years younger than me, we had to keep the thing of Santa going, and so Dad still brought my presents into my bedroom and put them at the foot of the bed. Well, I caught him; I heard him this time. It was all wrapped up in paper, so it's all crinkling and he's trying to be so careful as he puts it in my room, and I woke up. As soon as he went out of the room, I said "Busted!" and, well, I knew who he was; I knew it was Dad.

But I didn't know how to tune the bottom two strings. Dad said, "It's three in the morning; can't you go back to bed?" "No, no, come on!" So he came in and tuned the two bottom strings for me. And from 3:30 in the morning on Christmas when I was eight years old, I haven't stopped playing since.

Even when I was five or six, I had this audio thing. If someone is talking to me and the TV is on and there's music, I won't hear what's being said, I'll be dissecting the music. Even if I'm talking to someone and there's somebody on the TV talking, I can't concentrate. I'm a mono guy.

When we first got our TV at Woodlea Drive, in the house that my dad had built, there was a variety show on. It was like a Sunday evening, Ed Sullivan kind of show. This guy comes on playing classical piano and there was this weird slapping noise every time he hit a few keys, and I go, "Dad, there's something wrong with the piano." And he said, "Oh, no, there's nothing wrong with the piano, it's fine." And I said, "No, listen, listen." But they couldn't hear it.

So I said, "Well, maybe I'm wrong"—but then right afterward, the announcer came on and said, "For those who heard it, we apologize for the sound of the piano; some sheet music had fallen inside and was resting on the strings." My mother went, "How did you hear that?" That was the first sign that I had this audio thing going on. I'm not going to say I've got special ears, but there's something about the way my brain receives and translates sound that is a bit weird.

Audio is my thing. I'm not good with aesthetics. But sound, that's my thing. That's how I played by ear so quickly, like when my dad showed me the chords to "Tom Dooley." By the time I'd done it a couple of times, I had it, even though I'd never played the banjolele before. And I'll take a long time deciding what sound I want for which song, which guitar and then what amp.

Mum and Dad were married during the war, or just before it, and their music was Hot Club de France, Django Reinhardt and Stéphane Grappelli. My dad had a huge appreciation of the guitar and great players. At college he played rhythm guitar in a Django tribute act, and there's nobody better than Django Reinhardt, especially back then.

We finally got our first record player, and Dad brought home two albums. One was the Shadows' first album and the other one was a Hot Club de France collection. I ripped the Shadows open and put it on straightaway. It was all new material on an album in those days—you made singles, and then you did an album of other stuff. So this album was all brand-new tracks. I was salivating, learning every note. And then every time I finished, my dad would say, "Are you done?" And then he'd get his Django Reinhardt and Stéphane Grappelli and put it on. I couldn't get out of the room quick enough. This was horrible acoustic jazz stuff—as my own kids used to say, "Dad's playing that silent movie music again."

So I'm learning the Shadows' new album and Dad's putting on this horrible music. But each time this would happen I would walk slower and slower to my bedroom to get away from it. I would wait and I would listen and at first I'd go, "Ooh, what the hell is that?" And then gradually, it became a two-album deal; I'd play the Shadows first, and then I'd say, "Dad, do you want to put on some Django Reinhardt?"

I started to understand the genius of his playing. I hated it to start with because it wasn't a Stratocaster through a Vox amp. But then I realized that there's so much passion involved in this music, and technique. I said it then and I'll say it now, I'll never be able to play like Django; no one can. So my first type of music that was old-school was jazz, gypsy jazz. And that opened my mind to hearing other guitarists from other genres.

There was a little bit of rock and roll on the radio, before the pirate stations started in 1964, which opened up everything.

There wouldn't have been half the bands that there are to-day if it hadn't been for the pirate stations. But it was really these three weekend TV shows—*Six-Five Special* and *Oh Boy!* and *Wham!!*—where I saw all the American artists. John Lee Hooker and all these blues guys came over and were on those shows. The TV show *Thank Your Lucky Stars* came a bit later.

I saw Eddie Cochran on *Six-Five Special*. And Cliff Richard, Billy Fury, Adam Faith, all the English guys. I saw Gene Vincent, who was American, then Buddy Holly. Eddie Cochran and Buddy Holly—those are my two favorites, because they both played great guitar. I wasn't interested in anybody who didn't play guitar.

John Lennon said that when he heard Elvis, the world went from black and white to color. But it was all pretty much in color when I awakened; it was already going on. In 1955, I was five years old, that's basically when Elvis hit England. Elvis was just before my time. I loved his stuff, don't get me wrong, but I wasn't mad about Elvis. I was mad about his guitar player, Scotty Moore—who I, in the end, became a friend of. It's just a crazy world, isn't it? That's so special, to have met Scotty, a lovely man, and just talk with him about those Elvis sessions—oh, my God!

I went to Pickhurst Primary School, from school years five to seven in the primary. On the same grounds was the junior school, Pickhurst Junior School, and you went there until you were eleven. Then everybody took the eleven-plus exam. By the time I got to the junior school, I was playing guitar. I would bring my guitar to school and the teachers would sometimes ask me to play a song at lunchtime, and I'd have a little audience.

The head of the junior school, Mr. Ginty—it's amazing how you remember these names; can't remember yesterday, but I can remember Mr. Ginty—he said, "Peter, you play an instrument, right?" And I said, "Yeah, I play guitar a little." He said, "Well, look, I'm going to have Mr. Ginty's end of term show; it'll be a kind of talent show, and it'll be for the school, we'll have fun." I said, "Oh, that'll be great, I'd love to play."

He said that he had a song by Paul Evans that he wanted me to do—and this was a big song at the time—called "Seven Little Girls Sitting in the Back Seat." The story is, the boy's got all these girls in the back seat. "Seven little girls sitting in the back seat, huggin' and a-kissin' with Fred." So I guess I'm Fred. I had to tell my mother I was auditioning girls—I had no interest in girls whatsoever at this point, I'm eight or nine. But we rehearsed in my bedroom and then went and stole the show.

Around the same time, one of my schoolmates said to me, "What are you doing Tuesday night?" I said I usually just went home and played my guitar. And he said, "Well, you do that enough. Why don't you come out with me? I'm a Cub Scout, with a bunch of guys, and we have a lot of fun." So Mum and I went out and bought the long socks, the cap, the shirt, and the shorts. My friend and I go Tuesday night, probably on our bikes, to this hall where it was held, and the first thing I noticed was that my shirt was pristine; there's nothing on it except the badge of what troop we are.

I said, "Everybody's got all these badges down their arms. What are these?" My friend said they were proficiency badges. "How do I get one of those?" He said, "You go to the scoutmaster and he'll give you a list of subjects that you can choose, and you can do whatever you want." I said, "Give me some ideas. What's an easy one?" He said, "Well, survival is good."

I went to the scoutmaster and told him I'd like to try out for my proficiency test, my survival one. And he said, "Okay, here you are, Frampton. I'm going to give you two matches. I want you to go outside, I want you to get some twigs together, I want you to get some leaves and some wood, and I want you to start me a nice campfire." Well, it's November, in England. And it's raining.

So I came back and I said, "It's windy and wet and the wood's wet and everything's wet—it's not gonna work. Can you give me something else?" He said, "Well, funny you should mention it. I hear you play an instrument." I said yeah, I play guitar. He said, "I'll tell you what, bring your instrument next Tuesday and at the end of the day you'll get up, sing us a song, and if it's good, if we like you, I'll give you your badge." So I brought my guitar and I played "Peggy Sue" by Buddy Holly, and guess what? They all gave me a rousing round of applause and I got my badge.

Many years later, a man named Peter Bradley called me and said, "Hi, Peter. I run the Buddy Holly Educational Foundation in England. His widow, María Elena, would be very interested in you being part of our project, because we know you're a big Buddy Holly fan." She had these guitars made, exactly like Buddy's Gibson J-45. On the headstock and inside each guitar was the name of a song. So he said, "What Buddy song would you like to sing?" And then I would get the guitar with that song title, sing the song, record it, and then give the recording to them. The guitar would be mine to keep.

So I said, "Well, the very first song I ever played in front of anybody other than my family, at the Cub Scouts, was 'Peggy Sue.'" He said, "Oh, um . . ." And I said, "Is that a problem?" He said, "Well, umm, we've actually promised 'Peggy Sue' to Paul McCartney."

I said, "Oh, well, not to worry. Anything—'Maybe Baby,' whatever." I'm such a big fan, I was honored just to be asked.

And, of course, a Beatle must have everything he needs, as quickly as possible.

So three months went by, nothing happens. The phone rings again and it's the same guy again. And he says, "Hi, Peter, how you doing? Got some good news for you." I said okay. He said, "Are you still interested in 'Peggy Sue'?" I said, "Yeah—what happened?" He said, "We couldn't get ahold of Paul McCartney." And I wasn't gonna tell him that I had his phone number in my phone! So I ended up with "Peggy Sue." I think Paul ended up with "That'll Be the Day," so it ain't that bad. When I first got "Peggy Sue," I'd look down at my phone every time it rang. If it came up "Paul McCartney," I wasn't going to answer that one. Inside the sound hole of the guitar is one of Buddy's original frets, used when he wrote all those songs. It's a bit hard to see it, but I know it's there because sometimes I put my finger in my hole and I touch it!

The thing that I feared most at the high school was calling my dad "sir," because I knew everyone was gonna laugh at me at lunchtime. "You call your dad sir? Weird."

"Well, I have to here, don't I?" Everything was going swimmingly well—Mr. Eckersall was dad's assistant, the other teacher in the art department, and Dad made sure that my classes were taught by him. But then one day Mr. Eckersall got ill. So for one lesson, I had my father as my teacher, and I was petrified.

My brother went to the school after me and loved it, had no problem with it. But for me, it was sort of embarrassing to have my father there. You go to school to get away from your parents, not to spend more time with them. Luckily, my father was well liked, one of the most popular teachers. His initials are

O. G. Frampton, and my classmates couldn't work out what the O was, so his nickname was Ozzy. I would say, "That's not his name!" And they'd reply, "Oh, yes it is."

The reason why I left the school was not great. I knew the gym teacher as Uncle Ted, but now I had to call him by his last name, Mr. Ward, or call him "sir." I joined the gym club after school. We'd just got a trampoline, a big one, and I was mad about it. I was the first kid to do a front somersault; I was also the first kid to do a backward somersault. I was into it. And rope climb, jumping the horse, whatever; I was part of the team.

So one day I'm one of the last out, and I'm changing and putting my stuff in my gym bag. I've still got shorts on and I've changed my shirt and these two boys—two who didn't like my dad—were waiting for me. And they were gonna beat me up. They said, "Hey, Frampton!" I thought, "Hello, what's going on here?"

In the corner of the room, there was one of those big wooden crates or tea chests, as we used to call them, for storing stuff like bean bags. Originally, you had to use the crowbar to take the top off—they had these big metal clips over them that you'd force off, and there were nails sticking up all around the top edge of this thing. One of these boys lifted me up and put me in the tea chest and the nails went all the way up the back of my legs, from my shins to my butt. I think they just wanted to put me in there to scare me. I don't believe they planned on drawing blood, but they did. They saw the blood and they ran. I climbed out and I had to crawl to the headmaster's secretary's office. I literally crawled to the office, leaving a trail of blood.

They called my dad. He came running down to take me to the hospital. And he said, right in front of the secretary, "That's it! You're going somewhere else. We're not going to have this, you don't need this." He felt guilty that the only two pupils he had an issue with came after me. They were suspended from the school. My injuries turned out to be superficial, thank goodness, but it was scary.

After the gym club attack, my father, knowing the school system, was able to set me up to take an entrance exam to Bromley Grammar School. I never asked if I actually passed or not, but I did end up at the school, away from my father. But when I got there, it was more academic. I was very hands on—woodwork, metalwork, music, and art. I thought I would be able to continue all these at Bromley Grammar.

The first day I was told, "Okay, you can choose between art, religious instruction, music, woodwork, or metalwork." I said, "Excuse me? I'd like to do all of those except religious instruction." I thought, I'm okay with music; I won't do the music in school, I'll do what I love to do apart from music—which was woodwork. My dad was great at it; he was a fully trained cabinetmaker, which is like a master craftsman in the US.

I started doing the woodwork syllabus, which was three years. But in the last year, I said, "What the hell am I doing woodwork for? I want to go to music college." So I told my woodwork master and he was so pissed off at me that I wanted to change. He said, "You won't get it; you don't have enough time." But I joined the music class anyway, and I had only a year to catch up. I scraped by, because there was a lot of music history, mainly about Haydn, but I passed my music GCE exam. Soon enough, though, even music college would lose out. I wanted to play music of my own.

Chapter
Two

I started my first band at the technical high school—a piano player, a bass player, and me. I still had the generic acoustic, but I'd sent away for a pickup, so I could actually plug it in, and we did an end-of-term concert. We did a Shadows number, "Apache," and of course "Peggy Sue," and probably a Cliff Richard number.

Around this time—I'm twelve or thirteen now—my dad said, "This has become all-encompassing for you. If you're going to do this, because it's getting serious here, you need to go to guitar lessons." They were willing to pay for it, so I said all right.

I went to a guitar teacher named Susan Graham. It was classical training, but it taught me to read music. And even though I don't use it and am a very slow sight-reader, I could do it if I practiced. It also taught me scales and different positions on the guitar neck.

I met a guy called Terry Nicholson while still at Bromley Tech. He invited me around to his place and we started jamming; he was playing bass and I was playing guitar. We put a band together called the Trubeats and this was primo Shadows time, maybe a year before the Beatles. We were playing every Shadows number known to man, plus I was writing my own

21

instrumentals and we played those too. We'd do a couple of songs, but basically a lot of instrumentals. And then the Beatles came along and we had to start singing, for real. I remember we did Roy Orbison numbers like "Dream Baby"—Terry would sing that.

The Trubeats were all in the age range of ten to fifteen when the Beatles came out. We were doing all these local gigs. There were lots and lots in South London, and we were going for it. And then the Beatles broke in England with "Love Me Do"— way before "I Want to Hold Your Hand"—and that's the moment when I said, "Everything has changed now." The first time I saw them on television, doing "Love Me Do," I said, "This is something different. This is phenomenal." They're singing upside-down Everly Brothers harmonies, but they're playing through Vox amps like the Shadows, and it sounds great, and they all sing.

As soon as the Beatles hit, it was bing, bang, boom—all these new bands were on TV. The Merseybeats, Gerry and the Pacemakers, Freddie and the Dreamers, Billy J. Kramer with the Dakotas. It was just one after the other, but they were mostly from Liverpool or somewhere up north. But then bands came out from other places, like the Dave Clark Five and Herman's Hermits. It was all happening. There was so much creativity at that time, and they were all great, too. They all had good songs. It was all singles at that point, and you'd learn them all.

I was just a couple of years behind everybody, and I was watching all these incredible bands that seemed to come out at once. They would play locally and we'd go see them. I never saw the Beatles, but I saw some incredible bands that came right after them—the Who, the Small Faces, the Rolling Stones.

In America, it must've seemed like every week *The Ed Sullivan Show* had on another new English band.

Margaret Harvey was my first girlfriend. Unbeknownst to me, her father was involved in something to do with TV and films. *Dr. Kildare* was huge in England—much better than *Ben Casey*. I went over to Margaret's house one afternoon and Dr. Kildare himself was sitting in the living room—my God, it's Richard Chamberlain! This is awful, but I get introduced to him and I said, "Hi, so nice to meet you. My mother says you're a terrible actor." I somehow stayed friends with him after that and went to see him act on Broadway—and he's actually a very good actor.

But I said to Margaret, "We're playing at the church hall on Saturday night. Do you think he'd come down and just come on stage and say hello to everybody?" You know, it was just me being Pushy Pete again. And she said, "Oh no! Nobody knows he's here." So I go, "Okay, that's fine." We're halfway through the show and there's this hubbub, and the seas part. It's packed with people and I see Margaret and her dad and, oh, there's Richard.

He came up onto the stage and he couldn't say anything; it was like the Beatles, it was incredible. The crowd was screaming, pulling at him. They had to get all these ushers around him and get him out of there as quickly as possible, because they were after a piece of him. That was the first time I'd ever seen that, which was scary; it was pandemonium.

It went from "Ahh, nice show everybody" to *wow!* Everybody was pushing on the stage, people were getting crushed, and that was a little window into my world to come, I guess. They got him out of there and that was it. But even after I told him my mum said he was a bad actor, he still came to the show.

I told Mum what I said, and she was so embarrassed she wanted to kill me.

The local band that David Bowie played with then was called the Konrads, with a K. I first saw the Konrads on the steps of Bromley Technical High School—before David and I were both going there—playing a garden fete, raising money for the school. I remember going there with my dad and mum and brother, and I looked on the steps and I saw this boy with hair sticking straight up playing a sax and singing Elvis Presley songs.

He was just mesmerizing, so I said, "Dad, who is that? I want to be him"—but I want to play guitar. And he said, "Oh, that's Jones—yes, he's pretty musical, I think." So I got to know him before I went to the school, because I became a Konrads groupie. They would play school events, and also go to other schools, and I would follow them wherever they went, go see them in clubs and things like that.

When I finally went to the new school, the first day at lunchtime I made a beeline for Dave. I wanted to talk, hopefully play music, and hang out with him. He was in my dad's art course for three years, and I knew Dad could see that he was different. Obsessed with music like me, but also very much into art. His last name was Jones, which he later changed because of Davy Jones in the Monkees. Later, of course, everyone knew him as David Bowie, but I always called him Dave, because I knew him as Dave at school.

My father's passion was teaching art. He could see those students who had the eye and the excitement to learn when they walked into his classroom. Dave Jones was one of those. In later years, Dad and Dave kept in touch through me. Dave invited Mum and Dad to see him when he was in *The Elephant Man* on Broadway.

When Dave announced the Glass Spider Tour in 1987, we did a couple of performance/press conferences, one in New York and one in London. After the one in London, Mum and Dad came backstage, and after a while I couldn't find Dad. I asked Mum where he was and she said, "Oh, he and David disappeared off somewhere, I don't know." When Dad passed away, Dave was the first person to call the house.

Through Dave, I met George Underwood, who was also in Dad's form at the school. George is a phenomenal painter who later designed album covers, including Dave's *Ziggy Stardust*. He and Dave were best friends, until the day Dave died. So we wanted to bring our guitars to school, and Dad suggested we put them in his office. At lunchtime, the three of us would pull out our guitars and sit and play on the stairs of my dad's art block. The stone steps made for a phenomenal reverb. Always in search of the perfect sound . . . even back then!

I would play them a Shadows number, and then they would show me Buddy Holly's "Maybe Baby." "Do you know this one?" "No, don't know that one." I went to George's house one day and he lent me—which I still think I have—his original Coral label *Buddy Holly* album with all the biggies on it. Dave and George were three years my senior, and normally there would be an age disconnect when you're that young. But music is a powerful uniter for all ages!

At some point, Dave started working on Saturdays at Furlongs, a tiny music shop next to Bromley South station. Vic Furlong, the owner, had given Dave the job of selling singles and guitar strings, with enough pay for the day to maybe buy an album or a set of guitar strings. Dave eventually asked me if I'd like to take over for him, as he wanted to move on. He introduced me to Mr. Furlong and I got the job.

I can't remember now how or why I left Furlongs, but I got another Saturday job, this time in Beckenham, close to where I was born, polishing the guitars, restringing them. Local musicians would come in on a Saturday and hang and jam, and I would sit in and join them. The person who hired me was Dave Hadfield; he had played with Cliff Richards but was also the drummer of the Konrads. He had found David, as well as this incredible guitar player, Nev, and bass and keyboard players. David had left the Konrads by this time and gone on to form his own band. So I had known Dave Hadfield since the first time I saw Bowie play with them on the school steps. Anyway, he was now managing this high-end music shop within a department store called Robertson's of Beckenham.

Dave Hadfield said to me, "Nev's going away on vacation for ten days and we've got three or four shows. Do you think you'd be able to fill in?" I said, "Yeah, but I've got to learn everything." He said, "Well, you've been to enough shows." So I went to the next few Konrads shows and took notes. I went up to Nev and I said, "What key do you play so-and-so in?" And he says G, or whatever, and I say, "And the part that you play at the end of so-and-so, what string is that that you . . ." And he says "It's the B string—why do you want to know?" I said, "Dave asked me to fill in when you're on vacation." He got really pissed off, and I don't know what happened there.

The biggest gig of them all was the Beckenham Ballrooms. We're playing the gig and it's going really well. I'm doing all the solos—I don't think I did any singing, I was just trying to keep up. There's a DJ on another stage, and in between numbers he starts talking and he says, "People, let's give whoever this young guitar player is a hand." So everybody stopped dancing and they're watching me, kinda like I was watching David. I got this huge round of applause and I went completely red. Now I'm being picked out, and I just thought, "Thank God Nev's not here."

That was the first sign to me. I've never forgotten it, that I was now singled out publicly as being a young upstart guitar player. Because I've never thought I'm good enough at anything, you know? Especially playing; I've always got to practice to be good, better, better. I'm my own worst critic, a perfectionist, so it was kind of hard to take that kind of praise. It was an interesting ego boost, but sort of embarrassing all at the same time.

Dave Hadfield got fired from Robertson's for whatever reason. They brought in some other guy and he really didn't like me. My job was keeping the guitars clean, restringing them if they'd been played a lot, and then being behind the counter selling strings, sticks, whatever. I wasn't paid very much, but there were some nice guitar strings there, and occasionally a set would just fall into my bag. I don't feel good about it, but I did it. The new manager (who, as I said, didn't like me anyway) busted me and went straight to the department store manager. I got called on the carpet and was fired. I was in tears and said, "I'm so sorry." It taught me a huge lesson.

While I worked at Robertson's, Tony Chapman—the drummer of a very popular local band, the Herd—would sometimes come in to buy new sticks. I had already sat in with the Herd at least once at Justin Hall in West Wickham. Tony was actually the original drummer of the Rolling Stones. While he was in the band, they were looking for a bass player, and Tony knew Bill Wyman, because they went to school together. So he introduced Bill to the Stones.

The Stones had a residency at the Flamingo Club on Wardour Street—which I went to all the time, underage; I snuck out of the house and went there—and supposedly, the promoters had said to Mick and Keith that they could have the residency, but not with this drummer. So then Tony wasn't in the Stones anymore. But Bill, obviously feeling very indebted to Tony, said, "Look, put a band together, I'll help you. I'll produce it and help as much as I can."

So one day Tony came into Robertson's for some sticks or drum skins, and he said to me, "Look, I'm leaving the Herd and putting a new band together called the Preachers; we're all semipro, all from different big local bands in the area. Would you like to be part of this band?" I said that I was still in school. And he said, "Yeah, well, we'll probably do Friday and Saturday nights, is that okay?" I said I would have to check.

He said, "Come over, I'll give you a bunch of albums and write down everything that I want you to learn for the first rehearsal." So he gave me a stack of albums—everything from Otis Redding to Roland Kirk to Mose Allison. I'd never heard of Mose Allison before and just fell in love with all his stuff.

I pretty much learned everything that I was told to by the next week's rehearsal, and we started playing with Tony on drums, and also Peter "Moon" Gosling on vocals and keyboards and Pete "Face" Attwood on bass, and Ken Leaman on sax—he played two saxes at the same time, because we did those Roland Kirk numbers. And then we got a trumpet player as well, so we could cover it all; we could do Stax, we could do Motown.

I remember singing "Comin' Home Baby" by Mel Tormé and "Hide Nor Hair" by Ray Charles.

We did the Rolling Stones' "Get Off of My Cloud." Well, the only lyrics that you can understand on that record are "Hey, you, get off of my cloud." The rest is just Mick mumbling. So I sang it like that on stage—I didn't learn the lyrics, because I couldn't understand what they were! Now all of a sudden I'm a comedian as well, and people were stopping and watching, because it was like "You gotta have nerve to do that." So that was when I realized I could be funny, as well. Self-deprecation always wins.

Tony told me the story of the Stones and Bill, and said that we were going up to London with Bill next week; we had our first recording session. We're going to do this number that Bill wants us to do called "Hole in My Soul"—a jazzy type of 6/8 song that had a great scat vocal part with guitar. So we had this horrible Austin van and we were all sitting in the back on our way up to London and we stopped in Penge, where Bill still lived in an apartment over a filling station. Bill got in the front seat, so all we can see is the back of his head and we're all whispering, "That's a Rolling Stone!" We have a Rolling Stone in the front seat, you know?

We got to the studio. I put my hand on my guitar and this engineer came over to me and said, "Hi, my name's Glyn." "Oh, hi, who? Glenn?" "Yeah, Glyn Johns." "Oh, okay, nice to meet you." I had no idea. My first engineer happened to be Glyn Johns. Not a bad way to start.

I had been in the studio one other time before the Preachers. There was this band called Denny Mitchell Soundsations, and they were *this close* to making it. They were on TV shows and stuff, but never quite made it. I would go to a place like Justin

Hall, or wherever they were playing, and I was pretty pushy—I was like twelve or thirteen and I would bring my guitar and say to them, before they went on, "You should have me sit in." I would never say that now, but then, I was like, who cares? What have I got to lose? And they said, "Okay, kid, c'mon." Then they would ask me to come, bring my guitar, and sit in again. These were some of the people who ended up in the Preachers, so it was a very small scene.

Their record producer, who just got them on TV, came to me and my parents and said, "Look, I would very much like to take Peter in the studio and do an instrumental"—because they were still big then with the Shadows—"and have Denny Mitchell Soundsations be the backup band." So we went to this local studio—not in London, down in Kent somewhere, RG Jones studio—and he's the engineer, it's all his equipment, but it's straight to two-track or straight to mono or whatever it was back then. We all had to play everything at the same time, which was great.

I'm playing and they're backing me up on this song called "True Blue," and then I had an instrumental I'd written called "Fretting Around." I taught that to them and we recorded that as well for the B side. We did the two tracks but nothing ever happened, no record company ever went for it, but that was my first entrée into the studio.

But now I'm up in London with the big boys, and I've got Bill Wyman producing and Glyn Johns engineering. We did almost enough for an album, not quite. But then we went on TV. The Stones took over *Ready Steady Go!* for an episode; we called it *Ready Steady Stones*. Each of the Stones chose an act to come on, so Manfred Mann and Goldie and the Gingerbreads were also on.

Here I am, in this big TV studio. I'm there with Stu, Ian Stewart, the Stones' piano player and road manager, a sweet man. He's there changing strings for Keith right on the stage, and I helped him out. We're on the show as the Preachers and we're doing our "Hole in My Soul" song, and we played it live. I'm fourteen. The Stones did "Satisfaction" for the first time, I think, and it was freaking me out!

After the show was over, everyone that was on got invited into the office of Michael Lindsay-Hogg, the director, to watch the taped show. We're watching the show and Keith's here and Mick's here and Bill's over here and I'm just peeing myself. They're watching me on TV and I'm watching them. Everyone was taller than me. Wherever I looked, I was in this cocoon of famous people, people who I admired.

Bill and I got to be really good friends, and he started inviting me up to London to play on other people's records with him. I forget what session we were doing for some American girl singer that he was producing, but I was up in IBC Studios, which is such a famous studio. At this point I'm fifteen. We went to the pub for lunch and that's when I started to get to know Glyn. He said, "So you're still in school, are you?" They found me interesting, I guess. I didn't realize until later on how incredible that whole period was. I can only put it down to how small the scene was, and the fact that I guess I was noticeably good at that young age.

I'm sixteen and the phone rings and it's Bill. He says, "Let me speak to your mum, all right?" "Mum, Bill wants to speak to you." "Bill who?" "Bill Wyman—he's in the Rolling . . ." Oh, the Stones, ooh. They thought the Beatles were great, but the

Stones, they're filthy, dirty. Look at them, ugh. I think the Stones had just been caught pissing up against a garage wall somewhere and had gotten really great bad/good publicity from it.

Bill says, "Mrs. Frampton, would it be all right if I come around and pick Peter up? I was going to go up to the Bag O'Nails club tonight and I thought he might like to come with me. He's not been up to the clubs." I was way underage. And she says, "Well, yes, Bill, but he's got to be home by midnight." Bill comes around in this MGB, and I thought, "Wow, all this is fantastic."

We tootled up to town and went to all these clubs—the Scotch of St. James, the Bag O'Nails, and others on different trips. I'm at the table with Bill and everybody's in his face. Jimi Hendrix was there. He got up to play and took the right-handed guitarist's guitar, turned it over, and played it left-handed. And I thought, "Oh, my God"—he wasn't just good, he was amazing. Then he came over to see Bill and I got to shake his hand— but it was that time, you know? John Lennon might be over there, Mick's over there, all these people who I've seen on TV or listened to. So I was really privy, at an extraordinarily early age, to this fishbowl of very successful English rockers.

I'm realizing that this is what I want to do, for sure, and I'm learning how big-time musicians act by watching all these famous people. Everyone I got to know through Bill was always down-to-earth; all these big stars were really nice people—Jimi couldn't have been nicer. We're all the same; we just do different things for a living, you know?

Here I am hanging with these incredibly successful people who I'm a huge, huge fan of and it's crazy. How did I get here? It's a new experience for me, but I'm accepting it as I go along.

Okay, I've been accepted at this level, too—they don't know what I do, but Bill does. I was listening to every word Bill was saying. I'd go to his house and hang out there, and he'd give me his hand-me-down clothes because he is thirteen years older than me, but we were the same size. All the stuff I wore with the Preachers was Bill's old jeans and stuff.

Bill saved everything. And I mean *everything!* He was nuts about it—you went into his living room and it was like a record store. In the middle, there were two bins all the length of it, and all the way around the room was albums. And just inside the door was a little box with index cards, and he had every album alphabetized and cataloged, and he's still like that. I thought, wow, Bill's really into detail.

I'm asking about touring and what they do and everything, so I'm learning how a successful band works. But just seeing this person who's a Rolling Stone, who's now my friend, and he's friends with my parents and was this regular guy—so okay, I don't have to be something other than who I am. It was kind of like an apprenticeship. I was learning as I went, and I'm getting these amazing opportunities along the way.

I was now finding great guitarists to listen to—Wes Montgomery, Kenny Burrell, Joe Pass, a very young George Benson. I was broadening my listening. At that point, when John Mayall's *Blues Breakers with Eric Clapton* album came out, everybody wanted to play and look like Eric Clapton. They had the sideburns and the hair sticking up and the sneakers and, if they could find a *Beano* comic book like he's holding on the album cover, they would be reading it. You're starting to see "Clapton is God" written on the bridges and on the closed-up shops, and every guitar player is trying to sound and look like Eric.

The blues thing was my speed, and I could see I would become instantly addicted to it. There were all these players with
finesse, like Eric and Peter Green and Mick Taylor. All of a
sudden these English blues players were taking American blues
and redoing it their way. I listened to it—I was listening to
Blues Breakers, listening to Cream. It's hard not to when you're
a guitar player, because it's such great guitar playing.

But I said to myself, "I don't think this is the way to go." It's
such a seductive style that Eric has, it's hard not to reference
him. And I do—we all do, because it was his translation of this
music into a style that was very exciting. But I said, as much as
I love that, I'm gonna go the other direction; I'm gonna listen
to a lot of jazz players.

So that's when I really started listening more to Django again
and to Miles Davis, sax players and trumpet players and all sorts
of different instruments. Not for the technique, that would
be different on guitar, but for the melodies and the choice of
notes over different chord sequences. Then I would try to put
it together for myself. I'd maybe write a little something, a few
chords, record it on my tape recorder, and then play my own
lick over the top, probably after I had learned the Kenny Burrell
part on something. Kenny was the man for sound and choice of
notes; no one can beat him.

One night, Bill spoke to my mum and said that we wouldn't
be coming back that night, I'd be staying at his apartment. Mum
didn't want me to, but she said all right. So we went up to London. We go to this club, and he introduced me to his girlfriend,
Astrid. Astrid had a girlfriend who she brought, who was very
nice. But at the end of the evening, we don't go to Bill's apartment, we go to Astrid's apartment and this is her roommate, I

guess. So there were two beds in a very small room. Bill goes to bed with Astrid and I go to bed with this girl, and this is all phenomenal for me. This is a fringe benefit I could get used to.

Bill took me home in the morning, and I obviously don't tell my parents. Ten days go by and I'm getting a little itchy and I look down there and I swear I can see something moving. And I've got to tell my mum, because I don't know what to do here. I don't know what this is or how I got it. I was totally naive.

So I went, "Mum, can you come and look at this?" And she took one look at me, looked up, and went, "That Bill Wyman!" She was furious and marched me up to the end of the road to Mr. Dickinson, the chemist, and there were people in there and she loudly goes, "Mr. Dickinson, he's got crabs!" I'm like, Argh! This is horrible! You pay for what you play, you know? So that was the height of embarrassment—"Wait until I tell your father!"

It was all very difficult because I'm still at school, and I'm playing with the Preachers. First it was Friday and Saturday night, then it was, "Do you think you could do one Sunday?" I said, "I have a math test at nine every Monday." But my parents allowed me to play Sunday—so now I'm doing terrible at math, which I'm not that great at to start with. The neighbors are going to my parents, "Why do you let him do this? We understand he's very talented, but he's only fourteen." My mother's standard line was, "Have you ever tried to stop Niagara Falls?" She just said, "He's a force to be reckoned with, he's gonna do whatever he wants to do. Maybe it'll be later, but he'll do it."

They both knew before I did that I was destined to play music for a living, but I think Mum knew before Dad. She had a plan, it was just down to when she would put it into action by talking Dad into letting me do it. They were together until they passed, and from my point of view, I believe they were the perfect couple. They had spats—but nothing like I've had!

I finished school and I was hoping to go back to the sixth form, get my A levels, and go to music college, hopefully at the Guildhall School of Music. I wanted to be able to be an arranger for sessions. Had no idea, at that point, that I would end up a professional musician.

I'm playing with the Preachers at a gig, and two of the main players in the Herd, Gary Taylor and Andrew Bown, were in the audience. I knew them and I had already sat in with them at least once or twice by then. After the show, they sat me down and said, "Look, what would you think about playing with us for this summer, because we're making some personnel changes and everyone's changing instruments." I said, "I'll check with Mum and Dad, but I need to know the schedule, and as long as I'm not missing any school, that'll probably be great."

I started playing as the rhythm guitarist. But after I officially joined, Andrew Bown went from bass to keyboards, and Gary Taylor went from lead guitar to bass, so I was playing lead guitar and singing some. Now it's a foursome and we're playing all these gigs—still local, but we've got quite a following throughout the country. At the end of the summer, close to when I was going back to school for another two or three years in the sixth form, Andrew and Gary said, "What do you think about leaving school and joining the band for good?" I said, "Oh, I would love that!"

But I didn't think it was gonna happen. My dad's a teacher and my mother works at a school, you know? But my mother loved stage and film, and I'm sure she was a great actress when she was young. One time when she was acting in a school play, she was approached afterward by one of our most famous actresses of that era—someone with "Dame" before her name—and she said, "I think you have a great future, I'm going to award you a scholarship to RADA," the Royal Academy for Dramatic Arts. My mother was so excited. The Dame said, "Yes, you'll go there for free. Would you like that?" And she said absolutely, so she rushed home, told her mother and father, and they said, "Are you crazy? Actresses are regarded like prostitutes"—that's the way they were thought of in the early 1930s, as trollops, tramps. "You'll go and find a nice secretarial job, earn some money and bring it home." I'd call that the end of Mum's dream.

So she became a very good secretary, working in London for the Americans during the war, her acting plans dashed. Now we get to this point with me—this is like I've just been offered a scholarship to RADA and Dad's grumbling, "Never in a million years. You've got to go back to school and you're going to music college." But Mum gives me the "Leave it with me, Peter" look.

I think she saw that I had this natural gift for music, as she had for acting. And since she was stopped from doing what she really wanted to do, she was going to make sure that I was able to follow my dream. So I have my mother to thank.

The next thing I know is that Mum and Dad sit me down, and my Dad's slightly red-faced, because he's still not thrilled about this. She said, "We've decided to let you do it. But Dad has worked out what you should be paid; if you left school right now and went to work for the post office, you'd get fifteen pounds a week. So if they can afford to pay you fifteen"— which was the minimum wage at the time—"you can do it." The Herd weren't earning enough to pay any of them fifteen pounds a week!

My dad met with Billy Gaff, who was the Herd's manager— who later ended up being the manager for Rod Stewart and John Mellencamp—and Dad said, "Look, we've decided to let Peter join the Herd, but he's got to receive fifteen pounds a week." I'm sure Billy was like, "Well, the guys don't make that much right now." But Dad said take it or leave it. So they paid me fifteen pounds a week, and I didn't realize they weren't making that much. I didn't know. But within a year, we got a residency at the Marquee Club and we were earning a lot more money—now I'm still getting fifteen pounds a week, but they're all getting thirty-five pounds a week! So in the end, it all evened out. But I fired my dad as my manager as quickly as possible.

So it starts at Robertson's, with Dave Hadfield, and then Tony Chapman, and then Bill Wyman. I didn't really have to look for work after that. It all kind of came to me. Getting to play shows with the Konrads was the very first thing, but when I joined the Herd, that was it. Once I started playing with the Herd for that summer, that's when things started to happen for me.

Chapter Three

When I joined the Herd in '66, Billy Gaff was managing them. He was a good friend of Andrew Bown's and they actually opened a club together in Bromley called the Penthouse; I saw Cream play there. When we met record producer Steve Rowland at the Marquee Club, he introduced us to the very successful managers Ken Howard and Alan Blaikley. This was curtains for Billy, but it was the best thing for the band.

Howard and Blaikley were responsible for the Honeycombs' big hit, "Have I the Right?," and all these pop singles. They had this other band called Dave Dee, Dozy, Beaky, Mick & Tich. They were huge in England. Steve Rowland said, "Why don't we let the Herd do some of Dave Dee's demos, so we'll find out what they're like in the studio?"

We went in and did all these demos for Dave Dee and his band, and then Rowland said to Howard and Blaikley, "You should write some songs for these guys." We pretty much wrote our own stuff, but we also knew which side our bread was buttered on, or could be, possibly. So they came to us and said, "We love what you've done in the studio with our songs. We'd like to write a song for you and take you in the studio with

Steve, and we'd like to become your managers. Is that okay?" So now we've got a record producer, two managers, and along the way we inherited this business manager named Ronnie Oppenheimer, who was a friend of, and the business manager for, Steve Rowland. He was a shady character. So we had everything . . . even the obligatory shady character!

I never really wanted to be the front man; I just wanted to get in a band that was successful and be the lead guitarist. That's all I wanted to do, maybe do "ooh" and "ahh" occasionally, but not be the singer. So I was not the singer of the Herd—Gary Taylor and Andrew Bown were the lead singers. I did one or two numbers, and they did the rest.

Howard and Blaikley had us come into their office and said they'd written a song for us called "I Can Fly," and they played it to us on acoustic. We weren't thrilled, but it was okay—if we must, yeah. I was trying to work out what we were going to do with it and they go, "And Peter's gonna sing it." And I went, "What? No, no, no—Andy and Gary are the singers; I'm just the guitar player." "No, no, no, this is going to be perfect for you." And I immediately felt an uncomfortable vibe within the band. This is before we had even recorded a note.

I didn't understand why they had picked me to sing. My parents and I talked and they said, "It's probably because you're cute-looking, the girls will like you." Maybe that was it, who knows? Because I look cute? And that's been the bane of my existence ever since. It always got in the way. But this time, it was a means to an end.

We recorded "I Can Fly" at a studio called Ryemuse on South Molton Street, and I think we put one of our own songs on the B side. Tiny studio; control room's across the hallway.

We're recording during the day and Cream was recording their first album there at night and we're using the same engineer, John Timperley.

When "I Can Fly" was released, there was this gentleman in London who knew that only certain businesses, retail shops, and record stores reported to the music charts. This gentleman was Yes's manager, and he had two names—when he was the chart fixer, he was Harvey Freed; and then he changed it to Brian Lane when he became a manager. It was very strange. Anyway, I believe he would give the list of stores to the artists' managers.

So if we were playing in a city that had a shop that reported to the music charts, we'd go in and order and pay for two hundred singles. All it does is get you into the very bottom of the charts so that you're eligible for a spot on *Top of the Pops*. I wouldn't be surprised if it doesn't still go on digitally today. I mean, we're talking about buying a couple of thousand singles, but it got you there.

So "I Can Fly" made the bottom of the charts. Then Howard and Blaikley wrote "From the Underworld" for us and, again, they wanted me to sing it. This time it's not even the band in the studio, it's an orchestra—our drummer's playing parts on it and I'm playing on it, and that's it. I guess it was cheaper to go in with hired session musicians than it was to have the band record it first and overdub the orchestra later. Maybe they thought we would mess up, because we weren't tried and tested. Really, though, we would've been fine, because we were all such good players.

We finished the recording and next we were going to do a tour of Ireland, but right before we left, we got on Simon Dee's TV program called *Dee Time*; he was a DJ who got his own TV show and they had a house band. It was our first time miming or lip-syncing to our record on TV.

Before the show our managers came to me and Mary Lovett, my girlfriend at the time, and said, "We need you to wear something that's memorable," and I said, "Well, what do you mean?" They said, "Why don't you wear a black long-sleeve T-shirt, but cut one arm off and then put frilly lace around the shoulder where the sleeve had attached. And maybe you can put some of those same frills down your fly as well?" So we bought a T-shirt; Mary sewed it up, put the frills on, and when we walked out—it must've been during a commercial or something—the house band lost it when they saw me, because I looked ridiculous.

So we did this thing, our first performance on TV of "From the Underworld," and it went really well. We got in the van that night and we went to wherever you go to get on the ferry to go to Ireland. I guess it was a ten-day tour. By the time we came back from Ireland, things had changed. The Simon Dee program had gone over big. I should've started my own clothing line at that point—the Peter Frampton one-arm frill shirt.

When I had been asked to join the Herd, I thought we were very good. I had no idea, but I thought we could be a successful band. When we were first on TV and started to draw a crowd, that's when I realized I really was the guitar player in a great band; but unfortunately, now I was the singer as well, and it wasn't what I wanted. Don't get me wrong—there's nothing like going out and singing your hit for the first time, doing the show, and girls screaming at you. That's quite an experience and it makes you feel good. But also I could see it was pulling the band apart, I could feel it happening.

The single went crazy, goes up to number six, so we're in the top ten, we're on *Top of the Pops* every week. Years later, when I did the show *Biography* for A&E, they interviewed Bowie. He said something like, "It was Thursday night and I put on *Top of the Pops*. I'm just looking through and it's good. Wait a minute! That's Peter! What's he doing on TV? He should be at school!" I was on TV before he was.

This is when I first met the Bee Gees, the Foundations, all these big English acts. We were starting to do incredible business, going from clubs to theaters, and then we got an offer to do our first package tour with the Who. We were second on the bill, "From the Underworld" had got us that. Marmalade opened, then us, and then Traffic ended the first half; and then the Tremeloes and the Who played the second half.

I met Keith Moon and John Entwistle, who both became longtime friends. They kind of took me under their wing. Keith was a lovely man—not when he was out of it, but the rest of the time he was a lovely guy, a very warm person, and so was John. They had this driver named John Wolff, known as Wiggy. He had a wig, but he never wore it. He would drive Keith's Bentley, and Keith would be in the front seat, me and John in the back. I basically didn't travel with the Herd at all that tour.

The first time we went out of town, they picked me up in London and took me up to Newcastle or somewhere like that. Obviously, the Who were staying in really good hotels, but Keith and John lied to me and told me that there weren't enough rooms where the rest of the Who was staying, so we were going to have to stay at kind of a bed-and-breakfast place. I thought, well, this is normal, you know?

So we went to the bed-and-breakfast place this first night, and I'm writing a letter to my girlfriend, and I heard this giggling outside my door and then stomping as somebody runs away. I opened the door, luckily I had shoes on, and I put my foot outside and I stepped on a stink bomb. I broke the glass and—oh, my God, sulfur.

Keith and John were on the floor right underneath me. They gave me the single room, and I think at least two of them slept in one room, and maybe Wiggy got the other. I'm trying to write this letter home—"Yes, it's wonderful, I'm traveling with the Who"—and then I heard this noise and I don't know what's going on downstairs. My window was slightly open and again I heard giggling, and Keith was trying to aim bottle rockets in my window. I didn't get much sleep that night. And then the second night, it was the same thing. Not the best.

Then we stayed in one of those big rooms that's split into two, and you can pull the partition apart or lock it together. I didn't know they were next door, and so I'm asleep now and I suddenly hear loud music. The partition slammed open and John and Keith are dancing a show for me. I'm asleep. It's just insane. And then, as usually happened, they bumped into each other. Then Moonie started bleeding from his eye. They were probably out of it. I didn't realize that, either. I was naive—but quickly picking things up, I might add. So I was kind of their plaything. I loved it, though. I felt like I was the apprentice again. Whatever it is, I'll take it.

We get to the next gig and our dressing room is up about the fourth floor, and all of a sudden, everyone's in our dressing room. Keith and John come in and then Pete Townshend and Roger Daltrey came in and we were all in this one room, the Herd and the Who, and there's hundreds of girls outside. Keith pokes his head out and they start screaming, and he says to me, "Go on, Pete, stick your head outside for a minute"—screams. The next thing I know, I'm outside the window being dangled by Keith and John by my feet, literally all the way out. This was hilarious for them. And I had to put up with it. That was the scariest thing for me, the dangling. They weren't druggified at this point. Some alcohol obviously, but no one was crazy; everyone was just having fun.

There are two Whos. There's one in the studio and then there's one on stage, and they're both phenomenal, but I prefer to see them live. Great records, don't get me wrong, but there's nothing like seeing them live. I've felt that way ever since I saw them do "My Generation" playing live on *Ready Steady Go!*, the energy and the angst on top of the great songs and playing.

Pete would smash his guitar every night, but he'd have certain ones that he'd save. So the following day, Pete would be in his dressing room putting together all the bits to make one that he could break again. I was in there while he was putting it all back together, just watching him do it and we were talking, and it was all quite amazing to me. That night, I thought I'd go out in the audience and see if I could catch a bit of the guitar shrapnel. I stood near the front, at the side where he was, and when he did the "My Generation" smashup, bits came flying and I caught a PAF humbucker pickup, still with some wood around it in the screws. As a good deed, I brought it back to him and he said, "Nah, keep it," so I did.

At the end of their set one night, Pete and Rog were caught outside the curtain. The house dropped the curtain on them. And Pete and Roger got into a full fistfight. I didn't know whether this was part of the act or if it was for real! I remember thinking that only a short time ago I was at school, but now here I am, sort of a fly on the wall hanging out with the Who.

The touring wasn't that grueling. No one likes the travel, but by this time the Herd had a separate car for the band, so we weren't traveling with the gear; we had a road crew of one. It was all exciting to me. I'm walking past an open dressing room and there's Stevie Winwood and Jim Capaldi from Traffic sitting there, and their room always smelt pretty heavy. But Winwood was my idol, from when I first saw the Spencer Davis Group—you've got this sixteen-year-old kid singing "Georgia on My Mind" like Ray Charles, and playing Nina Simone numbers on the organ. It just blew me away.

We didn't hang out too much, all the bands together back then. I was basically just traveling with Keith and John and Wiggy. But it was exciting; it was all new to me. It was probably only ten shows—you can cover England with that.

The Herd did one album that came out, called *Paradise Lost*, and the title track was the single after "From the Underworld." Next, "I Don't Want Our Loving to Die" came out as a single, and that one went to number two in the charts. It was more poppy. Howard and Blaikley wrote that one, too.

Then we were on the Kinks package tour, with the Hollies, which was when I first met Graham Nash and Allan Clarke. The two of them would come into the dressing room, Graham with the black Gibson acoustic, and they'd sing Buddy Holly songs, and those two voices, Allan and Graham—I was speechless, they were so good, and with such ease.

It was interesting spending time with Ray Davies from the Kinks. I knew Pete Quaife, the Kinks' bass player, and that's how I met Ray. Ray and I would hang out. I think I said to Ray one day, naively, "This is a great tour; the last one we did was with the Who, and I kinda think Townshend's one of the best songwriters out there," and Ray just went, "I'm not sure I'd agree with you there." And then I realized what I'd just said. Because they're equal, both completely different and unique. Both are great.

After that tour, *Sgt. Pepper's Lonely Hearts Club Band* came out and I got a mono copy, before it was released. Mary and I went up to the Petticoat Lane Market on a Sunday—secondhand clothes, records, books, china, whatever. It's a nice little fair kind of thing. We're looking through the records, and *Sgt. Pepper* wasn't due out for another week, and the guy says, not looking at us, "You want to get the Beatles' new record?" What? "I happen to have a couple of copies." A couple of copies? He had a few boxes back there. So something had fallen off the back of a lorry on its way to the record shop. Who knows?

So we got a copy of *Sgt. Pepper* the week before it came out. We got back in the car, I drove as fast as I could back to Mary's place, and I remember both of us sitting on the floor and we just kept listening to the first side, the second side, the first side, then we lifted the arm up, first side again, first side again, second side. Until it was dark.

This was a major change in music. It was just incredible. And the techie side of me wanted to know how they did it. It was such a major jump, and they'd done it with fewer tracks than the Americans had. The Americans had eight and sixteen tracks, we still had four. The Beatles would fill all four tracks up, mix it down to two tracks on another four track, fill those two tracks up, and do it again. Unbelievable. I bet Giles Martin, when he remixed *Sgt. Pepper* in 2017, was able to go back to those original four-track tapes for each song and unwrap the previous mix downs. Discovering buried treasure.

We didn't tell anybody; we thought we'd get into trouble. Then Graham invited me and Andrew Bown to his flat in London—Graham called me up and said, "You know what I've got? I've got the very first *Sgt. Pepper* in stereo." I said, "You're kidding me." The Hollies were with the EMI label, too, and Brian Epstein had given Graham a stereo copy, on reel-to-reel tape. So there we are, taking turns listening to *Sgt. Pepper* in stereo. Even though, as time would bear it out, it wasn't very good stereo. But it was still the first one when they didn't have the drums on the right and the bass on the left or whatever; it was actual stereo and things moved around.

When "I Don't Want Our Loving to Die" went to number two, that's when things started to deteriorate with the Herd. The "cute" thing was still causing problems. *Disc and Music Echo* magazine came out with a cover that proclaimed me "The Face of '68." That was Penny Valentine's piece. She was a lovely lady, and it wasn't her headline, but the big article that she did came out, front page, with "The Face of '68" and there I am. The result being that now it's causing major discontent and jealousy in the band, and I knew that it was a sinking ship.

The band wasn't thrilled with me getting all the attention, obviously. I wouldn't have been, either. I never asked for it; I just got pushed out there by the management and I wasn't gonna say no. Then another writer with *Disc and Music Echo* hid himself behind the door in our dressing room, and the band was kind of arguing. The headline the following week was "Trouble Ahead in the Herd Camp," or whatever it was.

The Herd's successful years weren't a very enjoyable period for me, because there wasn't really room to play. We were now a pop band being screamed at, and that's fun for three weeks and then it becomes boring. You can't hear yourself play and it becomes a chore to be in a teenybopper band, which is what we'd turned into. We were playing the same set every night; we weren't doing any bluesy stuff or jazzy stuff anymore. It was the first time when I was singing with the guitar slung behind my back, and that's not why I got into this.

After "I Don't Want Our Loving to Die" was so big, I learned that we weren't making anywhere near what we should have financially. The person who told me this is now a not-so-loved figure named Jonathan King. He was a nerdy-looking guy with horn-rimmed glasses, and his big hit was "Everyone's Gone to the Moon."

Jonathan invited me up to town and I wasn't that naive—I knew he was gay. But I realized that he was a very influential person, so I was thrilled that he'd invited me. He had a TV show, which the Herd went on. He had a 45 record player in his car; he had an MGB GT. I think he had designs on me, which I kinda realized and sort of cut that off. Because later, unfortunately, he went to prison for doing things with underage boys and stuff, which is very sad.

We were sitting in an Italian restaurant in Soho, and he had an envelope or a napkin and he's saying, "Okay, so what are you earning per night? How many shows are you doing? How many people are in the band? Yeah, yeah, yeah. Are you paying the agent this? Management this? Okay. You're missing this much. This is what's going astray." So I went to the band and showed them the piece of paper. We had known there was something wrong, but Jonathan spelled it out for us.

Someone was screwing us, but we didn't know who it was. We repudiated our record label contract, our management contract, and our record producer contract, and gave notice to the business management that we weren't using them anymore.

You know that expression "If you leave us, you'll never work in this town again?" Well, we kinda didn't. You've got this team, a hit team: Steve Rowland, who'd produced all these big hits in England, Howard and Blaikley, Philips Fontana Records, and this accountant/business manager guy, Ronnie Oppenheimer. Basically we found out that it was Ronnie Oppenheimer taking all the money in and divvying it out. Which we kind of figured.

Fontana signed us back directly, without management. I don't remember how we settled with the management, how we got out of that, but we did. We started doing it all ourselves. We started a new album, and that's when Steve Marriott and Ronnie Lane from the Small Faces called Andrew Bown up and said, "We know what's going on; we heard that you're being screwed and you've got rid of everybody, and we've been through that a couple of times. We're with Andrew Oldham now at Immediate Records and we're loving it, everything's good. Is there anything we can do to help?"

Andrew Bown and I went down to Marlow off the M4, where Steve and Ronnie were both living in a cottage with their ladies. They were very forthcoming, very helpful as to what they went through—and, oh, my God, it was even worse than what we'd been through! They recommended Oldham to possibly be the person to help us.

I don't think we ever got that far, though, because they helped us produce a couple of tracks, one of which was a single, "Sunshine Cottage." It came out and went straight down the toilet. We didn't have the team, we didn't have the support, everything like that was gone. And you know that Howard and Blaikley and whoever weren't going out of their way to stop saying bad things about us, I'm sure. They weren't making it any easier, and they were very well respected; we were just another band, as far as everyone was concerned.

When we started playing to smaller audiences, everything started to die off again with the Herd. At this point, I was ready to leave the band. After Andrew and I went down to Marlow that first time, I just kept going back to see Steve Marriott every weekend, and we started jamming. Steve and I just hit it off. Ever since I'd seen the Small Faces on *Ready Steady Go!*, I had that same feeling like when I saw Bowie on the steps—I'm looking at Steve but instead of thinking "I want to be him," I was thinking "I want to play guitar with him."

Chapter Four

Basically, Andrew and I went down to Steve and Ronnie's place, and Andy came back and I didn't. I met Steve Marriott, started playing with him, and we're going great guns. He was still in the Small Faces, but I'd now left the Herd and he was helping me put a band together. Jerry Shirley was a stand-in drummer for Kenney Jones in Small Faces, so Steve said, "Go see Jerry." I did, and I loved his playing. Then we were looking for a guitar player and a bass player.

Johnny Hallyday, the French Elvis—dear man, God rest his soul, wonderful guy—hired Glyn Johns to produce him. Johnny loved the Small Faces and wanted them to write some songs for him. So Ronnie and Steve wrote some stuff, one of which we did on the first Humble Pie album, actually.

Johnny said, "Glyn, can you find Eric Clapton or Jeff Beck or Jimi Hendrix—I need a 'tres grand' guitar player." So Glyn says, "Johnny, they're all busy, but how about Peter Frampton?" "Who?" But I got a call from Glyn, and he said that Steve suggested I go to France—and, of course, this is my second go-round with Glyn, so it's all old home week. I went to France and I recorded with the Small Faces and became part of the band for a week. And this is my dream come true.

Johnny Hallyday is singing and we're playing—Ian Mc-Lagan, Kenney Jones, Ronnie Lane, me, and Steve. How did I get here? This is unbelievable. I just kept being given these great opportunities. I guess there's a reason for it, but all the time I'm never thinking that I'm good enough. Maybe it comes down to my being intuitive, because I'd listened to a whole lot of different music. I think that really helped me be ready to do whatever—I'm always listening and playing, listening and playing, copying this, copying that.

When we got back, I was at Glyn's place, and he said, "Do you want to hear this band I've been working with? We recorded and mixed the album in about ten days. They're called Led Zeppelin; it's Jimmy Page . . ." "Oh, yeah, I know Jimmy." "And John Paul Jones . . ." "Oh, I've done sessions for him!" I listen to the first side of *Led Zeppelin 1* sitting on the floor with Mary, in front of the record player, and it's another *Sgt. Pepper* moment for me.

When we heard the Zeppelin album, we were speechless. What stood out to me was John Bonham. I'd never heard a drummer like that before, not that powerful. I couldn't get enough of it. I had a cheap set of drums and I wanted to learn how to play, so during the day—we were in a basement, so it was okay—I'd just play drums to that album, and also *Beggars Banquet* with "Sympathy for the Devil" and all that. Bonham was a major influence on me. I had to learn why it was so good, what he was doing. He was a whole different animal from so many drummers before him; he really reinvented rock drumming.

While we're there at Glyn's place listening to Led Zeppelin, the phone rings, and Glyn says, "It's Steve, for you." Steve said, "Hey, mate, I've just done me last gig with the Small Faces. Can I join your band?" I said, "Really? Are you sure you want to leave?" He said, "I just walked off the stage—that's it. And Greg Ridley's ready to leave Spooky Tooth . . ." I said, "Oh, my God"—because I knew how good he was.

He said, "You, me, Jerry, and Greg, how about that? Let's start rehearsing." So I came back in the room and said, "Steve's left the Small Faces and we've just formed a band." And Glyn asks, "Really?" I don't think he thought it was a very good idea.

The following day Ronnie Lane called me and asked me if I would join the Small Faces. I said that we could've all been in a band together with Steve, but now it was too late. Steve and I were forming a band. I could never fill Steve's shoes in the Small Faces, that wouldn't work; it took two people to replace him in the end, Rod Stewart and Ronnie Wood, and they did a wonderful job giving the Faces a great second act. I think Steve had wanted me to join the band, but they didn't want it, so he left—I guess after they had negated his idea, he wasn't enjoying it anymore.

Steve said, "I've got this place down near where I live called Magdalen Laver Village Hall, and we can rehearse there." Greg and I would get in the car together and drive from London all the way to Essex, where Steve and Jerry were living.

I knew what our strong points were, that's for sure. Having already played quite a bit with Steve, as just two guitars jamming, I was very excited because I knew that I loved his style. I started writing these heavy riffs, so it brought out all sorts of things in me musically that wouldn't necessarily have been there had it not been for Steve.

When we met—Jerry, Greg, Steve, and I—we were all listening to different albums, but there was a bunch that we were all listening to. One was *Music from Big Pink* from the Band, and then Steve turned me on to Taj Mahal. I think Mick or

Keith had lent Dr. John's *Gris-Gris* album to Steve. Keith wanted Steve to be in the Stones, but that didn't go down well with Mick, I guess.

Our first rehearsal as Humble Pie was in Jerry Shirley's mother's living room. We set up there with little tiny amps and Jerry's drum kit, and we jammed on "We Can Talk" and "Chest Fever" by the Band. Steve said, "How about that song on *Gris-Gris*?" The song he meant was "I Walk on Gilded Splinters." It became a long song on the *Rockin' the Fillmore* album.

Years later, in the '80s, Jerry Shirley and I were at an event in New York, and Dr. John was playing. We went up to him and said, "We just wanted to tell you what big fans we are." And he said, "What band do you say you're from? Humble Pie? I've got to thank you. I had some problems back in the day, and I was sitting in jail on a drug charge. I couldn't afford a lawyer. You did that cover of my song and that was a hit album, your album. Then I could afford to get me a lawyer and I got out of jail thanks to you!" He gave us a big hug, and Jerry and I were just speechless after that.

We started working on the songs for the *As Safe as Yesterday Is* album, plus a few covers and whatever. We signed with Andrew Loog Oldham, with Immediate Records. Andrew, a dear lifelong friend, started off as the publicist for the Beatles, then managed the Stones. He said to us, "I think the way to announce this band is at Ronnie Scott's club." "Well, that's a jazz club," we replied. "Yeah, hear me out—it's a small room and we'll fill it with press."

Before that first show, we were backstage in an office somewhere; there's no dressing room. We were supposed to start at a certain time and it's half an hour after that, and the bar is closed, but Andrew's put champagne bottles on each table and he keeps replenishing them. He kept going out there and checking and coming back, "Not yet, not yet." And when the audience temperature was right, he said *go!*

It was one of the most incredible experiences, because the audience had all forgotten they were journalists and went back to being fans, and we wowed them. It was really incredible. We weren't loud; we were still with the small amps, but it was a great sound. We were already doing some of the more heavy, bluesy stuff. And we got the best write-ups that champagne could buy.

So we were off. We released "Natural Born Bugie," which went up to number four, and then *As Safe as Yesterday Is*. We recorded the album with Andy Johns, Glyn's brother, at a place called Morgan Studios. It was just a lot of experimentation. The first album was really quick; we pretty much had it all ready to go.

I think that it was all the influences that we'd been listening to throughout the years. Now we were able to put it all together. We had my whole library of riffs and things that I'd listened to on one side, and Steve had his riffs and licks, and I'm learning his and he's learning mine. His is much more angular blues, dirty; mine's more lyrical, if you like, but we were both writing heavy rock songs. A lot of people think, "Well, Pete just played his solos over there," but "I Don't Need No Doctor" is my riff. A lot of times I would bring a riff to rehearsals and we'd jam on it and all of a sudden it would turn into a song.

Steve and I shared solos—he'd do half, I'd do half. There was a healthy competition, and I learned so much from the way Steve rehearses, the way he writes and everything. He would never sing at sound checks or at rehearsals. We would just play, and then when we would get up on the stage, he would sing. It was so weird; it was perfect.

We were able to start fresh. What it enabled us to do most of all was to start over, on a musical level rather than on an image level. This was the first band in which we were all able to do exactly what we wanted to do. It was a totally democratic band, at the beginning. Any one of us could bring in a song, and if we all liked it, we would record it. It was a band, all for one and one for all! It was the whole idea of doing something different, with the interplay of the guitars and Steve's voice.

We didn't really realize what we were doing, but we were enjoying it. One of the reviews of *As Safe as Yesterday Is* was horrible, but it did say, "This band could be classified as heavy metal." I think that's one of the very first times that phrase got used—even though we weren't, really. Later on maybe, but we weren't anything like Pantera.

But I was playing louder than I'd ever played before. We never played the same thing twice in the solos. It was a lot of make it up as you go along, which I love. Our numbers could be four minutes one night and seven minutes the next. There were no rules in Humble Pie. If you wanted to go on and on and on, if Steve wanted to play a harp solo for thirty minutes, go do it. No one was gonna tell us different at that point.

I really shouldn't be a guitar player. There's a story I heard somewhere of a music teacher: to find out what instrument would be best for you in the school orchestra, he would hand out pieces of paper and say, "I want you all to draw around your hands and fingers, and then sign it and give it back to me." He would have a class of thirty students, and he'd say, "Okay, Beasley, small hands, flute. Brown, long fingers, double bass for you," and so on. When he got to Frampton, it would be, "Okay, Frampton, piccolo"—something small, because I don't have very long fingers. That's why I've always favored guitars with smaller necks.

But I didn't know that, and I never thought about it until I was forty years old. I'm so glad no one told me this when I was starting to play. Phew! So there's another reason why I play the way I do. All these great blues players, they've got fingers out to here, they're huge. I remember shaking hands with Freddie King once; well, it was like my hand disappeared.

It was during Humble Pie when all of a sudden I realized, "This is me now; this is my style." Listening back to "Stone Cold Fever" on the *Rock On* album, that solo is pretty jazzy. I remember coming in and listening to that and thinking, "Wow, that's different, I've moved on."

I didn't necessarily want to be a jazz guitar player; I just wanted my own style. I wanted to be one of those guys who, they play one note, and you know who they are. And I got there, but I had to do a lot of work. I was compiling, I was taking notes—it was a thesis on a guitar style, if you like. Listen to everybody, learn everybody, and then Humble Pie comes along and, all of a sudden, I'm able to put it all together because there's room.

Steve Lukather from Toto (and a million other sessions) says I was the first cat who went outside the box with notes that weren't regularly played in rock and roll solos. But I didn't want to play normal rock and roll solos. I didn't want to play like anybody else; I want to play like me. I woke up one morning, went to a rehearsal, played a gig with Humble Pie, and came off and said to myself, "Wow, that's me now. I can feel it; I've invented me, by listening to the world."

The sound of the guitar is in the fingers. If you took Jeff Beck and Eric Clapton, and you said there's Eric with his Blackie and his amp, and Jeff Beck with his white Strat and his amp, and then you have them switch positions and guitars, the sound would follow them. It wouldn't matter which guitar they were playing or what the amp was. When I met Eddie Van Halen for the first time, I picked up his guitar and it sounded like me. It didn't sound like him. And then he picked it up and instantly it's Eddie.

When I met Eddie, he played one of my songs on his guitar. It was "Nowhere's Too Far for My Baby" from the *Frampton* album, and he said, "I played that backwards, and turned it into a Van Halen song." I was honored and thrilled that I had inspired him. I think he's phenomenal, but I could see he's a fan of my playing, too. I never think that I could be inspiring the great players I admire—I always think the other way around. But we do all inspire each other.

When David Bowie started to become more famous, around the time of "Space Oddity," he was Humble Pie's special guest on the Changes '69 tour. It was just him sitting on a chair with a 12-string acoustic, that was it. And it was phenomenal. He was just great. He was number one with "Space Oddity" at the time, and we were number four with "Natural Born Bugie," so it was a good tour. Dave Edmunds was in Love Sculpture, who were also on that show. Another great player!

We weren't thinking that David was going to be one of the all-time greats. I just thought that he was mesmerizing on stage, even then—he was special. I had no idea he would go on to do what he did. I'm sure he had it in his mind, like I did, but none of us knew what was coming. It was like, "Well, Jones is in a band and Frampton's in a band." That was about it.

Andrew Oldham lent us Eddie, his driver, and his Phantom V Rolls-Royce for this tour, so we were traveling in style. It was in the winter, because I remember it was always raining, so the windows were always up and everybody was smoking cigarettes and smoking pot. I was not partaking at that time. On one trip up to Newcastle, Steve and Jerry and Greg were smoking something that made me feel like I wanted to throw up just smelling it.

Whether I liked it or not, I was getting high. By the time I got to the gig, I was wobbly. I didn't feel good at all, and I turned white, then green, then white again. I walked into the backstage green room and David said, "What's wrong? What's wrong?" I passed out onto a couch. His girlfriend, who was very well endowed, I fell on her—woke up with my head in between her breasts, literally. Dave's going to Steve and the other guys, "What have you done? What have you given him?" He was always very protective of me.

By this time, I'd already tried pot, but every time I smoked it at Steve's, I would pass out and end up in the rose bush outside the kitchen, because I felt I needed air and had to get somewhere cold. So this wasn't for me, it wasn't my drug of choice. God—that was horrible!

I was barely drinking. I think I was still drinking shandy at that point, and we'd started drinking Mateus Rosé. Early on in the Herd, Andrew Bown drank whiskey and I tried to keep up with him, and I couldn't do it. Before the hits, we were in Belgium playing, and one night I was out of it, and our drummer, Andrew Steele, dressed me down and I took it to heart. That's when I said, "I can't compete, and this is not doing me any good," so I stopped.

In England, as soon as we had the hit with "Natural Born Bugie," we started getting screamed at again. Remember how I was "The Face of '68?" Well, Steve had been "The Face of '66," and the fans just couldn't get over it. But it was only at shows that we would get screamed at. I pretty much lived a normal life.

The first place Mary and I had together was in Hammersmith; not a great part of town. And then we had a basement apartment in Westcroft Square. The bedroom was upstairs, with barely enough room for a bed, and there was a small basement living room, kitchen, and bathroom.

When I was still living with Mum, Dad, and Clive, the milkman once said to Mum, "Where's his Rolls-Royce then, Mrs. Frampton?" This is while I'm sleeping, and they're both pointing at my Morris Minor 1000 that I bought as my first car for thirty pounds!

I've always been able to support myself and pay the rent and utilities. And I've never had a "real" job! I'm laughing because a lot of people who are not in this business think it's all like being on a luxurious spring break. If only!

When I left home to move in with Mary, I never had to go, "Hey, Mum, could you lend us a fiver?" I'm proud that I was able to do that. After our first hit with the Herd, each week I could afford to pay my rent and maybe get one shirt from Carnaby Street or King's Road. Dandie Fashions was my favorite. We were on TV, but we weren't wealthy people. You don't make a lot of money from a hit single in England.

We were very prolific in Humble Pie, and *As Safe as Yesterday Is* and *Town and Country* came out pretty close together. We would first go down and jam at Magdalen Laver Village Hall, and then we got to the point where we would go straight into the studio. Each of us would bring in songs, and whatever we all liked we would record.

We were on the road, so we didn't have as much time to prepare for *Town and Country*. A lot of that was rehearsed in the studio. One day I would play drums, Jerry would play piano, then Steve would play drums. Or I'd play organ, I'd play guitar, Steve would play Wurlitzer electric piano. We all played everything, so it was really enjoyable. Any one of us could say, "I've got this idea!" and "Go and do it" would always be the band's reply.

Steve played less guitar on that record and more keyboards. We did "Every Mother's Son," which is kind of a country song that's just him and me. "Take Me Back" is the first track, which is very acoustic. Just me on guitar, and the three of them sitting around me playing percussion instruments. "Heartbeat" was a Buddy Holly cover, but Greg, me, and Steve all sang the verses together in harmony, so it was very different from Buddy's version. Pretty eclectic, how the album moved around. A mixture of styles.

We mixed *Town and Country* at Olympic, in what was called the reduction room. I wanted a master copy of the mixes before it was actually mastered. Andy Johns set it all up, and he said to this intern, who was there with his girlfriend, "Okay, can you just do this?" I was watching these two Studer tape recorders, and they've both got the red light on, and I said, "I think this is wrong." He stopped it, and we discovered he had erased the intro of the first track, which was my song "Take Me Back." I went running, yelling, "Andy! Andy!" "Don't worry, don't worry, I'll remix it."

It wasn't until after I'd finished the *Wind of Change* album with Chris Kimsey that I realized that the intern had been

Chris! He never said anything, but I figured it out. Of course from then on, Chris and I have been friends. But at the time I had no idea who this guy was, I just wanted him to fall off the face of the earth . . . gently!

As soon as the screaming girls thing started with Humble Pie, Steve and I looked at each other and said, "Let's go to America." Greg had been there before with Spooky Tooth, probably supporting Joe Cocker. We went for our first tour there, and we opened for Mountain a lot.

The very first day, I woke up in Manhattan, in the Holiday Inn on Fifty-Seventh Street and Tenth Avenue. As I walked out of the hotel for the first time, I turned around and looked up and gasped, because we'd seen it on TV, but you don't experience Manhattan until you're standing in front of the skyscrapers and you're looking up and it seems like they're toppling down on you. I've never forgotten that. It seemed like I was looking through a fish-eye lens at them all, they were so huge.

I decided that for breakfast I would just go to the coffee shop in the hotel. I'm this polite nineteen-year-old, and I find a space at the counter. It's a regular New York coffee shop. And there's so much action going on. You know, it's fast—"Gimme this! Gimme that! Gimme this!" I'm going, what is this "gimme" business? So I'm going, "Excuse me? Hello?" A guy came in after me and he gets his food, and I'm still going "Hello?"—the polite Englishman. So in the end, I said, "Gimme coffee," and I got coffee. You learn that you can't be bashful at the counter in a New York coffee shop. You've got to be demonstrative. This was a US learning curve for me.

That's also when I learned how to say "butter" in America. I've got the coffee, I've got the eggs, and the toast is there, but it's not buttered, so I said, "Excuse me, could I have some butter?" "Some what? What are you saying? You speak a foreign language or something?" And he said, "Oh! Butter!"—like b-u-d-d-e-r, *budder*. So that was my introduction to the different language and culture of America, even though I thought we both spoke English?!

One of Humble Pie's first shows in the US was at the Fillmore East, opening for Santana. We then did a bunch of dates, starting in Boston with Mountain. Even though we had done a lot of gigs, we had no idea what our place was in the hierarchy. No one told us how long to play. So we came on and did an hour. Mountain were very nice, because they loved our band. But Gary Kurfirst, their manager, had a word with us and said, "You're only booked to play forty-five minutes, and if you go over, we can't get to the second encore." He was very nice. "Oh! You mean there's a limit on how long we play?" We were coming out and doing our acoustic thing first, as if we were the headliner.

That first tour was about six weeks, sharing rooms in Holiday Inns. I'm sharing with Jerry, and Greg's sharing with Steve. The big thing was every week, we would all meet in the same room because *Star Trek* had just started and it was shown in the States first. We had only seen a couple of episodes in the UK. These were all first-run showings of the original series. Spock's ears were still a work in progress. Humble Pie were true Trekkies!

We had a lot of great times, just the four of us—I'm not even sure if we had a road manager. We were doing well, theaters and big clubs, like the Boston Tea Party, and the one in New Orleans, the Warehouse. We were going down really well, but it wasn't a very cohesive act at all. We were just doing what we wanted to do, without considering that if you move one number, it changes everything, the vibe changes and the show energy changes. We had a lot to learn, put it that way, but we were a great band full of angst.

A strange thing happened one day. I'm a huge Peter Green fan; his sound and his fluid style with the early Fleetwood Mac was very seductive. A beautiful guitar style. So I was in New York playing with Humble Pie. Our wives and girlfriends didn't want us staying in Manhattan, because they didn't want us hanging out in the city that never sleeps! So our manager put us at a hotel just over the Tappan Zee Bridge. I thought, "I'm not digging being stuck out here."

I had met a girl in New York, so I borrowed a car and went to her apartment. She said, "I know Peter Green, and he's in town. Do you mind if he comes by?" I said, "Not at all! I've always wanted to meet him!" I don't know how much time went by, but Peter Green turned up. He had his Les Paul with him and I had mine with me—never without it—and he said, "You wanna jam?"

You have to understand, this was a huge deal for me. Peter Green was already on the same level as Eric Clapton and Mick Taylor. All three had been to the School of John Mayall. And now, Fleetwood Mac had formed and was starting to have major hits.

So we get our guitars out and we rest them on something wooden, like a cabinet, that's got some resonance, because we've got no amp. He's there on one side and I'm on the other, and we're resonating through the cabinet, chest of drawers, whatever. And I was loving it. We're this close, and we're playing along, and he lets me solo for a while, I let him solo for a while, and I thought he was kinda digging it.

Then he stops and he asks, "Tell me, what sign are you?" I said I was a Taurus. He said, "I knew it." He packs up his guitar and he gets up and he walks out. "I don't like Tauruses." I didn't know whether it was that or the fact that maybe he had dated this girl, and I wondered if it was wrapped up with that. I don't know, but he didn't like Tauruses—that much was very clear.

I don't think we spoke for a while after he left. It was just like, "What was that?" Of course, I know now why, because we've all learned about Peter's problems and mental health issues.

We have recently lost him and even though it was a strange encounter, I will always remember our jam and what an incredible guitar player he was.

We got to LA, to a Ramada Inn, and that was it. We went out to breakfast, came back, and our bags were outside in the hall. Basically what had happened was that Immediate's money had been frozen because they went Chapter 11, bankrupt. The money ran out and Andrew Oldham couldn't afford to pay the hotel bill. Gigs were canceled, and we left with our tails between our legs—luckily, we had our return tickets back to London.

When we got home, Andrew took us aside and said, "Look, I can't release you from the publishing deal." But he did let us out of our recording contract. And for that I always thank him, because then he told us, "Go see the majors—Warner Bros., CBS, Atlantic, and A&M—and this is what you ask for. Ask for like $250,000–$300,000 for eight albums, two per year." So we went into Atlantic, we met with Ahmet Ertegun and Jerry Greenberg in London. Ahmet said, "We're gonna make good music together." I loved Ahmet. We were close; he was a dear friend to me. He said, "Jerry, let's go, we got these guys signed up." And we said, "All right, okay, we'll get our lawyers onto it."

We had one more label to go see, and it was Larry Yaskiel at A&M. We'd been saying the same thing to each company when the money issue came up, but when Larry asked, "So how much do you want?" instead of saying $300,000, Steve said $400,000. I'm trying not to change my expression. Larry said, "Okay, I have to go and call Jerry Moss now. I'll be right back." I said, "Steve, that's like a hundred grand more—what the fuck?" And he said, "He can only say no." We'd already got an offer from Atlantic, which is where we wanted to be, because of its history and all the great Atlantic artists.

A few minutes later, Larry came back in the room and said, "We've got a deal. But Jerry would like you to use Glyn Johns as producer." And we said no problem! So we were to receive a hundred thousand dollars each over four years.

Steve said that we should go to the accountant that they used with the Small Faces, who was a good man, Howard Marks. We went in and Steve starts, "We just want one company; all the money will go in there and then we'll each have checkbooks on it." And I said, "I don't think so. We'll have *four* companies and *four* checkbooks"—because I thought it might save some in-band fighting later if one of us spent more than their share. And so we made four separate companies.

Fast-forward to after I left the band. The members were persuaded to use one company name, which turned out to be a disaster. I'm sure Steve came up with the name, Oven Development (oven, pie, get it?). Jerry Shirley told me years later, "Guess what happened?" I didn't have to guess; I knew what happened. There was no money left, because Steve had spent it. Jerry said, "You were so right at the time; why did we change that?" Don't get me wrong, I've made my own share of fatal financial mistakes, just not that one.

We originally had our four companies based in the Channel Islands. So the money came from America, was split up four ways into our four accounts, and then we were only taxed on what we brought into England. It was a lot of money back then. We would've all gotten $25,000 each year for four years. So we all bought cars! I bought a 1965 Aston Martin DB5, the James Bond model, for £1,750. Steve got a DB6, Greg got a Bentley Continental—all secondhand—and Jerry got a Rolls. And this is before we've made any music for A&M.

Mary and I were childhood sweethearts, we met when I was fourteen, and we were a great team, we really were. She was modeling at the time and was in TV commercials and stuff like that, so while I was away touring, she was doing that. She also wrote a cookbook, in which my one recipe contribution is scrambled eggs.

We managed to buy our very first house, right off Abbey Road, at 9A Bolton Road. It was a four-story townhouse, and that was phenomenal; now here we are living in St. John's Wood. We were quite a social couple; we had lots of people come around. Mary had lots of friends and so did I, so we were always having dinner parties and going out to dinner. I've often said that I believe Mary has stayed in touch with everyone she's ever met. Mary was a very positive thing in my life, always very supportive. She was a constant for me. We're still best of friends.

When Glyn came in, he said, "This is your first album for A&M. They've hired me to be your producer"—not that we didn't love having him there—"but I've got a couple of things to say. Your first two records are fine, but they haven't done anything and I really think you ought to look at your MO.

"I think you've been diversifying too much and doing every-body's material and everybody's singing and you're not taking advantage of your plusses. This is the way I see it—Jerry's the drummer, Greg's the bass player, Peter's the lead guitar player, Steve's the singer and guitar player. That's it. All right?"

This didn't bother us at all. I still sang my one or two on each album, which was great. People have said, "Oh, didn't you want to do more singing?" No, not when I had Steve Marriott right there, that's the last thing I want to do; I want to play guitar, do some harmonies with him, sing a verse here or there, but why not just play guitar and listen to him?

But we definitely did change our direction a little bit. It took the next album, then touring some more, and then the *Rock On* album—which is our best studio record while I was still with the band. Steve and I were doing a lot of guitar work together; Glyn would say, "Okay, for this solo how about you and Steve work out and play a solo together, maybe some harmony?" That's where all that came from.

On the Beardsley cover album, Steve's vocal on "Live With Me" is so good. "Live With Me" was me switching to organ; I didn't play guitar on that at all. Steve plays the guitar solo and it's so cool. We probably started recording with "I'm Ready," because we'd been doing that in the live set.

At Olympic Studios, Glyn had us all set up in a line, as if we were on stage, and Jerry was on a wooden drum riser facing the control room window. When we came in and listened to the first playback of the track, I just remember saying to Glyn, "How did you do that?" The drums sounded incredible. So did everything else. Great quality sounds are so inspiring to me. I'm so lucky to have been able to work with Glyn so early in my musical journey.

There were things he was doing as an engineer that I was picking up on—he would record the drums with a little bit of plate reverb, but then when he would play them back they would come through the same faders, and it would go through the reverb again and it would flange. That's difficult to do; you've virtually got to do it the same day because the chamber might never set exactly the same again.

I came up with the "One Eyed Trouser Snake Rumba" riff and played it at rehearsals, and Steve started singing a melody over it. It was so cool when I'd come in with something and Steve would add his part to it, and with Greg and Jerry my little idea sound would become, you know, wow! We had our ups and downs, but you listen to Steve and you want to hug him. He was just brilliant; there was so much I learned from him.

Glyn was very instrumental in helping us with our direction. But at the same time, it was the beginning of the end for me, because I loved what we were doing, but I wanted to do acoustic numbers, too. We had started out recording more of a balance of acoustic and electric. The songs I was writing and singing were more acoustic.

This is also when Greg, for good or bad, said, "I know this American manager." Spooky Tooth were with Chris Blackwell's label, Island Records, and Chris would use Dee Anthony as the co-manager for all his English acts when they went to America. Greg said, "Dee is awesome—I think he's the man for us."

Right before we got to San Francisco, I swapped my SG for a Gibson 335, the big-bodied one, with the F holes and everything. Of course, Humble Pie played so loud that every time I turned up for a solo it was all feedback and sounded like a bunch of noise, and I was so pissed and embarrassed. I couldn't turn it up to be heard.

I had a friend in the Bay Area named Marc Mariana. He came out to one of the Fillmore shows, and said to me after, "Couldn't help notice you had a little problem." Very diplomatic understatement. And I said, "Yeah, I should never have got rid of that SG. I didn't realize that the 335 would feed back so much." He said that he had a guitar that I might want to use for the rest of the shows, a Les Paul. I wasn't really big on Les Pauls, I'd had a couple of bad experiences with them, but what the hell, this is an emergency—yes, please, thank you.

He came around breakfast time to the hotel coffee shop and had this brand-new guitar case and opened it up. Out came this black '54/'55 Gibson Les Paul. Originally, it was a Black Beauty, so it would have had the old P90 type pickups. Marc wanted three humbucker pickups, because there's this wonderful album cover of Smokey Robinson and the Miracles with their guitarist, Marv Tarplin, holding a beautiful Les Paul '57 custom with three pickups, and every guitarist just loved that. After Marc put in these humbucker pickups, he sent it back to Gibson and had it refinished black. And it looked brand-new, except it's this vintage guitar. Today, of course, we wouldn't touch it—if you refinish it, you ruin the value.

Marc and I took it up to my hotel room and I started playing. He'd hand-sanded the neck, so it was much thinner. I have short fingers, so it was like it was made for me. At the end of the fourth night, I gave him the guitar back, and I said, "I can't thank you enough. You don't think there's any chance that you'd ever want to sell it, would you?" And he said, "No, I don't think so—but I'd like to give it to you."

I put cream surrounds on the pickups, which gave it a different look. And that Les Paul was pretty much the only guitar I played from 1970 to 1980. Just about everything I did, I used that guitar. A little later, I got one other guitar, a 1955 Red Fender Stratocaster. I bought it from a great guy in Chicago called Bumble Bee Bob; a great blues harp player. But it became more and more difficult to play any other guitar than that Les Paul.

Chapter Five

Dee Anthony flew over to England and we were all kinda wowed by him— the archetypal big, burly American manager guy. Once we signed up with him, he got us in with Frank Barsalona at the Premier Talent booking agency. We were already signed with A&M, so we were set for records, which Dee was kind of pissed off about, because he didn't get a percentage of our royalties, for the first four years, anyway. We had signed the record deal with A&M before he took over. After I left, Dee renegotiated Humble Pie's A&M deal, and from that moment on he took 20 percent of the Pie's record royalties and publishing, and 20 percent of all tour gross.

We opened for incredibly large acts in incredibly large venues straightaway because of Frank's clout. Everybody who was anybody was with Premier Talent. Frank was a very clever man, and a lovely person. A gentle guy; you look at him and you might not think that, but he was a gentle, sweet teddy bear.

Dee and Frank came to see one of our very first shows at the Fillmore East, and we went down well. In between sets we went to Ratner's—the Jewish deli next door. The second set wouldn't start till 11:30 p.m., 12:00. So, the band, Dee, and Frank were all sitting at a table in Ratner's, and we said, "So what did you think, Frank?" He said that one of the best numbers we had in the act, "Hallelujah I Love Her So," was in the wrong place. He said, "I think you should move it here and do this other one up earlier." He manhandled our act for us, in a phenomenal way. We went on for the second show, and what a difference! That was our first lesson about building a show.

At first, Dee was like a coach. He was very excitable, very passionate, and he loved Humble Pie—he just loved that band. He was also co-managing ELP at this time and J. Geils, who we played with so many times. We were all impressed with Dee, that he was this powerful go-getter kind of guy. But he always looked like a Mafia guy to me.

He had a wild temper and he would shout at people, scare people to death. He traveled with us, stayed in the same shitty hotels as us—not all the time, but at the very beginning, to kind of whip us into shape. He would always give us his critique, he was like our football coach and would even blow a whistle from the side of the stage.

We had no money for touring when we started, so A&M was giving us tour support, which would obviously come out of our record royalties later. Dee was also doing some funding for us. We'd get paid through Dee's office—we were getting gigs, but we weren't making enough to cover all the expenses. There was no need to get an accountant at that point, because we weren't making any money at all.

Dee handled everything from the beginning, so all the money went to him. The only thing that came directly to us, because of yours truly, was the yearly A&M recording advance that was split four ways. We were living on those annual advances.

His tried and tested method was to have us play in front of as many people as possible in the shortest space of time, always.

We became known as the best support act in the business, because we were good and sold tickets. There you go, that's the criteria right there—are they going to add ticket sales? The special guest/support act was on the bill to sell tickets, and our agenda was to steal as much of the headliner's audience as possible. That was the game plan. "Tonight you're on with ELP? Go out there and make sure that when the audience leaves, they're gonna go 'ELP was good, but that band, Humble Pie, they were *really* good.' That's what you're looking for. 'Hey, I've got to check their album out.'"

After the first album with A&M, we did a couple of tours in the summer. We were stationed in New York and would get sent out on gigs wherever we were needed. When we went back to England to record *Rock On*, we were ready to move up to the middle spot on a three-act show. That placement is actually the best spot anyway, because as it gets later, the audience gets more tired or high. So given the choice of a spot, I'll always take the middle one. There's no pressure, you've just gotta go out there and burn and steal.

Rock On was the most enjoyable record I made with Humble Pie. It really showcased Steve and me on guitar, and of course Glyn made it sound great. Glyn was in the studio trying to guide us to our strengths, which he did.

They were much better songs, more cohesive. "79th and Sunset" is me and Jerry playing piano. I'm playing the top part and he's playing the bottom—I'm doing my best Nicky Hopkins. It was just more of a rock and roll direction; even my song on that album, "Shine On," was more of a rock piece rather than acoustic.

Everybody knew that not everyone was going to have a song on this album. It was going to have whatever was absolutely the best, which was a different MO for us. Before that, it was,

"Jerry's got to have a song, Pete's got to have a song, Greg's got to have a song." Well, that didn't happen; and I think that's why *Rock On* was so good. It was definitely more cohesive than the Beardsley cover album, and more angled toward stage-y stuff. Then that led nicely into the live album.

But I could also see where this was all going. When I met Steve, I thought, "If we form a band, I don't have to sing anymore if I don't want to." That was the situation that I thought was the best for me. But then I realized that the songs I was writing weren't gonna fit now, because we'd done the first couple albums where it was acoustic and light electric, and now we're getting heavier and heavier. When we did "Shine On" on *Rock On*, Glyn thought it should be the single, with me singing, and Steve said, "No, that's not the single," because it was too poppy for him. Humble Pie never played "Shine On" live.

Rock On started getting some airplay in America and our reputation as a live act kept growing. Now we had either Dee with us or John Doumanian, who was our road manager. John, who has been a dear lifelong friend, has worked with Woody Allen for years, been friends with him since the '70s. In *Annie Hall*, there's a scene where a drug dealer comes into the apartment. He's got a big 'stache, and he says how much it is, whatever, and Woody just looks at the coke and sneezes so all the cocaine instantly goes airborne. The dealer is John. He's in just about every one of Woody's films, like the way Alfred Hitchcock always turned up in his own movies.

He had all these Americanisms that we had never heard before. "What kind of diet are you on, John?" "I'm on a seafood diet—when I see food, I eat it." A very funny, warm, and caring person, a really nice man. He would call you up in the morning—"Are you up? Have you had your breakfast yet?"

"Yeah, it's in my room." "Did you finish it?" "Well, there's an egg, I think . . ." "I'll be right over!" He'd go to each member of the band and finish our breakfasts. But we were all learning about America from him, how things work.

With the band, there had always been more smoking hash than drinking. Toward the end of my stay with Humble Pie, I noticed that they were getting into coke. I wasn't smoking pot, doing coke, or drinking that much, if at all—that all came later. Up until that point, I'd dabbled but wasn't interested. I don't remember Steve ever being drunk on stage or anything like that. Maybe he'd have a shot before he went on, but never drunk.

There was one time at the Whisky a Go Go in Hollywood, though—one night when we saw Steve's self-destructive side. He blew a show. He didn't speak to the audience, or if he did, he was rude. He was just not on; he was in a bad mood and we were livid, and we told him so, and Dee told him as well. "There's three other guys up there with you. You want to do that on your own, that's fine, but you've got three other guys that are trying to do a great show here and you're disrespecting them." So obviously the next show was phenomenal and we got over that. When you're that talented and charismatic on stage, you're allowed to have an off night. That was it, though; I otherwise never saw Steve do a less-than-stellar show while I was still in the band. His performance would always give me chills.

I was staying in a hotel in Manhattan and Dee said, "I want you to meet someone, come on over." I would just go hang with him, because he was a good hang. He was just a fun character socially. I pulled up to his Park Avenue apartment, and there was a limo outside with a huge guy standing next to it, and there's another huge guy with an ill-fitting suit by the door. I went inside and there's another guy by the elevator, and then I went up to Dee's floor and there's *another* one there. Guy knocks on the door, opens the door, there's another one inside. So I'm going what's going on? These guys look awfully mafioso to me.

I come in the room, now I'm a little nervous. We go sit in the den and Dee said, "Peter, I'd like you to meet Joey Pagano." "They call me JP, Peter—Joey P." I said, "Oh, okay, hello." And now it's all coming together; I'm thinking this guy was a hit man for Lucky Luciano. Holy crap! We're sitting there and he's telling me how great Dee is and everything—"Peter, you stay with this man; he's a good man, huh? He'll make you a lot of money." And then he says, "Peter, I have to speak Italian with Dee for a second here. Do you mind?"

I guess at that point I should've said, "Would you like me to leave the room?" but I was kind of naive; I didn't. I had never seen Dee that quiet or subservient, ever. It was the only time I'd seen him like that—very quiet, in the presence of the head of one of the five families, and they were incredibly powerful then.

Joey P leaves and I said, "What was all that about?" And Dee got out his cigarette holder, stuck a menthol cigarette that's out to there in it, and lit it up. He said, "Well, Frank Barsalona won't take Mafia acts." I said, "Good for him." He said, "Hmm, not so good for him sometimes, because they're going to kill Frank." What? Dee said, "Well, they aren't now, but they were going to kill Frank, because he won't take this act that they want him to take, and they want me to talk him into taking the act."

As the story goes, there was a Muhammad Ali fight coming up at the Garden. Dee was going to be sitting next to Frank, and they were going to give him the shiv in the back, the ice pick or whatever, right in the neck or however you do it. Dee was to get up and leave. Well, that didn't happen, so I realized Dee had saved Frank's life during that "Italian" conversation they had that day in Dee's den. At that moment, I really wished I had taken Italian at school.

He was letting me in, right? He wanted me to see how powerful he was. But I didn't see his power—I saw this other guy's power, and Dee was almost like a blubbering idiot. But still, he was able to negotiate that situation.

Until now, nobody knew that story except me. But gradually, everybody who was around me would tell me when Dee called them and said to them, "I'll have your legs broken if you mention a word to Peter about this." He would do a lot of that. I was completely in my own bubble; I wasn't allowed to know anything that was going on. And I didn't really care. It was all too much for me anyway. I didn't want to know how much money I was earning, because it was just overwhelming. My father was a teacher—I was expected to earn thirty pounds a week after my music career didn't work out.

Apparently, Dee had John Gotti meet with Steve Marriott, because Steve said he wanted to leave Dee. So they had a meeting with Steve and threatened his life. Scared the shit out of him. He wanted to go solo, and do his own thing; he didn't want to be with Humble Pie and wanted to leave Dee. And none of that was going to happen.

Rodney Eckerman, my road manager for many years—who ended up being a co-president of Live Nation before it was called Live Nation—was threatened more than a couple of times by Dee, because he was the closest to me. No one wanted any trouble, so no one told me anything.

My theory is that Dee was hired by the Mafia to be Tony Bennett's road manager. This is how Dee started in the business: His job was to carry the one monitor speaker, make the arrangements for the band, and be the wig cleaner, the toupee cleaner. Tony was managed by the mob, and one day—this is Dee's story—Tony had earned enough money where he came to Dee and said, "I've bought myself out and I want you to be my manager."

So Tony made enough money to buy himself out from the Mafia, but Dee never did. They stayed friends, though, because years later, at Michele Anthony's wedding—Dee's daughter, who became a huge record label executive—Tony was there, and Don Rickles, Bob Newhart, and many more. It was at the Pierre hotel, the meal's going on a bit, and Don Rickles shouts out, "Hey, Dee, can we have the boy singer sing now?" Meaning me, the boy singer—from then on I was always the boy singer!

Then it was, "Ladies and gentlemen, the show is about to begin," and the curtain comes away and it's Count Basie. There's Freddie Green playing rhythm guitar. It must've cost a fortune—well, I found out how much, because after they played, Dee said, "You want to meet Count Basie and Freddie Green?" So we went into a stairway behind the kitchen and there's Count Basie and Freddie Green, and I get introduced, "Hi, kid," one of those. And then Dee proceeded to get out this wad of hundred dollar bills and just kept handing them over until I thought he was never gonna stop. And of course, it was all my money.

I met and befriended Bob Newhart that night. His *Button-Down Mind* album was unbelievable. We had it at home, and it was the album that knocked the Beatles off number one. He's a wonderful man and even to this day, when I'm in LA, I'll call Bob and we'll go for lunch. When I'm paying, we go to the

Four Seasons, and if he's paying, he takes us to McDonald's, because of course he's really just an accountant.

So as long as Dee wasn't earning any money, the Mafia didn't bother him. But then, all of a sudden, he's got ELP in America, Joe Cocker, Ten Years After, all these English acts. He's got to steal something from the bands to be able to give the Mafia their piece.

I first started to wonder about this a few years later when we played two nights at Wembley Arena in London.

John Doumanian said, "Dee has me flying back to New York tomorrow after the first show." The promoter had been told by Dee that he needed so much of my fee up-front from the tour, and John took the money—all in cash—back to New York. That was when I started going, "Can't you just wire that money?"

Those Wembley shows were also memorable because on the afternoon of the first I cut myself with a butter knife, right through my finger to the bone. I had to play both shows with a plastic skin covering—I signed a tambourine in blood with my name and tossed it out. The show must go on!

John would tell me things, because he was a great guy and couldn't stand seeing what Dee was doing. But they still all worked for Dee. We all did. That's the way I felt; I was working for Dee, Dee wasn't working for me. Whereas ever since I got rid of Dee, people work for me and I've been in charge of my own destiny 100 percent. Mistakes and all!

I wish Bill Graham was still here. I really do. I miss Bill. It's not the same without him. He was a rogue, but he was such a lovable rogue. He invented the staging of a rock and roll show. He knew how to do it.

I remember the first time we played the Fillmore East as Humble Pie. The roadies had to get the gear there at a certain time because there were carpenters who would make little plinths on wheels for all the amps. This modification was needed because there were two shows a night, sometimes four acts, and they all had to come off and on; it was like a TV show, and I'd never seen that before. Bill Graham was there in the afternoon, watching everything—"Why hasn't that got wheels on yet?" He pulled it off; every show was on time.

For a while we seemed to be the house band at the Fillmore East—we wouldn't necessarily have a lot of dates booked, but things would come in while we were staying in New York. We'd base ourselves out of New York, and off we'd go to do these dates. But if we didn't have anything going on, Frank would get a call from Bill Graham, "An act dropped out, send the Pie." So we built a phenomenal following in New York.

We loved the Fillmore. Certain venues are just special, not only great for the band sound-wise but also great for the audience. I might upset people here—Red Rocks is wonderful looking, but it doesn't sound so good on stage. It sounds good out front, but on stage the sound is a bit weird.

Winterland was another one. That was everybody's favorite San Francisco gig—a ballroom, basically, that sounded great, and it was big. I believe it holds more than seven thousand people. There are these specific places around the world that just have this thing about them, going back all the way to the Marquee Club, which was great, and Eel Pie Island, a club on an island right in the middle of the River Thames in Twickenham—great places to play or see someone, if a little worse for wear (and with that lovely touch of damp smell).

The *Rockin' the Fillmore* recording was just another show, but it had an aura about it that made you realize that it was a special gig. Before every gig you get nervous; otherwise, it's time to give up or stop, because if you're not nervous, then you don't care. But we played there so much that it just became a normal show for us. That's why we were so comfortable, and we recorded the whole album in that one venue, over four shows in May of 1971.

"I Don't Need No Doctor" is a great story. We were playing Madison Square Garden for the first time, opening for Grand Funk Railroad. And we actually got a sound check, which was unheard of in those days. Our crew was getting our gear ready. Jerry's drums are set up, my two Marshall amps are on, Greg's ready, Steve's ready, so I just picked up my guitar and started messing around. Steve's out at the front-of-house mixing console, and it seems like he's like a mile away.

We're looking at this huge place and I'm just playing one chord; it's echoing back, and so I keep playing it and hearing it bounce off the back wall. I started playing first a loud E chord then a G and finally an A chord. Then Jerry goes, "One, two, three, four," and falls right in playing with me. It happened just like that; that's no word of a lie.

Greg jumps on the bass, and then I see Steve running from the mixing board to the stage. He doesn't even pick up a guitar, he just grabs a mic and sings, "I don't need no doctor," right over it. He said, "Hold on the A, hold on the A!—'I don't need no. . . .'" We did it that night and it killed. And from then on, we did it every night.

It's just magic when that happens. We had no idea that he was gonna come up and sing, or if he was gonna sing, and we just all went, "Wow! That's incredible!" It's a pretty involved arrangement, but we came up with it at that sound check and played it that same night, fully formed.

We played with Grand Funk a lot. Terry Knight, their manager, was basically learning everything from Frank and Dee; he was watching what they did. We did a European tour with them and kind of blew them off the stage. We were doing really well at this point. Then we did the American tour, and the first show was at Shea Stadium—we were the first band on that stage since the Beatles. In fact, the show sold out even faster than the Beatles' did!

The way stages were in those days, there was no roof. It was just a platform with lights. We had just flown in from England, and the airline had broken the neck of Steve's guitar. So we had a dear friend who had helped us out before, Frank Carillo from Long Island, and he could fix guitars quick. So I called him up and said, "We got a show tomorrow; can you fix Steve's guitar?" He said, "Sure—we need longer for the glue to dry, though." I said we didn't have time and he said he would do the best he could.

He clamped it till the glue had dried, and Frank brought it back for the sound check. We went out for the show, we got on the stage, played ten minutes, and it starts to rain. We're slipping all over the place, and all of a sudden I hear Steve's guitar going out of tune. It's going flatter and flatter, and the glue's coming undone and the headstock is bending. The worst thing that could happen. It had been in the back of my mind that it could happen, because now it was humid as well as us not having enough time for the glue and the clamp to do their thing. Steve quickly changed guitars, but that's what I remember most about that gig. There were sixty-five thousand people in the audience! It was incredible, the most intense experience audience-wise that I'd had up until that point.

We loved the guys in Grand Funk. We were good friends. Terry would try to enforce discipline; there would be lights out and they would have to be in their rooms. Then they would sneak out of their rooms and come and hang out with us after lights out, and we thought this was all hilarious. I'd never heard of anything like that before. They were a fun bunch, and after I left Humble Pie they asked me to join their band, but I said no. I was honored that they had asked me, but I didn't want to be in another band. It was time to make my own album.

We played Hyde Park in London with them, which probably had more people in the audience than Shea, actually. Grand Funk weren't anywhere near as big in Europe. That's why they wanted us on the bill. That was our finest hour, basically. A lot of the pictures on the *Fillmore* album, the daytime shots outside, they're taken from that Hyde Park show.

After we cut the *Fillmore* record, we took it home to England to mix, but we buried the audience and the vocals weren't loud enough. I felt that. I didn't really like the way it was mixed. We sent it to Dee and he said, "Where the fuck's the audience? There's no excitement. It's a live record; it's not a studio record!" So we brought the tapes to New York and got Eddie Kramer in to remix it. I don't think the band really wanted to remix it, but I could see it. So Steve, me, Eddie Kramer, and Dee were in the studio listening to tracks and working out where the audience should be and all that. The voices were louder, the audience was louder, and now it sounded like a live record.

When it was done, Dee came over from New York to London. The other guys all lived out of town, so I went over to his hotel to look at the *Fillmore* cover. I thought it was fabulous; it was a great cover. He said, "Well, you guys are gonna headline now, you know that. This album is gonna do it; I just feel it."

And I said, "I know, yeah. I just got something I need to tell you. I'm leaving the band."

Chapter **Six**

It was the best time for me to leave Humble Pie, because we were ready to dive off the diving board. I knew the live album was going to be successful; there was no way it wouldn't be. And I thought, "If I don't leave now, I'll get sucked in and I'll have to stay." I knew it was my time to leave the band and become a solo artist—I knew that's what I wanted to do.

Dee said, "Well, you better call them." So I called Steve from Dee's suite, right then. I think he was with Jerry, and they were both really pissed off and I don't blame them. But when I make my mind up, that's it. Big decisions are always easy for me—small ones, no, but big ones, I make those easily. Whether that's good, I don't know. It's good for my survival, and I have always been a survivor. But still I was sad. Humble Pie was the best band I was ever part of, but I just needed to start my own.

The whole Humble Pie period was basically two and a half years. We formed in '68 and by '71 I was gone. Three albums—it all happened in a short space of time, but it seemed endless while we were touring. I don't know how many tours we played of America, but it was a lot. We might as well have just gotten a hotel at Heathrow.

But we rose to the challenge, and that's probably why it all happened so quickly. We were like the Who inasmuch as we made great records, but we were something else live, much more bombastic. The energy was very, very high.

It had been decided that "I Don't Need No Doctor" would be a single, but we had to do an edit on it; it's seven minutes long. Either my guitar solo or the harmonica solo; there's gotta be a cut. I said, "We can't cut the harmonica solo, it's so phenomenal." They said to think of this single as a trailer for the *Fillmore* album. Okay, so, bitching and screaming, all right. In the end, it worked; it got us on the air and album sales started going crazy. *Fillmore* became Humble Pie's first gold record. It was a big success everywhere, and having just left the band, I thought, "I've made the biggest mistake of my career."

But it was time for a change, and that was it. I was giving up the certainty—as certain as one could have been at that particular moment—of success with Humble Pie, and that wasn't necessarily an attractive thing to me. I also thought my timing to leave would be all right for the band, because they could get somebody else in before the album came out, then bingo, they're ready to rock. They brought in a great guitar player, Clem Clempson, and they'd actually started writing and recording the next album, *Smokin'*—which turned out to be their biggest one of all and my favorite Humble Pie album.

I could also feel while on the tour, when we recorded the *Fillmore* album, that I was becoming less tolerant of Steve. That tour was the beginning of more drugs and drinking. Steve was driving everybody crazy. I wish he hadn't been crazy, but then maybe he wouldn't have been so hugely talented—you can't change one part of someone without losing the other. Everyone put up with it because of his talent.

But that wasn't my reason for leaving, really. I just wanted to be in charge of my own destiny. I didn't want to be in a band at that particular moment. I'd had my fill of bands and I thought, "Now's the time. I'm not enjoying being in the band. Steve is becoming a little bit more out of control, and the writing's on the wall." So during the tour I made the decision. I came home and I told Mary. I don't remember if she thought I was crazy or not.

Right then I didn't have any foreseeable income. Because I left the band, I didn't receive the money from the fourth and last year of our advance. So I started looking for more session work, which had really kicked in with George Harrison in 1970.

Mary and I had a great friend named Terry Doran; we had met him at a bar, La Chasse, on Wardour Street just a few doors down from the Marquee Club. He was George Harrison's personal assistant and had worked for John Lennon before that. We would be up in town and often meet with Terry. One time, I was in La Chasse with him and he said, "Would you like to meet Geoffrey?" So I said, "Who?" He said, "George"—each Beatle had a code name. I said, "You mean Harrison?" He said, "Yes; he's doing his first production for the new Apple label, the Beatles' label, for Doris Troy, and he's at Trident." I said, "I know Trident Studios, it's just down the road."

At Trident, you walk in from the street and you're on the control room level and the studio is down below. So I walked into the control room and George was standing behind the mixing board, and he looked up and said, "Hello, Pete." And I swear, I wanted to look behind me to see if Pete Townshend had walked in.

But I guess I'd been on TV; I guess he knows of me, right? You just don't think that—a Beatle knows who you are. I have to say your knees do buckle a bit the first time you meet "one." So he came over and said, "Well, would you want to play?" And I said, mumbling and stammering, yeah, sure. He said, "Come on down."

I go down the stairs into the studio and he hands me this— very famous now, I didn't realize it—red, refinished Les Paul. He gave me this guitar and plugged me into a little Fender amp and he said, "Okay, this is how it goes," and he showed me the chords. It was a track called "Ain't That Cute." It was for Doris Troy, who wrote "Just One Look," which she released in the US and the Hollies put out in England. She also was one of the background singers on "Shine On" for Humble Pie, so I knew her. "Oh, Doris, I'm so thrilled, it's great to play on your record now."

We started the song, running it down, and I'm playing rhythm very quietly. This is the Beatles' lead guitar player, so don't make waves. I'm just thrilled to be here. Klaus Voormann is playing bass, Nicky Hopkins is playing piano. Barry Morgan, who owns Morgan Studios, is a top session drummer and there he is. George stops, he says to me, "No, no, no. I want you to play lead."

Now my mind is totally blown. So I end up on this very first session, that I wasn't booked on, playing the lead intro and all the main lead guitar parts. George did a little solo in the middle, but I'm doing all the other lead guitar parts. And it was good, it was a great track. At the end of the session, he says, "Can you make all the other sessions now? I'd like you to play on everything." They'd already done a few tracks, but I ended up playing on six or seven others.

Mary and I would go down and hang out at George and Pattie's house called Friar Park. Klaus was living in the guesthouse— the gatehouse, I think. I remember at George's one night, Klaus saying, "I heard the finished album; I love what you're playing." On all the other sessions, it was Ringo playing drums. That's half the Beatles!

I made friends with Ringo, too, and went over to his house, a huge place in Hampstead, and met Maureen and the children. We hung out together, and I got to play his drums, and we just became really good friends. We remain friends to this day, fifty years later. We wrote a song called "Laughable" together for one of his most recent albums. Now if you think I was a trifle nervous driving to his house that day, well then you would be correct. "I'm writing with a Beatle!!!"

While we were remixing *Rockin' the Fillmore* in New York, George came into town to do the Bangladesh benefit concerts and he was staying at the Pierre hotel. He invited me up to the suite and so it's me, him, and Pattie, and he's got a couple of amps, couple of guitars, every Beatles record, and a record player.

He didn't tell me why, but he said, "Can we just run through a couple of songs?" I said sure. So we're running through "While My Guitar Gently Weeps" and whatever he was gonna do in the concert. I had already asked him, "Do you need an extra guitar player?" And he said, "I wish you could, Pete, but Leon Russell is bringing Jesse Ed Davis in," and I said, "Oh, it's not a big deal." Hey, I was thrilled to just be a part of what I'd already been a part of.

So we ran through quite a few numbers, and I'm wondering what's going on. I'm not playing the show with him; he's already told me that. We finished playing and sat down and we're having a glass of wine or a cup of tea, the three of us are just talking. I couldn't pass this opportunity up, so I asked, "George, can I ask you a few questions about all those records over there?" I said, "I love the guitar on 'Taxman' . . ." He says, "That's Paul." I'm really putting my foot in my mouth here, but he doesn't seem to mind.

I left and went back on the road, still playing dates with Humble Pie before the album came out. I would fly back into Manhattan to do more mixing with Eddie. We were working during the day, so I went to the nighttime Bangladesh concert. After the show, I made my way back to the side of the stage and I saw Terry Doran. Terry's going, "Where have you been?" I said, "I was on the road—what do you mean?" "George has been looking for you everywhere!" I asked why.

He said, "We didn't know whether Eric was going to make the show 'cause he was so strung out." So I said, "Oh, my God— you mean, George wanted me to play?" He said, "Yes, we were trying to find you. So stay here just in case!" If you remember the movie, Eric Clapton is leaning against the amp. I felt so bad for him, but I had no clue what was wrong. Apparently, they had to give him a shot of something to get him through the shows. He played great, but it wasn't his finest moment. I saw George there, and he says, "Where were ya?"

George asked me to play acoustic with him and Badfinger on *All Things Must Pass*. I played on about five tracks—"If Not for You," "Behind That Locked Door," and a few others. A couple of weeks went by and George called me again and said, "Phil wants more acoustics." I said, "You're kidding me!" He said, "I know, but we gotta do what he says." So it's just the two of us in Abbey Road, the huge *Sgt. Pepper* studio, on two stools, facing the glass, and there's Phil Spector on the other side of the glass. Might I say, I have always thought of him as a killer producer!

They're putting up all the tracks that I played on, and some that I didn't, so I'm not even sure how many I played on the final album. I know that I tracked five, and then with George, it might've made six or seven. He showed me the chords, and I'm a quick study. This was one of the greatest moments in my life, sitting on stools in Abbey Road, in front of Phil Spector. As they're changing tapes, George and I are jamming. Now, it doesn't get better than that.

Spector was quiet. He did keep on complaining about his stomach ulcer, but otherwise, he didn't say much at all. Not to me, anyway. His normal rule was artists are supposed to be in the studio; producers and engineers are in the control room. Well, that didn't fly with George Harrison.

Every time we'd do a track, we'd all go into the control room—two drummers, the rest of the band, maybe seven of us total—and Phil would look very uneasy. Well, Phil always looked uneasy. But, boy, once you opened that door and walked in, it didn't sound like seven guys, that's for sure. The first track I heard when I walked into the control room the first day, before we recorded anything, was "Isn't It a Pity." Hearing it on the EMI Abbey Road speakers, it sounded like eight thousand people—it was the Wall of Sound right there; there it was! Every tape machine is going with delays, echo everywhere. And it sounded phenomenal.

George was very, very excited about making a solo album. He was very happy. This was before Pattie left and she and Eric Clapton got together. Pattie, George, Mary, and I had all become really good friends and hung out quite a bit together at that time.

I've no idea why I'm not credited on *All Things Must Pass*. Must've been an oversight. I don't know. I never asked George, because I never wanted to bring it up. We lost touch when I moved to America, which I'm very sad about. That was my fault. I was in this other world all of a sudden. As soon as I moved to America, it all took off, and I wasn't going back to England that much. George was very kind and a dear friend to me, and I'm sorry I didn't get to see him again before he left us.

That's one of my disappointments in myself, that I didn't stay in touch with a lot of people who I'd met along the way. I've made up for it since, but that period was like being in a hurricane for me: '75 to '79 was just nonstop and I wasn't, obviously, in the best state mentally. I guess it's just the way I'm made, that I turn these corners and I start again. Which is good and bad.

We started playing "While My Guitar Gently Weeps" at a charity show I organized in Cincinnati in January 2002. We had lost George Harrison on November 29, 2001. The night before our show, I called the band and asked them all to listen to the track. Maybe we could try it at the sound check and play it that night as the last encore, as our tribute to George. Well, we did, and the crowd loved it. I had to convince them to leave. We have played George's song at just about every show since, and it always gets the same reaction. I miss you, George, and thank you so much.

The sessions for *All Things Must Pass* were also when I was introduced to the talk box. There's an audio clip on YouTube of the very first time I heard it, when Pete Drake was first making this crazy sound, and you can hear George talking and me laughing.

We had done a couple of tracks already and then George said, "I've got Pete Drake coming in from Nashville." Pete was a pedal steel guitar player who played on Bob Dylan's album *Nashville Skyline*—he was part of Nashville's legendary A Team of studio musicians. During the '50s, '60s, and early '70s, you name a classic country track, it's the A Team! (My longtime friend and cowriter Gordon Kennedy—who is a phenomenal guitar player, writer, and singer—his father, Jerry Kennedy, was one of the main guitar players of the A Team.)

During that session, Pete set up his pedal steel right in front of me—there's George to my right and three members of Badfinger to his right. Pete sat facing me, and we did "If Not for You," and it's blowing my mind to watch him do this. I couldn't get any closer if I tried. They had to change reels in the control room, so we had a moment, and Pete says, "Peter, I want to show you something."

He got out this metal box, put it on the edge of his pedal steel, put this wire here, plugged this in here and that in there. Then he got a plastic tube out, a clear plastic tube, and fixed it onto this new-fangled gadget. He then put the tube in his mouth and the pedal steel started singing to me. The sound is coming out of his mouth. And I'm going, "Holy crap, that's the sound from Radio Luxembourg!"

When I was young, there was this radio station called Radio Luxembourg. It wasn't supposed to be picked up in England, but from seven o'clock to midnight every night, they played rock and roll—American, English, you name it. So when it was lights out, I'd turn the transistor radio on and listen to that.

Their number was 208 on the AM dial, and their call sign, every fifteen minutes, was "Fabulous 208" with that talk box sound—I believe what they used in those days was called a Sonovox—oh, but that sound. Being a tech guy, I'm asking, "How did they do that? What is that sound?" And now here it is, right in front of me, the same sound—the circle is complete! How do I get one? Pete said, "I made this one myself."

That actual box that he demonstrated to us, his wife lent—with Pete's permission—to Joe Walsh to record "Rocky Mountain Way." Joe said to Bob Heil of Heil Sound, "Hey, Bob, this talk box is too quiet to use on stage; can you make another one that's louder?" Bob said, "Yeah, I can do that." So he made the Heil Talk Box. My then-girlfriend Penny McCall spoke to Bob, and for Christmas 1973, he gave me one.

I went to a rehearsal hall—it happened to be Foreigner's rehearsal hall, in their management office in New York—every day for a couple of weeks. I'd go in there and I'd plug it up and, on my own, learn the ways of the talk box. It wasn't easy to start with, but once I got it down, it got easier.

After I'd learned how to use it, the first number I used it on live was "Do You Feel Like We Do." And that first time we did it was the most incredible experience, because it got everybody's attention immediately. It felt like the whole audience instantly moved forward twelve inches. The connection between me and the audience got much closer straightaway. I'd just say, "Hello," or whatever I would say, and they started screaming—"*What is that?!*" For me, it's the humor; it was a humorous way to communicate with the audience, as another entity.

Joe used it for the sound, whereas I heard Pete Drake talk and sing through it. Stevie Wonder used something by the amp maker Kustom called the Bag on *Music of My Mind*; all the background vocals are done through the talk box with a synthesizer. Jeff Beck used a talk box on a Beatles cover, "She's a Woman," and that was the Bag, too; Stevie Wonder must've shown him one when Jeff played that great solo on "Lookin' for Another Pure Love" from the *Talking Book* album. But when I introduced it into our show in "Do You Feel," that took it to an H.N.L.—'hole 'nother level.

In 1972, Harry Nilsson called me up, and it was the same as when George called me. He said, "George speaks so highly of you, would you come and play on my record?" These were heady calls, I must say! I went down to Trident Studios again and it's all the same guys—Ringo, Klaus, Nicky Hopkins. Chris Spedding was the other guitar player. It felt as if I had become a part of this session team. Harry sort of took me under his wing. He was another one who became an instant friend. I'd hang out with him, and he was the most charming, gentle, caring person. Even when he had a few, he was still the same; he was just a little bit more gregarious.

He played us the songs for *Son of Schmilsson* on the piano or on the guitar. No demos—we'd stand around the piano and he would sing them to us. One he played went, "You're breaking my heart, you're tearing us apart, so fuck you!" And we thought, hey, you're going to change that, right? No.

Harry had all the songs finished, he knew what he wanted, and we all came up with parts that he liked. My favorite—and I can still see us in Trident Studios—I'm playing my Les Paul and Harry is playing acoustic right in front of me. Klaus is playing bass sitting to my right and Nicky on grand piano is to my left. It was just the four of us tracking the song "Turn on Your

Radio." I wanted to do seventy-four takes of that song! I still don't have words for the experience or the song.

After the Nilsson sessions were over, I got word from Ringo that he and Harry were making a movie called *Son of Dracula*. He said there's a band in the film called the Count Downes, and he asked if I'd like to be the guitar player. Harry was playing the Son of Dracula, "Count Downe" himself, and Ringo was playing Merlin.

There were two days of filming for the band, and the first was in a warehouse at the Surrey docks. It was a small stage where the band gear was set up, and the whole place was constantly being sprayed with fake cobwebs and, of course, fake smoke. But there was nothing fake about the Count's backup band. On the first day, Klaus Voormann was on bass, with me on guitar, John Bonham on drums, and Rick Wills, who played bass in my band, on rhythm guitar.

I had my Les Paul with me, but Rick needed a guitar. Our crew for day was the lovely Mal Evans, the Beatles' road manager, so I asked him if he could rent us one more guitar. There was enough time because filming always takes forever. Mal came back with three or four guitar cases, and we thought he'd called a rental company to send some over. But these weren't rental guitars. These were the Beatles' guitars (insert brief pause for reader to breathe).

Rick ended up playing John Lennon's red Rickenbacker—and if that wasn't enough, when I picked it up, I saw there was a piece of paper taped to the back; it was the set list from the Beatles' very last concert. John had given the guitar to Ringo while they were making the *White Album*. Recently, Ringo had a huge auction benefitting his and Barbara Bach's Lotus Foundation, and that red Rickenbacker sold for $910,000.

The second day of shooting was at the Speakeasy club in London. Our drummer du jour was . . . "Ladies and Gentlemen, please welcome Keith Moon." Of course, Moonie and I been friends since the Herd days, and it was great to get to hang out again for a day. This time we also had a famous brass section, with Jim Price on flugelhorn or trumpet and Bobby Keys on sax. Rick was playing the million-dollar Rickenbacker again all day.

In 1972, we had no idea what Beatle memorabilia would eventually sell for fifty years later. Guitar collectors love to say, "Give me $10,000 and a time machine." Think how many 1959 Les Paul Standards you could buy back then with that much money. Now they're each worth $500,000 and up.

Working on these sessions, I became really good friends with Nicky Hopkins. He played on a lot of my early studio records, and I played on his solo records as well. He taught me so much about piano—not that I could ever play like him, but I would watch and nick little bits he'd play. He was so sweet; he would come over, "Oh, Pete, that's it, you've got it!" Very endearing, quiet, soft-spoken.

Most great musicians or artists of any kind are usually modest or insecure or both. This is something I've found in my life: When you have someone like Nicky Hopkins, one of the few genius piano players, you know he will raise the level of your track just because of the unique parts he will bring to the song. Yes, he knows he's good, but by playing this amazing take and with a cheeky smile at the end, he doesn't need to tell you. When you have someone who thinks they are the bee's knees and tells you how great they are—it doesn't always follow. But most tremendous players don't think they are. They keep getting better because they're always striving to go somewhere new musically.

Ringo and George just loved to play, and this was a new playground for them because they had their own label; they could do whatever they wanted. Being with them together in a room was daunting. You get used to it, because they're just normal people, but that feeling never really goes away. Even to this day when I'm with Ringo, he's still a fucking Beatle.

John Entwistle had done most of the *Whistle Rymes* album, and he wanted to do one more live track. But first, he said, "I've got this other track, would you come and do a solo?" I brought my Les Paul and an early '60s Ampeg Reverberocket. I played the solo and John seemed to really like it, and then he said, "Do you mind playing on all the other tracks now?" The guitarist who had already played on the tracks was a good player, so I felt weird, but I did play quite a few solos that day. After that we laid down a track all together, played live, so yeah, I got to play with The Ox. That was fantastic—another dream come true along the way. I expected to just come in and do one live track, but I was there the whole day.

It was just an honor to work with these people. We're all fans; musicians are all fans of other players, and we all have people who we really look up to, and when you get to meet them, and actually work with them, it's the biggest thrill. I remember coming away from that session feeling totally elated, because so much more had happened in the day than I expected.

John was a sweet man. Quietly crazy, but sweet. In 2002, my band and I came in to play Las Vegas. My son, Julian, was with me and as soon as we arrived at the Hard Rock Hotel, where the Who was staying, a fan came up to me and asked if I would sign his guitar. Then he asked if I had heard that John Entwistle had died in the hotel the night before. We were in total shock.

Wherever the Who stayed on that tour, John had been selling his artwork. I had been so excited to see John and the lads; now this had become a surreal and very sad day. So I went into the shop in the hotel lobby where all his paintings were and I bought one.

It was Mary who played me the first two Tim Hardin albums and I was instantly in love with his writing and singing. Some incredible songs, like "If I Were a Carpenter," "Reason to Believe," and "Misty Roses." I covered "Hang on to a Dream" on *Frampton Comes Alive II*. I got a call in early 1972 from Tony Meehan, the original Shadows drummer, saying he was producing and playing drums on a new album with Tim, and would I be interested in playing guitar. Being such a huge fan of both Tim and Tony, it was a no-brainer. I couldn't wait to play on the sessions. It was in the new Apple Studios in the basement of the Apple building in Saville Row. We only recorded covers of other people's songs, though I was really hoping he might have a couple of his own new songs, too.

After one of the sessions, Tony asked me if I could stay behind one night and sit with Tim and help him finish any of his half-written ideas. I did sit with him at the piano with me playing guitar and asked him to play me any of his unfinished pieces. He had come to the UK to be part of a methadone program that was not available to anyone in the States. He was trying to get off heroin and was not able to concentrate on one song idea for long. So he would give up and move on to another. The short pieces I heard were potentially really great songs, much like those on *Tim Hardin 1* and *2*. I so wanted to help him finish a new song, but it wasn't to be.

He was a lovable, crazy genius with drug issues. After the session, I asked him where he was staying. He didn't sound too thrilled with where that was. So I said, "Come stay with us tonight." We got nearly all the way to St. John's Wood and he remembers he left his methadone by the piano. Back we go to Apple! Eventually, we were home, and I remember he stayed with us for some time.

After I left the Pie and I was doing all these sessions, I was in charge of my own finances. I did quite well, actually—but not legally. I didn't know; I was so naive. There was an offshore financial banking system that was the brainchild of Andrew Gordon—I'll never forget his name.

Of that yearly advance from A&M Records, I only had £3,000 left. That was it! I had left the band and also the last yearly advance. So I said, "I gotta do something. I need to make some money, because I need a nest egg here while I'm working out what I'm going to be doing next." Somebody said I should go see Andrew Gordon, who had worked with Robert Stigwood.

I went to his place in Mayfair—of course—a huge brownstone, and he said, "Oh, yes, Peter, come in." He knew me from the Herd. He said, "How much have you got to invest?" I'm talking to this guy who invests in the hundreds of millions. I said I had £3,000. He goes "Oh." Big rock star.

He said, "That's okay, we're buying this company and when we buy it, the stock price will go up and then at a certain point, I'll tell you when to sell." I said okay, and I had no idea it was illegal. I gave him the £3,000. I gave him everything. Idiot—but it turned out I wasn't.

I keep looking in the papers. My £3,000 went up to £4,000. Up to £6,000. It went up to over £20,000. He called, I sold. Unfortunately, I forgot to call my mum, who had bought a little bit of it, so she lost out. I felt so bad. But anyway, I was okay now. Talk about luck, you know? I should be in prison. But I had no idea. I believe now they call that pump and dump!

Chapter **Seven**

As soon as I had that meeting with Dee in 1971, when I phoned the guys and told them I was leaving Humble Pie, I started to work on material for my first album, which would become *Wind of Change*. I had quite a few songs—I was writing stuff that would've been apropos for *As Safe as Yesterday Is* or *Town and Country*, or even *Rock On*, but it was not where Humble Pie was going. At home, I had my little music room upstairs, a studio with two Revox recorders and a little homemade console, so I was putting these things down. I called Glyn Johns.

Glyn came over to our house in St. John's Wood, the house I had bought with the money from Humble Pie. I played him six or seven tracks and he said, "Well, they're all love songs. I don't think we've got anything here." I was very disappointed because I'd been friends with Glyn for years, but he was telling it like it was. He wanted another Zeppelin or Eagles, so I guess I understood a little bit. But that was not a thrilling moment for me.

Life goes on, more sessions, I'm writing more stuff, and I get on a plane either to or from New York and there's Chris Kimsey, Glyn's assistant engineer on the *Rock On* record, and we finagled it so we sat together. I told him I was doing my first solo record and that Glyn wasn't interested. He said, "It's funny, because Glyn just told me he's throwing me out of the nest—he wants me to go; he thinks I'm ready to be an engineer."

So that was that, we decided that my first solo record would be his first album as an engineer. And it was one of the most enjoyable records to make, because it was the first one where it was all whatever I wanted to do, and Chris was a wonderful partner.

Chris was still working with Glyn, so I had to wait until he had free time. We would sometimes work from midnight to six in the morning, and sometimes it would be an ungodly hour in the morning the other way around. It took about six months to do that record. Of course, the A&M folks decided to turn up on the day that I had Ringo, Klaus, and Billy Preston come down for the song "Alright"—"He's got a Beatle, an honorary Beatle, and a bass-playing other Beatle!"

I was so nervous sitting down with Billy at the piano. I'm playing the chords and singing the melody, and he's starting to get into it and all of a sudden he comes up with this piano part that dominates the whole track. Then Klaus came up with a great bass part, and Ringo was Ringo and played great. My friend Frank Carillo, the guy that fixed Steve's guitar at Shea Stadium, was playing second guitar. Just an unbelievable session.

The first band, Frampton's Camel, really started in the studio on *Wind of Change*. One of my favorite drummers was Mike Kellie from Spooky Tooth. Rick Wills was someone who Jerry Shirley introduced me to, and he was a friend of David Gilmour. I remember jamming with Rick at Dave's house around that time. So for most of *Wind of Change* the band was Mike Kellie, Rick, Andrew Bown, Frank, and "yours truly."

On "Fig Tree Bay," I put my guitar through a Leslie speaker cabinet, and Chris had this tape delay going on it, and the vibe of it was just so cool. I remember singing it live, in the room with all the guys. I'd realized that overdubbing later is a pain in the ass, because there's something about the moment when you are recording the track and you're all playing together. That's when it's all going down, because you're a part of a team, and when it's working, when it's all gelling, you don't think about what you're playing, you just do it. And that's what you always hope for.

I had to listen to the live vocal that I did with the band to get back the vibe, but finally I found the mood of it again. It was very difficult, but I'm very pleased with the result, and that was when I realized this was working for me and it was something unique. And Chris chose it to be the opening track, because it had this draw-you-in, spacey mood to it.

I was playing with different players for the first time, and they played so great together. The music was vastly different from Humble Pie, and I was starting to feel like I was creating "me." Maybe it wouldn't be a hit, but that's not what it was about. It was about making my first solo album of the best songs I've got and the best playing, the best of everything, for my first release. The more we got into it, the more confident I got that each track was turning out better than I'd thought.

Andrew Bown from the Herd came over before a session and I said, "I've got this song I want to do, but maybe we should do a cover of something today, just try something different." He says, "Well, how about 'Jumpin' Jack Flash'? You love that song." I said, "Yeah, but the Stones—can't do that." He said, "No, no—play it like Wes Montgomery, your style, like in octaves, and have a jazzy tone; don't rock it out so much." We did it that way, and that was another one when I went, "Wow, this is pretty good," and it became a staple of the live act. (Through a friend of a friend, I later got a message from Keith Richards thanking me for including "Jumpin' Jack Flash" on *Comes Alive!*—he said it helped him buy his new house.)

I smile when I think of it, because the vibe on the sessions for *Wind of Change* was a discovery. That's what it was—a discovery of what I could do as this solo artist now. The songs were working, and of course Chris brought so much that he had learned from Glyn and he was creating himself as well, as an engineer. We were both discovering what we were going to do for the rest of our lives, and he and his wife, Christie, are lifelong friends of mine.

The first show I did when I got my band together, after *Wind of Change* was recorded, was opening for Humble Pie on a tour of England. The first night, they all stood on the side of the stage and blew raspberries at me.

It was definitely a learning curve, because I was doing acoustic numbers on stage. It wasn't easy to do. When the band went off for me to do a number all on my own, and the crowd was ready for rock and roll, Mike Kellie came over to me and he says, quietly, "Good luck." It was a character-building moment, put it that way. I already felt uneasy, because I was opening for the band that I just left, so it was a little tense. But I had resolve, so I knew that it was the right thing for me.

I hadn't seen the bad side of Dee yet. None of us had at this point, not until money was being made later, so I wanted to stay with him. He said he'd be interested, but he just kept on asking, "Are you sure? Are you sure you want to do this?"

I felt lucky, because I was still with A&M, still with Dee Anthony, and still with the biggest agent in the world, Premier Talent. So Frampton's Camel were opening for ZZ Top, who were filling arenas, at the time of *Tres Hombres*, '72, '73. Most people didn't know who I was. There weren't really any shouts for Humble Pie. There were Humble Pie fans, but it was mainly the few people who had bought *Wind of Change*, and the rest were ZZ Top fans.

Then the next day, we'd be opening for the Moody Blues, Ten Years After, you name it, whoever was big. We were the opening spot—I'd gone down from the middle spot, back down the ladder to the opening spot, which was fine for me.

I hadn't been singing much in Humble Pie and I had no idea how to control my vocals. I knew how to sing; I just didn't know how to sing properly. We played one night up in New York State, in Albany, and I blew my voice out. The review I got for the show the next night was "It's uncanny how similar Frampton's voice is to Joe Cocker." For one night and one night only!

It was freeing, to say the least. I just felt like, at last I've got to the place where I need to be, where now I'm going to create for me. I'm going to do this whole thing for me, and if it doesn't work, I'll form or join another band. Because I'm someone with perseverance and never giving up—which I got from my parents—Frampton's Camel always went down well, but sometimes we went down *really* well. It was up and down.

Mary and I got married at a registry office. I felt that it was one of those things, marry her or lose her. We'd been with each other since we were very young, and to get that serious without playing the field, I think was wrong. Terry Doran was our best man, and afterward we went rowing on the Serpentine in

Hyde Park, London. There's a line in "Don't Fade Away" on the *Frampton's Camel*: "Side by side rowing with you, rowing with you."

We finished the tour to promote *Wind of Change* and then I went home and started writing material for *Frampton's Camel*. I'd split up with Mary, so I was basically living in New York, either at Dee Anthony's house, in his spare bedroom, or at Frank Carillo's place in Long Island. They moved his brother Andrew out of his room for me; he had to sleep on the couch. Their mother said, "Peter is not going to stay on the couch; he'll stay in the bed. Andrew, go to the couch." It was a very nice Italian family, great people, and they sort of adopted me.

I was in Andrew's room, writing "Lines on My Face," and I played it for Frank and his jaw dropped. He says, "That's a really good song!" I said, "Oh, good! You like it? In that case, let's try that one on the next record."

While I was staying at Dee's place, Mick Gallagher—who ended up managing and playing with Ian Dury, and before that also with the Clash; he's the keyboard player on "Rock the Casbah"—flew to New York and stayed in a hotel, and we were writing and arranging together every day at Dee's. "All Night Long" started with a great riff of Mick's; we finished that one together. This happens to be a song that was covered by one of my all-time favorites, Roger McGuinn. It was also the first time anybody covered one of my songs, ever, and he did it much better than I did.

We rehearsed at this place on the Old Kent Road, which was actually owned by . . . remember Dave Hadfield, back in the music store in Beckenham? Now he had a recording studio, and he's also got a rehearsal studio right next door. So, small world—here I am with Dave again, paying him this time.

One night before rehearsal, I came up with these chords, D, F, C, G, and it just went round and round and round and I started to sing to it. That was it; that's all I had. I went to the rehearsal and didn't say anything about it, didn't play it. We finished a twenty-minute jam and both Rick Wills and Mike Kellie said, "Wind that back like two and a half, three minutes, okay? You played a riff that we should listen to, because it was cool." We find it and Kellie said, "That's an intro right there— let's write a song."

We played that bit and I said, "You know what? I've got this four-chord thing, see what you think," and I just scribbled down the lyric "Do you feel like I do"—that'll work for now. They said, "That's perfect! That's a great chorus. Let's keep it. What are we gonna do for the verse?" I go, "Let's move it to A, and we'll make it simple, then go back to the chorus."

So we had the intro, the verse, and the chorus, but we spent a long time working on that intro because it modulates in the key—I think I said, "Let's bring it up a minor third, make it exciting there." And then it misses a beat, does a three-four bar instead of a four-four bar, a little bit of Zeppelin in there. No talk box, nothing; just extended solo at the end. It was a phenomenal day rehearsing. And by the end of the day, we had what was going to be our closing number. We played it at the very first gig we ever did. No one knew it was coming, and it went down a storm.

Going into the second record, there was no plan. I never plan anything. We needed a couple more songs. We had "Do You Feel Like We Do," which we did twice—the one you hear on *Frampton's Camel*, and one that was much faster. I don't know whether I chose the right one to this day, but I'd love to hear the faster one someday to compare.

On the Wind of Change tour, our drummer Mike Kellie had caught a cold. It was winter, we were playing places in America where it's really cold, and he's got one light jacket; that's all he's got, no coat, nothing. He would go off into the night to find things to elevate his mood. After a couple of days of this, he was walking around with just a jacket and we're all in big coats and he starts to get a really bad chest cold, so we called a doctor in and he said, "You've got pneumonia, you have to stay in bed. You can't even travel."

We all went into his room after the doctor left and started trying on his boots and clothes, saying, "Mmm, these fit me, you won't be needing these anymore." Then later the same day we all, except Kellie, went out to get a meal and see a show. On the way back, it's getting pretty late, and guess who we see on the street? In his jacket, freezing weather out there, it's Kellie with double pneumonia, looking for coke. So I thought maybe he wasn't going to be quite the fit for us anymore, and unfortunately I had to tell him that we were going to have to find somebody else to be our drummer. I loved Mike Kellie; RIP.

For the *Frampton's Camel* album recording sessions, I had decided to work with Eddie Kramer in New York. So I asked Eddie if he had a list of great session drummers, and he said, "No worries, we've got handfuls of great drummers here in New York. Here's the three guys I would say to call." I call the first one, no answer. I call the second one, no answer. No voicemail, no answering machine in those days.

So I called the third number, which was John Siomos, and he picked up on the second ring. I said, "Hi, my name's Peter Frampton and I'm going to be working on an album with

Eddie Kramer. Eddie is singing your praises and we don't have a drummer right now. Would you do the sessions with us?" He said absolutely. When I think back to how easy it was to reach John that first time I am so thankful he picked up. I don't believe he picked up any of my calls ever again. I could never get hold of him! It was a fluke that he answered the phone that one time, because you'd have to literally go to his place and bang on the door to find him—"Oh, I haven't paid my phone bill."

John was the first drummer I'd ever played with where we didn't say a word. He and I could just play together, guitar and drums, and we could write a whole symphony. Todd Rundgren said exactly the same thing about him, that he had a feel like no one else; John plays on "Hello It's Me" and the whole *Something/Anything?* album. I didn't realize that Todd had asked him to go on the road but that John had chosen to come with us, which was great. I didn't know that until much later, until I spoke with Todd and we talked about how great, how different John was as a drummer, how inventive he was—one of the all-time greats. Dan Wojciechowski, my dear friend, band brother, and amazing player, is the only drummer I've played with who can actually channel John when the band plays the pieces he originated. Yes, I'm one lucky guy!

The first track we did in Studio A at Electric Lady Studios was "Lines on My Face." It was a relatively short session and we had to be finished by six o'clock. So that day we only did the one track, and as soon as we started playing it, when I heard and felt what John was playing, it was like magic. The feel was just so unbelievable and easy. Everybody was blown away with how it was feeling; I don't think we did more than three or four takes.

After we finished the take we liked best, we all came into the control room and Eddie said, "So what do you want to do now?" I said, excitedly, that I wanted to play the solo. It was like 5:30, we've only got half an hour and we've got to be out of there. I went out into the studio with my Les Paul and this old 1960 Ampeg ET-1 amp that I'd had since Humble Pie, and I did one take of the solo and that was it. That's the one that's on the record. After I finished playing—and I can still remember the feeling at that moment—I looked up and everyone in the control room was whooping and clapping. That's one of the best recording moments in the studio for me.

It was a wonderful feeling when things like that happened, and "Lines on My Face" became such an important song in my live show. When talking about feeling a sense of achievement and where we were going, that track was very important. It enabled me to become more relaxed and creative, knowing that what I'm playing is working.

Stevie Wonder's *Talking Book* had just come out, and "I Believe (When I Fall in Love It Will Be Forever)" just slayed us. Mick Gallagher and I were playing it and we just went "Holy crap! We should do that one!" We had so much bravado— covering a new Stevie Wonder song?! But when we went to record it, no John. His drums were there, but no John. We called him, he doesn't pick up. So I took the plunge and played the drums. I was proud of it, and it takes a large pair of balls to do that number! And I wasn't finished with Stevie Wonder songs, either.

John didn't turn up the next day, either, so I played on a track called "White Sugar," which was not about cocaine; it was my answer to "Brown Sugar." It was about sugar in general and how bad it is for you—it was my health statement of the day. Playing drums on that one was hard, and there was no guitar recorded yet. Just me on drums, Rick Wills on bass, and Mick

Gallagher on piano. I had to put the guitar on afterward. But now I was really getting into this drum business.

After we had finished all the tracks, I started mixing with Eddie in Studio B. We finished "White Sugar," which sounded great, but I felt I needed to take the tracks home to England and go back to Olympic Studios to finish mixing the rest. I mixed all the other tracks on *Frampton's Camel* with engineer Doug Bennett back in Barnes, London, in the reduction room at Olympic. That's when I first felt I'd earned my wings as an engineer.

While I was in my relationship with Mary, which is mostly true of every relationship I've had, I never took advantage of the core of groupies, or any outside interests or fringe benefits! When I sign on to a relationship, it's monogamous. The music was all-important. But there was kind of a switch that was thrown after Mary and I got married and things started to go wrong. I said, "Okay, well, I'm not looking, but if something comes along . . ." I was ready to move on. So it really affected me that way.

I had first met Penny McCall a while before. She was the wife of Mick Brigden, who used to work for Mountain as tour manager. I had known him since our first trip to the States in 1969, when we opened for them. When I left Humble Pie, he was hired as their new road manager. They were in Japan touring, and one night I was playing in New York at the Academy of Music. After the show, I was the last one to leave the dressing room. Just before I left, Penny comes walking in. I knew her because I'd known Mick for a few years by now. She walked in and said, "You wanna come for a drive out to the country?" I said, "I'm not working tomorrow."

So she drove me out to their apartment, and I stayed the night. All of a sudden, I'm rather attracted to this person. This was an experience for me, new stuff—she was a bad girl and I knew that, but that's probably what attracted me. I'm Mr. Goody Two Shoes here. Not anymore.

One night we went out to her apartment in Bedford, and I just got this feeling. I said, "Do you speak to Mick on the phone?" She said no, the phone wasn't working. I said, "You're kidding me! What if he's at JFK, and returns home tonight? I have to leave, I don't feel good about this at all." She drove me back to my hotel. No, I didn't like that side of it; I'm sleeping with the wife of someone who is a friend of mine. It's horrible to think about now. Here comes the "but" . . . but I was twenty-four, and this was becoming a very exciting relationship.

I would end up writing two successful songs about her. "Baby, I Love Your Way" and "Show Me the Way," and later "I'm In You," which was originally part of the "Ways" series, first being titled "I'm in Your Way." She inspired another couple, too. "Baby (Somethin's Happening)" was one of them and pretty much spelled it out—there was something happening! No secret about "Penny for Your Thoughts," the acoustic instrumental piece on *Frampton* and later *Frampton Comes Alive!* Meanwhile, though, what happens when Mick gets back? And from here on, it gets dark.

Even though I had met Penny before we recorded *Somethin's Happening* in 1973, this wasn't one of my better creative periods. I barely had enough songs for a record. It was album, tour, album, tour, album, tour—there just wasn't time. You had three weeks to write. It was the worst received of the first three albums; it pretty much tanked.

But "I Wanna Go to the Sun" started out on that record and I still really love the take we kept. It took a while to record because I wrote it on piano and wanted to sing it live, but then again, I'm a guitar player! So it wasn't until the second day of recording that we got the take I liked. I remember my dear friend Alvin Lee of Ten Years After coming by to visit the first day for encouragement. It's still a very unique track with just me, John Siomos, and Rick Wills. The live version with Bob Mayo on piano and me on guitar is altogether a different animal.

We went back to the US and did a lot of touring. I was moving up occasionally to the middle spot, so we're obviously selling tickets. The trajectory was a mirror image of Humble Pie, the MO was exactly the same—play in front of as many people as you can in the shortest space of time, and steal the headliner's audience by being really good. You want their audience to remember you. We were building a following, and at this point my first headline show as me solo came in New York at the Academy of Music.

So I knew that the next record had to be good—we were doing so well live and I was in love or in lust, whatever it was, and Penny was my muse. It was very exciting. It was all the things you're not supposed to do, "Thou shalt not sleep with another man's wife," but I found it all very exciting. She taught me how to drink. I had always hated it before. Also, I started smoking a little pot for the first time since I gave it up early with Humble Pie.

It was time for the next record and I was very inspired. I wasn't going to have a lot of time to write again, so I thought I better go away for a while and sequester myself. I went down to Nassau, Bahamas, for three weeks on my own and borrowed

Steve Marriott's cottage on the beach. I took my acoustic, an electric, my boom box, and lots of legal pads.

When I arrived at the airport, I saw Alvin Lee and his wife, Suzanne, at the baggage claim area. From the moment I hugged Alvin and Suzanne and we said "hello" till they left two weeks later, none of us remember a thing. We had started having a great old time and I'm thinking, "Oh, dear, I'm not getting any work done." Then they left and I've got nothing I like. Now I only had eight days left to write the whole album. Uh-huh, yep, that'll happen.

The day after they left, I got up and thought that I really needed to get my skates on and write some songs. So after some Corn Flakes or Raisin Bran, within about twenty minutes I had written the chords and melody to "Show Me the Way." It just happened. I thought, "Oh, this is better than all the other crap I've been writing; this is good. I like this." The chords came first and then the lyrics were, "I want you"—Penny—"To show me the way." I wanted to know how she was feeling, because I couldn't call, she was probably with her husband, and it wasn't easy to communicate in those days on the phone from the Bahamas to New York.

So I wrote the first verse and the chorus lyrics and put it down on my boom box. I made sure I had a good enough version on the cassette so I could come back to it later and finish it. This boom box was a Sony 550A, and I used to love the sound because it had a really cool limiter/compressor built in that made anything I played on acoustic, piano—well, anything—sound really great. (There was an early Sony cassette recorder with a flatter shape that I had, and I believe that's the one Keith used to record the acoustic on "Street Fighting Man." It's such a cool intro to that song, and then Charlie Watts comes in playing on the first beat of the bar instead of beat two, where you'd normally play the snare off beat. Unique.)

A little later that same day I went for a swim, had some lunch, and then took my guitar outside—little table, legal pad, under a huge palm tree—and I started finding the chords to "Baby, I Love Your Way." As the sun began to get lower in the sky, I remember sitting there as I was writing, watching shadows moving across the page—so it really wrote itself: "Shadows grow so long before my eyes, as they're moving across the page." Oh, that's good! Once again, I wrote the first verse and the chorus, and felt it was time to move on.

Before I went to bed, I thought, "Well, let's try writing on my electric," and I tried an open A tuning just for a different inspiration, and came up with the chords and riffs for "Nowhere's Too Far for My Baby." So I quickly put that down on my 550A recorder, no melody or anything yet, but that's two and a half songs in a day. Which sort of put me back on track. But, as Bob Dylan says, sometimes you're in input and sometimes you're in output.

I had seven songs by the time I left Nassau, and I wrote the others later—some of them, I hadn't even written most of the lyrics when we recorded the tracks; I'd write the lyrics the day I was going in to do the vocal. Some are okay, some I wish I'd spent a little bit more time on. With "(I'll Give You) Money," we were playing that night at the Wollman ice rink in Central Park, New York. At the sound check I started jamming this sort of Zeppelin chord thing and John Siomos started playing Bonham-esque drums, and that's when and where I wrote the song—on that stage.

Penny came over to England when we were recording the *Frampton* album at Clearwell Castle, Gloucestershire, England.

We used Ronnie Lane's mobile recording truck, Reels on Wheels, that Zeppelin had used recording their *Physical Graffiti* record. It was so cold in this castle; they were refurbishing it at the time. You would go to bed with a mountain of bed covers on top of you. It was very English weather—so cold, and did I say damp? And in the morning, you'd say, "I don't think I'll have a shower today," because you had to get up, get dressed, go to the bathroom, turn the heater on, come back, get back into bed, wait. And then before you got back somebody else was in the bathroom! And only a bath, no shower, if I remember correctly. Thankfully we were all British, except Penny, and used to the damp and the cold.

We had our amps and drums set up all over the castle. The drums were sometimes in the living room, or the kitchen, because we'd move them all around for different sounds. For the track "(I'll Give You) Money," John was playing drums in this huge living area, and we took the front skin off the bass drum, with no deadening at all, to give it that "cannon" sound you hear on the album track. Andrew Bown was playing bass—we started off with Rick Wills, but Rick is kind of accident-prone, and he'll be the first to admit that. One time I lent him my boom box—yes, one of my treasured Sony 550As. He put it on top of his car while he was cleaning it. So when the car was nice and clean, he got in and drove off. At the exact same time my 550A recorder made a funny crunching sound as it hit the road, breaking into a million pieces.

The first time we went down to Clearwell Castle we had to wait a couple of days for Chris Kimsey, who was finishing another project in London. We knew this, but I decided we should go down and check it all out and start working on the music. One day I was in the truck with the engineer and his assistant. Rick Wills was down in the basement recording area and I heard him talking over the live mics there and he started saying that he didn't think the songs were any good. There was more, but I got from the truck to where he was in about 0.2 nanoseconds and simply said, "You're fired!" The first track we recorded after he left was "Baby, I Love Your Way." But Rick did okay. After our band, he played with Roxy Music, and then with Foreigner for *Head Games* and *Foreigner 4.*

Sometime before the *Frampton* album came out, I was driving into Manhattan, I've got WNEW on, and I heard my name. I'm at one of the toll places and I had to pull over. I turned it up. "Yeah, so the short list for the Rolling Stones' new guitar player is so-and-so, so-and-so, Peter Frampton." "Oh, what? You're kidding me!"

I called Bill Wyman and I said, "What's going on?" He said, "Well, yeah, your name's in the hat, innit?" It was Charlie and Bill who put my name in that hat; they were my two closest friends in the band. But I knew; I had this feeling that it would be Ronnie Wood, because he's kind of another Keith. I think it was down to Ronnie, Harvey Mandel, Wayne Perkins, Jesse Ed Davis, and me. Which was a total shock, but I loved hearing it.

Later, while recording at Electric Lady for the *I'm In You* record, Stevie Wonder came down to play a harmonica solo on a track. When I arrived that night, I was met by Mick Jagger next to the Studio A entrance, where he was mixing a live Stones album. It was a thrill to see him, obviously. I took the opportunity to ask him if it was really true that I was on the short list for the Stones. He said, "Yeah, you were. There was five of you." And I said, "Well, why didn't I get the job?"—just joking. And he said, "Look what you went and did!" He said they could see that I was just about to break big with my own career. To be on the short list was definitely good for my credibility at the time, which I then proceeded to ruin.

Anyway, we finished recording at the castle, and Chris and I went back to London to work on overdubs at Olympic Studios. Penny kept calling and saying, "Are you finished yet? It's coming up to Christmas, I thought you'd be done by Christmas." No, no, it's going to take a little longer. I arrived in Mount Kisco, New York, on the 31st of December, 1974, and we checked into the local Holiday Inn because she was out of her relationship and I was moving in. We had to wait for our friend Mary Beth Medley to leave her apartment so we could set up shop. So we thought, let's go down to the bar; it's New Year's Eve.

We went down and there's a band playing and I suddenly realized I knew the guitar player. It's Bob Mayo—he was in Frank Carillo's band called Doc Holliday, who Chris Kimsey brought to Olympic and produced and recorded. They were all in these band outfits, so I go up to Bob and say, "Hey, Bob! How's it going?" He said, "Oh, I wish you wouldn't see us here." I said, "Well, I'm staying here waiting for our apartment to become available."

As I'm watching and listening to them play, I'm talking to Penny and I'm thinking, "God, he's such a great keyboard player and he's great on guitar, too. I wonder if he would join the band?" But Andrew Bown was playing keyboards at that time.

So when Bob had finished one of their many sets that night, we started to talk. I told him we didn't have a bass player, and he said he'd play bass if I wanted. But I had a better idea. I knew how great Andrew was on bass—he played bass in the Herd before I joined them, and had stepped in after Rick Wills took his leave on the *Frampton* album sessions—so I told Bob I would see if Andrew would switch from keyboard to bass permanently so Bob could play keyboards and guitar. Bob had a great voice, too. As soon as I could, I called Andrew in England and asked him if he wouldn't mind switching to bass and he said, "That's great." Bingo, bango! I had a new band.

Andrew played with the band for a few months in 1975, but left after the spring tour. He told me he needed to leave to concentrate on his own solo career, which I totally understood. He has always been a great songwriter, and I think our discovery and love of the same kind of music—especially the amazing organist Jimmy Smith with Kenny Burrell and Grady Tate on drums—led us to writing together in the Herd. That was my first pro band and Andrew definitely showed me the ropes. Not long after he left, he started playing with another band, Status Quo.

I was sad to see Andrew go, and it also meant searching for another bass player. I spoke with Kenny Passarelli, whose playing I really liked, but he was already working with Joe Walsh. He recommended that I look at Stanley Sheldon. I called Stan and asked him if we could meet soon and play a little. He seemed excited.

At the time I was staying in Los Angeles, and Stanley enters my hotel room wheeling an amp and bass. I had my acoustic with me and we played a couple of songs and I thought, "This guy's good—no drums and he's very good." So that didn't take long, and he wheeled the amp out and he's in. Now all the *Comes Alive!* players were in place, and within a few shows, I realized we had a very, very special band—John Siomos on drums, Stanley Sheldon on bass, Bob Mayo on guitar and keyboards, and yours truly on guitar.

I felt my playing and singing were definitely improving along the way, and things were definitely changing musically, like going into fifth gear, with this great group of players. All of a sudden, I was doing things, playing different solos, and Bob was following me and guiding me at the same time. I never play the same solos every night, and he would change whatever he was playing to follow me, giving me this great harmonic bed.

Bob Mayo was now a huge part of the feel of the band. When there are only four players, you all have to be in touch on a special level. But that only happens when it's the *right* four people. This was a dream band for me and all of us felt the same way.

John's playing came from somewhere so deep and was so soulful. He was an orchestral drummer with this totally intense feel. A one-of-a-kind player. Penny named Stanley "Shelly" because our road manager at the time was also named Stanley, Stan Coles—who then, a few years after he left us, changed his name back to Brian because Stanley was his *middle* name. I've always thought how much easier it would have been if Stan Coles had changed his name to Brian earlier.

More important, though, Stanley Sheldon was an incredible bass player who played fretless 100 percent of the time, which added to the unique feel and sound we had. He was a total lock with John, and so that completed the musical picture. It gives you a great feeling of "We're going somewhere right now. This is an amazing band." We were just killing it. Audiences were going crazy—we knew something was happening!

When the *Frampton* record came out, it sold three hundred thousand on its own, so it pushed us up from the middle spot to headliner in certain markets. Regional breakouts is what they used to call it, and now New York, Detroit, and San Francisco had become places where I could headline. It was exactly the same as Humble Pie, mirror image—*Frampton* was my *Rock On*. Same number of albums exactly, before the one that hit. And I thought, "Well, we're going to do a live album now. We're well-oiled—even though the band is technically a new band—we're ready to rock, we're doing incredible shows every night." Before the 1975 US tour had started, Jerry Moss, Dee, and I spoke and we all said, "It's time," and we knew what that meant.

Chapter Eight

I had very little confidence at first. I was enjoying what I was doing, but I didn't know where I was going. I had never really thought past this tour, this album. I've never been someone who worries about what's going to happen in twenty-five years, or even next week. I built this following on the road, playing all these gigs, and I got more and more confident that it was going to work.

The best teacher on how to deal with an audience was Steve Marriott. I learned so much from him. But every act we were playing with could fill an arena, therefore we were always in front of a big audience. We played a lot with Edgar Winter, and they had a great stage act. Peter Wolf, another terrific front man, was with J. Geils and the lads. He would call me Limey, which I always took in an endearing way. He actually presented me with a basket of limes on stage one night. We did so many incredible shows together. ZZ Top was another band we played with a lot. I love them because they're superb players, but their staging got more and more over the top. One tour, I swear I saw cattle on stage. They're very funny, too.

I learned something new from every act—how they got the audience going, how they built their set. I would steal stuff from everyone, watch how they would say certain things and what reaction they would get. It was a great learning curve for me, from '72 all the way through to *Comes Alive!* It wasn't until the tour for the *Frampton* album that I really felt prepared to be a headliner. I wouldn't have been ready before.

We could have recorded in New York, Detroit, or San Francisco, but due to the routing of that tour, it worked out that it was best to have Wally Heider's mobile truck come up from LA and record at Winterland in San Francisco. It was our very first time headlining in San Francisco, so the event was actually far more stressful than even the recording. We had done previous live recordings for the *King Biscuit Flower Hour*, among others, and for those I would immediately go to the truck when I got to the venue and speak with the engineer. We would discuss details like how many mic inputs and how to combine them on twenty-four analog tracks. But this show was so important, all I could think of was sound checking and making sure we all sounded as good as possible. It was a very nerve-wracking day but luckily the engineer, the late Ray Thompson, did an incredible job recording us that night.

We only had an hour of material, because we were used to playing the middle spot for just forty-five or fifty minutes max. I wanted to do an acoustic set anyway, so adding three acoustic songs, plus a couple more with the band, there would be enough to choose from.

That show was also the first time I ever did a bump of coke before I went on stage, which wasn't good, but it was just everywhere now. We walked on and I grew two feet from the ovation. I'd never experienced it before, nothing like this. It was unbelievable—over five thousand people and they'd all bought a ticket to see me and my band, for the first time. That's why that show was so special, because it was so important, and yet all of the nerves just dissipated as soon as we walked on stage, because you could feel the love from the crowd. It was my time.

We came off stage, and you can tell you've done a good show when everyone in the band says, "That was my best show so far this tour." You don't often get that, but everyone agreed that night. Usually one person will be, "Ah, well, I know it was good for you, but I had a couple of flubs." We went to the truck and Ray Thompson played back a couple of bits and we were just floored.

The following week, we were playing LA, supporting Rod Stewart at the Forum, and we went to Wally Heider's studio. Ray said, "I'm not even going to mix it; I'm just going to leave all the faders flat." Bob and me and, I think, Stan were there; we listened to a few tracks and it just blew us away. The energy, whatever it is about that record, hit us and we just went, "Oh, my God! This is amazing!"

We were walking on eggshells with A&M—*Frampton* did okay, but it wasn't gold, so I still felt like I was pushing my luck if I didn't deliver. Dee said, "Let's just do a single live album; don't do a double one, okay? That'll be better for Jerry; I think he'd prefer that." So we mixed enough for one disc, none of the acoustic numbers, no "Show Me the Way." I don't even think "Baby, I Love Your Way" was on there, because we didn't like the versions of those two we had from California. They were newer and we hadn't played them as much.

Chris Kimsey mixed what was to become *Frampton Comes Alive!* at Electric Lady Studios. We first had to choose the songs to mix that would fit on one record. Seventeen or eighteen minutes a side is optimum; even twenty is okay, but any longer and you start to lose volume when mastering. So I remember side one was "Somethin's Happening," "Doobie Wah," and "Go to the Sun"; and side two was "Lines on My Face" and "Do You Feel."

When we had both sides mixed, I wanted Jerry Moss to hear it. So he came to New York, we went to the studio to listen, and he sat in front of the console. The comfy couch was a step down in front of the console, so we couldn't see him while we played the tape. We played him both sides of the album and I'll never forget as, all of a sudden, his head just came up over the console, and he said "Where's the rest?" And I said, "You like it?" He said, "I love it! But where's 'Show Me the Way'? Where's 'Wind of Change' and 'Baby, I Love Your Way'?"

I told him I didn't like the versions we had of those; the rest of the songs were ones we'd been doing for a while, but the songs from the *Frampton* album hadn't found their live legs yet. And he said, "Well, go and do some more recording, but I would like a double album!"

So we did half a dozen more shows, and got a great version of "Show Me the Way" in Commack, Long Island, where Eddie Kramer engineered for us. Then we went to Plattsburgh, New York, and recorded at the college, with Chris engineering. From that night we got the version I liked of "Baby, I Love Your Way." So now we had the two we really needed. We'd gotten the acoustic numbers a couple of days before Winterland, at the Marin County Civic Center.

Chris Kimsey actually had to leave before we finished mixing *Comes Alive!*—he had another project starting and we'd run over a bit—but he only left me two tracks to mix, which were "Show Me the Way" and "Shine On." They ended up being the A and B side of the first single. We had been mixing for a while, so we had a game plan going; the board was pretty much set up, ready to go, but it was still me mixing. I've always been proud of that, I enjoy engineering. The way instruments can sound has always been a passion of mine.

So it was now actually finished! The master then went to the legendary Doug Sax, the incredible mastering engineer who had already done a beautiful job on the *Frampton* record. When we finally handed it to A&M and Jerry heard the whole thing, he was over the moon. He was very pleased.

I was in LA on the A&M lot to work on the cover. Roland Young was the art director and he had pulled a few live shots of me to check out for the front cover. I had a look and wasn't sure, so I called Jerry—it's so weird that you could do that, call the president of the company—and I said, "Jerry, can you come and help me? I need some help choosing this cover." He said, "Sure, I'll be right over." He comes to the art department and he looks at the photos with me, and he says, "This one." I said, "Yes, I like that one too, but it's up the wrong way, the aspect is wrong." He said, "Well, we've got a double album, gatefold cover, so how about we turn it like this." So it covered the front and the back of the cover. Great idea!

I looked at the photo and I said, "But it's got only one light behind me on one side; it makes it look weird, a bit one-sided." Jerry said, "Yeah, and it's not quite in focus. I tell you what we'll do—I'll have the art department paint another light there so it's balanced." My dear friend Richard Aaron, who passed away recently, took the original photo, and he said that his photography teacher told him, "You get a photograph on the front cover of the biggest-selling album ever and it's out of focus!" He said that he got a lot of shit for that. Rest In Peace, Richard. You did great.

I knew that *Comes Alive!* was coming out on January 6, and we weren't touring straightaway, not until the spring. I had decided that Penny and I should go on a vacation, so we went back down to the Bahamas and stayed in one of Dee's cottages for ten days. Before we left, I spoke to Dee and he said, "Cobo Hall in Detroit just went on sale, and it looks like it's going to sell out." I said, "Oh, my God! That's huge, that place!" So I left for vacation going, "Wow, that's pretty good."

We came back ten days later and Dee said, "You remember I said that show in Detroit was going to sell out? Well, we've added three more shows—and they're selling out, too." So we did four nights at Cobo Hall, two in January and two in February, all sold out, which was insane. The record hit and by April 10 it was number one. Dee called and said, "Are you sitting down?" I said, "I will be." He said, "You're number one! The album is number one in every paper—*Record World*, *Cash Box*, *Billboard*, and *R&R*."

Say what? Career-wise this was the best news I could ever hear—I was in shock, I really couldn't believe it. As happy as I was, though, I couldn't help listening to the man on my other shoulder whispering, "How are you going to follow this one up, buddy?" But it was the time to celebrate with the band and our families. Still, the first thing I did was change my phone number.

Cobo Hall was just the beginning, and then everywhere started selling out. There were a few dates we had to honor that had been booked the year before, in smaller venues, and they were pretty much bursting with people. And then every time I got in my car and turned on the radio, there's me. I was living in New York at the time and I would change the channel and it's me, too! Whatever button I pushed, there was *Frampton*

Comes Alive! And it wasn't just the singles, "Show Me the Way" and "Baby, I Love Your Way"—it was "Go to the Sun," it was "Money." WNEW was playing virtually the whole album.

Of course, "Baby I Love Your Way" and "Show Me the Way" had been released as singles a year before and nothing happened. Only three hundred thousand people bought *Frampton*, so the majority of people thought *Comes Alive!* was my first record because it was the first one they'd heard. It was incredible. I mean, "Do You Feel" was over fourteen minutes and it was being played in its entirety on a lot of stations. WPLJ was more of a hits FM station, so I was asked to do a "Do You Feel" edit. How do you edit "Do You Feel"? Well, I did one, which was released as a single. It went to number ten at a full seven minutes plus. (WPLJ did their own edit, too. Tut, tut, tut!)

The whole thing from then on became surreal, because people started changing the way they acted toward me and around me. All of a sudden, people I would meet got this deer-in-the-headlights look on their faces because now I'm "Peter Frampton"—that other guy.

That first month when everything was going berserk and all of a sudden everyone knew who I was, it was very exciting. When you're walking down the street and you know that everyone's turning around and looking at you, it's exciting at the beginning. But I was almost apologetic for it—it's just me here, Peter, you know?

One day, I was in New York City with Vince Morrow, a great longtime friend, who was one of the managers working with Dee. We were in a limo driving to an interview or something. We got a flat, so we had to get out of the car on Fifth Avenue and I'm standing outside the car and all of a sudden, I become the pied piper. People walking past me started turning around and coming back. We've got to fix the flat, there's no-where to go, so I became surrounded and I'm signing auto-graphs on Fifth Avenue.

On tour, I was used to going down to the coffee shop, having a meal with the guys, just hanging out in the bar after a show. Can't do that anymore. I was playing with Lynyrd Skynyrd, and I came down in the elevator on my own. The door opened and the lobby was a sea of people. Dee and Vince saw me, came rushing over, "What are you doing outside your room?" I said, "What do you mean? I can't come out of my room anymore?" They said, "Not really, no, you can't."

It was pandemonium. They were all pulling my clothes, whatever. I'd been through this with the Herd somewhat, so I knew what I was in for. I said, "Not again"; this is not what I wanted. They took me back to my room and said, "If you want to come out of your room, it's going to have to be a military operation from now on." We would take over a whole floor of a hotel, we had enough people with our entourage of band and crew, and we would have a guard outside the elevator. It's like going backstage and the off-duty cop is saying, "Sorry, you're not on the list." Of course, at first I was still putting my real name on the hotel registry. I hadn't had a problem till now.

As soon as we went out on the Comes Alive! tour, it was nuts. We had already been playing with huge acts. We played our first Day on the Green in Oakland in the summer of '75 with Fleetwood Mac and Robin Trower, who headlined. But then in '76, we played Day on the Green twice! So we played Oakland three times within a year; that's over 180,000 people.

We started flying in private planes after there was a situation when we had to play an afternoon show somewhere in the east and then pack up and fly all the band, crew, and gear to do an evening show somewhere out west. Pretty soon after that Rodney Eckerman, our tour manager, rented our own (British) Vickers Viscount four-engine turbo-prop plane. This made things a lot easier as we were playing every night. I never counted, but I seem to remember Bob Mayo saying one day we had done over twenty shows in a row, no days off! Our road crew was twice as big because now we were carrying our own production, PA system, and lighting.

Dee said, "Just accentuate your moves," because there were no screens in those days. It was the first time they had three-tier PAs. To actually become used to playing stadiums was strange, but you acclimate. It became the norm. One weekend when my parents came over, we played both JFK and RFK Stadiums, in Philadelphia and Washington, DC. One was 115,000 people, one was 45,000 people. Same weekend.

All the audience wanted to see was the live album, so we had to keep doing that same set. We were out west and Stephen Stills came and sat in with us, and he said, "You should change the act up a little." It got to the point where we were played out. It was okay, but we could do it in our sleep.

After a few months, I got another call from Dee with the same direction. "You better sit down." By this time, the album had been at number one for what seemed like forever. My life was changing quickly in many different ways. But when Dee gave me this latest news, it had a jarring effect. He told me my live album had now sold more copies in the US than the legendary album *Tapestry* by Carole King—which was the best-selling album of all time!

As I'm writing this, I'm re-experiencing this whole conversation and the feeling it instantly gave me. Being number one on the album charts was of course always a dream—a dream for any artist, I would imagine. If you're a writer, of course you'd like to be number one on the bestseller list, or if you're an actor have a number-one film.

But to have the biggest-selling album *EVER* brought on a different feeling. I got scared, because I knew that I had to follow up this live behemoth and obviously it couldn't be another live album. It had taken me six years to write all the music on *Comes Alive!* and I could already hear the rumblings of our team talking about the next one. And I think that fear had a lot to do with my starting to drink too much and do drugs. The thought of writing the followup was daunting.

After a show in Manhattan, we went to an ELO party. We were placed at the "to be seen" table, a big round table in this club, and there's ELO over at the other side. Well, there's no cameras around them at all. I think it was Stanley Sheldon's wife, Judy, who said, "Do you know that everyone in this room is staring at you?" I said, "Yeah, I'm starting to notice that, too." I could see all the photographers, and our presence was totally monopolizing this party. It was embarrassing, so we all got up and went over to talk to ELO, which moved the attention over there. That was the first over-the-top paparazzi experience we had—which is nothing like it is now, but it was still bizarre. The photographers were already inside the club, so I'm pretty sure they knew we were coming.

This new fame, the incredibly large audiences and ovations, it really did seem to happen very quickly—one day, nobody knew who I was, and the next day, the elevator operator was telling everybody I was staying on the third floor. And everybody wanted a piece of me.

Someone later asked Cameron Crowe, "What happened to Peter Frampton?" He said, "It was like Peter was strapped to the nose cone of a rocket. They shot him out into space, he landed on the moon, he got off, and there was nobody else there." I thought that was a really great observation. And because I was the only person up until then who had sold that many, played to that many, I could actually start to say, "I must be doing something right. Maybe I am pretty good."

I always feel that I'm not as good as I should be, but during the initial onslaught of "instant fame," I started to believe that everyone was right, that I was pretty special. I allowed myself to have a big head for about three weeks, and then I realized that I hadn't changed at all; it was everybody else who now saw me in a different light. I've always been pretty well-grounded, but this experience of becoming a household name, seemingly overnight, was a bridge too far. After experiencing this craziness for a while, a new normal developed and I became me again.

Musically, I've always wanted to learn something today that I couldn't play yesterday. It's not like, "I'm as good as I'm ever going to be today, stop, that's it, no more practicing. I'm just fan-bloody-tastic; I'm the bee's knees." I've never thought that, and I've always kind of felt embarrassed about the success and the adulation. At first when someone would say to me, "That was great, what you just did there was fantastic," I never knew what to say, because I was embarrassed. Eventually, I learned. I taught my children, "You just say thank you. That's all you say." But I had to learn that.

For me, it's always come down to the conflict between the looks and the playing. Always. Over the years it has made me angry, because I wanted to appeal to both men and women equally. Up until *Comes Alive!* I was known as a musician—okay, I looked good, too, but the crowd had always been an even mix of both sexes. But after the album and the photo shoots in various stages of undress, now the girls are at the front while the guys are at the back. Feeling demoted from musician to teen heartthrob always bothered me until the *Fingerprints* album many years later, which was when I was finally able to say goodbye to that feeling.

For the *Rolling Stone* cover, Jann Wenner wanted Francesco Scavullo to take the shot. I knew Scavullo was a very famous fashion photographer. So why is he taking my picture? "Well, it's an honor to have Scavullo take your photo." I'm sitting in the makeup chair and my hair looks fine already. I'd shower, shake my head, and it's done. Now this hairdresser guy, who obviously knows much more than me, all of a sudden has my hair out to here. And he puts some pretty heavy makeup on me as well, and I'm going, "I don't really look like me." I said, "Can you calm it down a bit?"

I'm fully clothed throughout the whole session, but half-way through, Scavullo, in a broken Italian accent, says, "Peter, Peter—for me, please, please, Peter, could you, just for me, not for publication, but could you please take your shirt off, for one shot, please?" I said, "No, no, I'm not going there; I'm not going there again." "Oh, please, Peter . . ."

So more shots, more shots, and then we're done. "Okay, we're finished now, very good. Peter—just for me, just one shot, please?" And I'm so naive, and I should have known better at this point, but I go, "Oh, okay, one shot." I take the shirt off, click, one shot. One frame—front cover of *Rolling Stone*!

I'm sure that Jann already had an intention for the piece; I'm sure he already had the title written, "The Pretty Power Rocker." I could've done without the "pretty." I was on a plane and, somehow, Dee had an advance copy of the cover. He didn't say anything, he just put it in front of me, and I freaked out. I said, "They can't use this! This is a teenybopper cover, not a musician." Even then, I realized, this could be a big mistake here. "Could be"—it *was*.

Dee went back to Jann and said, "Peter hates it and he wants to do another photo shoot." So they took me to the beach in LA with another photographer, and I wore a T-shirt and jeans and the guy took a shot from the sides with my hair blowing back. A better shot—for me, anyway. It wasn't really a great shot, but at least it was a guy in a T-shirt and jeans, which is who I was. So both covers went to the newsstand; it was the first time they ever did that. The Tale of Two Covers!

When I was in Scavullo's studio, I really didn't think he would use that shot. But he was given a job to do, and I'm sure Jann said "Shirt off," so he had his orders. Because he just wouldn't let me out of the studio without that shot. But I'm thinking, "I've seen this before," and that's when I hatched the theory that I've refined over the years: A pop star's career is eighteen months; a musician's career is a lifetime. And I'm a musician. Lucky for me that I have perseverance, because it could've been all over after *I'm In You*—I mean, it really could've.

When I played the Forum, Ringo and Keith Moon came, and I sat with them in the dressing room. Ringo said, "So is it last week you were at the Troubadour, now you're playing the Forum?" I said, "So what happens for me now?" And he said, "Well, it's different for everybody, isn't it?" When he said that,

I wished there were three other guys I could talk to about it all. I missed "the guys."

The guys in Humble Pie were great like that. When we released our first single in England, "Natural Born Bugie," we started doing some TV promo. We walked into photographer Harry Goodwin's room at the BBC *Top of the Pops* TV show and immediately noticed he had set up a table with a pie and four plates with knives and forks for us to pose with. Humble *Pie*. Well, I think you can imagine where the pie and plates ended up? Uh-huh, the walls, the door, the floor—everywhere but in a photo with us. In his heavy Manchester accent he said, "Well, lads I guess we better try something else."

I played Memphis and I got a huge bouquet of flowers from Elvis. And of course, guess who took the card? Dee. I wish I had that, even though somebody else wrote it, just to see "Love, from Elvis"—I mean, come on. But it's almost like I've paved over the feelings I had back then, because it was so hurtful when everything crashed. There were so many mistakes made that I let happen because of my naivete. I stuck to the people I knew because we had done it together, I felt. Everyone was responsible in some way: from me to Dee to Frank and Jerry. (Later, Frank was the only one who said I shouldn't do the *Sgt. Pepper's Lonely Hearts Club Band* movie.)

I felt they must know better. But my feeling now is that nobody knew better than me at that point, because no one had actually been there doing it. They're not me. So I should've used the word "no" a lot more.

So it was a multitude of feelings all at the same time. "Wow, maybe I am good—maybe I'm *really* good, but I don't feel like it." I felt the disconnect between the perception of me and the way I thought about myself. This side's going, "Yeah, you're doing okay, my friend; yeah, it's going good. You're the biggest star in the world right now." And this other side's going, "Holy shit! How do I follow up that album?" Fear clutched my heart, as John Doumanian used to say.

We were in LA and Rodney Bingenheimer, the famous DJ, was there with Steven Ford, President Gerald Ford's son, who was apparently a big fan. Steven and I spoke on the phone, and I said, "Well, you should come to a show." We had to empty a whole row for Secret Service and everything. He came backstage afterward, took pictures; he was just a huge fan. Steven came to quite a few shows and then he said, "Would you like to come visit the White House?" We said "Er, all right." I liked President Ford, even though he was known for being a touch clumsy.

We flew from New York in a Learjet to Andrews Air Force Base—me, Penny, Bob Mayo, Dee, his wife, Valerie, and his daughter Michele. We got the royal tour with Steven, and his brother Jack was there too, and we went all over the White House looking at everything. And then he said, "Dad wants to know if you'd like to come and say hi; he's in the Oval Office." We go in and meet the president and he welcomes us in and we all talk for a few minutes. Then we go off and tour the White House some more and have lunch.

Steven said, "Dad wants to know if you'd like to come and just have a chat with him in the private area." It was an apartment within the White House. We went up there, and there's a TV on and the actual butler—the very one portrayed in the movie *The Butler*—was still working there then. He came in, very nice, and said, "Mr. President, would you like your drink, sir?" He gave him his drink, a gin and tonic, I think, and he put it right on the arm of the sofa, and I'm thinking, "Please, don't knock it over." I just don't want to have to tell that story.

We're talking and President Ford says, "Excuse me, would you mind, but Walter Cronkite interviewed me today, and I just want to see how they edited me." So now we're watching Walter Cronkite interview the president and I'm sitting right next to him and it's a surreal moment. He's the president; it's not like you're watching a singer or an actor, this is the president of the United States. The interview was actually really good, and then the TV went off and I'm starting to feel more relaxed, but still you can't get over the fact that he's the president and you're sitting in the White House, oh just chatting.

He said that any support from me would be a huge help. I was the biggest rock star at the time, and I'm sure he wouldn't have had me there had it not been for Steven. He obviously told his dad who I was and what I'd done. The president was very complimentary to me and just a super nice guy.

I don't think it was until I left the White House that it dawned on me what we'd just done. While I was there, I told myself to just get on with it, get over your nerves and try to act normal. I don't visually remember a lot of things in my life, but I remember exactly what the Oval Office looked like, where we were standing. The official photographer took pictures of us all in the Oval with the president, but it took years to get those photos. I remember what everyone was wearing and the scenery and everything from the private residence, and I'm thinking, "I'm in the Oval Office right now!"

Now, I don't know if it's true or not, and this has been denied, but I was told at the White House that there's an area that only the president is allowed to visit. It's a few floors belowground. And down there, under the White House, is a fully manned submarine that has a passageway out to the Potomac. I doubt it now, but why would someone there tell me that? And is it feasible? I wonder if it's true—it would be great if it is. Very James Bond.

With Humble Pie, I had experimented with pot and it didn't work for me. Then with my own band, at the beginning, they were all starting to go off and do things in bathrooms and I thought, "Oh, God, this is not what I want."

Dee was the first one to offer me coke. We were in London, I'd come to visit with him, and he's talking with ELP's manager. The manager gets out this packet of coke and says to Dee, "You want some?" "Yeah, I'll have a bump." Then they looked at me and said, "You wanna try this?" I said, "What the hell, let me try it."

The first time you do coke, it's a whole new experience, because you're invincible for twenty minutes, and you have all these wonderful ideas, most of which are rubbish. You do a lot of talking—twenty minutes later, they're still talking and I go, "Excuse me, would there be any chance of getting some more of that?" They started to laugh because I'm a newbie. That's what happens when the high leaves—you crash and want some more, and on top of that I have an addictive personality.

When I met Penny, we smoked pot and drank. But then once you've opened that door, it's not so easy to close it again.

We would do coke after a show—never before, never drink before a show. As I said, the first time I ever did coke before a show was before I went on stage at Winterland to record *Comes Alive!* That's why we couldn't use the vocal from "Somethin's Happening"; I had to redo that because I couldn't sing properly. That's the only one, though. I didn't even do vocal exercises back then. Coke and vocal exercises, hmm, somewhat of a dichotomy?

But afterward, you'd come off stage, go into the dressing room, and there'd be four lines of coke that the road manager had put out, and a shot of brandy. So after "Do You Feel," we'd come off, do the lines, do the shot, and then go back out and do the encores.

Being on stage in front of that many people—you hear this huge roar and scream of the crowd. You finish the show, rush off stage, and moments later, you're speeding away in the car in total silence. That's the most surreal moment of the night, when your ears are ringing but it's completely silent in the car. You go back to the hotel and try to stay as high as you were on stage, which you can never do. The adrenaline of playing a huge show, even if there are no substances involved—you can't sleep for a good couple of hours after that.

I remember finishing a show, a stadium gig somewhere, with David Bowie on the Glass Spider Tour. I jumped in the car with Dave at the end of the show. We're driving back to the hotel that night. We were so elated, so high, just from the energy of the show.

Our ears are ringing and David sighs and asks, "What are you gonna do now, Peter?" I said, "I'm not quite sure." And he says, "I think I'm gonna have a bath." And we just started laughing. It was just like, of all the conversations you could have after walking off stage in front of a hundred thousand people. Five minutes after you come off stage, you've left it all behind and now it's time for a nice bath.

Penny taught me how to drink and drug, so I have to give her the credit, unfortunately—but, hey, I only have myself to blame, because you can take a horse to brandy but only he or she decides whether to drink or not. Well, I decided to try everything at that point. I don't know why, but I do know the future wasn't something I was ready to deal with right then.

Penny was hardcore with her drinking, and I wasn't at all; I was a lightweight. It didn't take much, and I was not a happy drunk, either. I could never tell when it would happen, but I would freak out, black out, and go crazy and trash stuff. I think it was all because I didn't want to deal with the fact that I didn't know what was going to happen next. Or maybe more like I did know what was going to happen next. I anesthetized myself. So '76 to '80 was berserk, a time of just trying to blot it all out.

One begets the other. You drink and things don't happen right. There are functioning alcoholics and drug addicts, but I wasn't one of those. I was a binge drinker. (Because I have an addictive personality, you can imagine that when I say I have finished Netflix, I really mean I finished Netflix.) I would never drink every day, never really drank that much at home. Maybe at parties, but it wasn't like, okay, I get up and start drinking. I was never one of those. Apparently, binge drinkers do more harm to themselves, but who knows?

But one thing I never resented, even if it became my signature at this time, was the talk box, because I love it. I love its humor; it's very funny, the whole thing is a joke. I don't care who you are and how many times you've heard Auto-Tune on the radio or on the records that you own, there's nothing like when the guitar starts talking to you. Like the guy on *The Simpsons* said when I was on the show, "Man, that guy's guitar is talking!"

One night, Billy Joel and I were both at JP's club on Thirteenth Street in New York. It was kind of a late club. I'd been down in the basement with JP and probably someone from my band, and then we came upstairs and we saw Billy. We knew him because of the song "Piano Man," which was a huge hit for him.

We were out on the sidewalk and Billy's got no car; he was hailing a cab. I said, "Hey, I've got a car." He got in and we're talking, "Hey, JP's club is great. Did you have a good time?" So he asks, "How do you make that sound? What is that thing with the tube? Can you put a piano through that?" I said, "You can put anything through it if you can amplify it." He said, "Oh, wow, I'll have to get one of those."

Well, he never did. So forty-two years later, he invited me to come out during one of his shows at Madison Square Garden, and it happened to be his birthday, so I'm going to give him a birthday present—I gave him a Framptone talk box. He tried it at sound check, and I wanted him to just say, "Hello, New York," if he could, but he was too nervous about it.

But I don't like to use it too much. A little goes a long way, and I used to have just the two numbers that I used it in. Now I have three, because when we were recording "Black Hole Sun" for *Fingerprints*, Matt Cameron from Soundgarden and Pearl Jam, a dear friend and great drummer, said, "Oh, can you just do a little talk box in it?" Even the drummer from two of the greatest bands ever wanted to hear the talk box.

Chapter Nine

As I said, though, I was scared because I knew that there was something about the live album that was special. I couldn't follow up a live album with another live album. I had to go back into the studio, and what took six years to write—the material on *Comes Alive!*—I now had to write in a few months. That's when I started heavily imbibing. That was when it got bad.

Everyone's going, "Are you writing? Are you writing? You've got to record again! We've got to get another album out!" And I'm thinking it's the biggest album in the world; why would I need to put another album out right now? My agenda was, "Give me time; it'll probably take me a couple of years." The old rules: you have a big hit, you put out another album six months later. But no one had ever sold this much before, so I wanted to take my time.

You would think that the Eagles have put out twenty-five studio albums, because they're so successful. But it's actually only seven—since they can't stand each other, they only go near the studio when they have great songs.

A&M had built a new building next to their lot for their publishing division, Almo Irving. They said, to my face, that it was known as The Frampton Building. Then A&M started profit sharing with their employees right after *Comes Alive!* Management's agenda was much different from mine at that point. I'm the goose that laid the golden egg, and they need another one!

It was a sinking feeling. I sensed that I just wasn't going to be able to come up with the goods for a studio album to follow this behemoth. And I was right, and I *knew* I was right, and I was scared. The thing about being number one and number two is that if number one and number two are in the room, people are going to be all around number one. Number two is picking up a girl, having a nice evening, casually talking, and heading home. Number one is still stuck in the room, signing autographs and taking photos.

In 1977, when *Comes Alive!* was still a huge hit, Johnny Carson's wife was the head of the SHARE charity organization in Los Angeles. At the time, the charity raised money and awareness for cancer, and I believe they do even more now. When I was booked to play the Forum in LA, Dee told me that he and Frank were donating their percentage from the show to SHARE and it would be great if I wanted to do the same. I thought it was a great idea, so I did and presented a check to Joanne Carson at a restaurant after the show. I often wondered how the suggestion of my donation seemed to come out of the blue.

Well, the next year I finally worked it all out, after Dee told me I was to get a star on the Hollywood Walk of Fame. How does that happen? It was also proclaimed "Peter Frampton Day" in Los Angeles the same day I was to get my star. My parents were there, and it was an amazing honor and yet another thing that I would never have imagined could happen to me. The proclamation listed quite a few things I had done or achieved, including my donation to the SHARE charity. Ahhh. So I believe the donation had played a part in me being eligible for the star.

We're sitting at a table at the ceremony and Milton Berle came up and sat right opposite me, and they introduced us. I knew he was a huge star, but I had no idea how legendary he was at the time. And his opening comment to me was, "How's your Hampton, Frampton?"—meaning Hampton Wick, which is rhyming slang for "dick." I wasn't expecting this and didn't quite know how to take it. I didn't see the humor in it in that exact moment. But I didn't know that Milton Berle was so proud of his own Hampton that he would whip it out anytime, anyplace—I was not aware of the American folklore of how big his dick was. He was maybe looking for an opportunity to whip it out and show us.

I'm privileged to have been born at a time when, with my success, I was able to meet a lot of these legendary people, and it was interesting to see how they acted in public situations. I learned a lot from meeting them, how they reacted, and if I saw a reaction I didn't like, then I wouldn't do that myself. I always watched how big stars acted, because we all have bad days and the last thing you want is for a fan to come up to you and you're in a bad mood and you're rude. I've been there, I've done that, and I hate myself for it. I always try to put myself in their position; they're nervous and excited and whatever I say or how I act in this one moment we meet will stay with them for a lifetime.

They say don't ever meet your heroes. Well, luckily, I've met a lot of them, and they're all nice, mostly. But I've met some, very few, who were not nice people when I went up to them, and got rebuked. So I know what that feeling's like, and I don't want my fans to ever feel like that. I think I do a good job, but I've had my moments like everybody else.

I went down to Mexico after the Comes Alive! tour, with Cameron Crowe and his then-girlfriend, Mary Beth Medley, and Penny. We went down to Las Brisas, where you have your little pool with flower petals. I remember playing Cameron some ideas for the next record. There were probably about half a dozen songs that were virtually finished. But, of course, I left the tapes there when we left and there was no backup. That was a major setback for me. I tried to remember what I had lost, but I'm sure there was stuff that I never did recall. So then it was kind of like starting from scratch after already a few months of writing.

I'm In You was a record that I didn't want to make. I didn't really have any material that I liked except the title track, so we were just jamming in the studio. It must have cost a fortune. Richie Hayward from Little Feat came in and played double drums with John Siomos, which was my dream, to have them both play together. We did this sort of mock Little Feat–type number that I wrote, "Won't You Be My Friend," but I knew that there was nothing else there that I liked. Why was I in the studio? Why are we doing this right now? I'm not ready!

We were in Electric Lady for, like, forty-eight hours one weekend. We locked the door and there was someone who was supposed to come in; it was Monday morning, and we didn't let them in. We'd been in there for two days straight, and then we went over to the Hit Factory and started there with Chris

Kimsey. Bob and I were doing background vocals or something and we were just stupid. We were out of it, getting high in the studio. You come in the following day and you listen and you go, "All right, let's throw that away," and you start again.

I'd bought a house in Westchester, and my parents came to stay with me and I mentioned to my mum that I'd really like Stevie Wonder to come in—it would be a dream if he'd come and play. She said, "Call him up. You don't know until you ask him. All he can say is no." This is my mum; see where I get it from?

I called Motown and I got a call back from Stevie Wonder. Oh, my God! I said, "I'm a huge fan, would you come and play some harmonica for me on this track? It's called 'Rocky's Hot Club' and it's sort of Django-ish." And he said sure. I hung up and I went, "Mum, you were right."

So one night at the end of '76, I walk down the stairs in Electric Lady, and Mick Jagger is standing there. He said, "I hear you've got Stevie Wonder playing harmonica. Would it be okay if I came in to watch?" I said of course, of course.

Stevie gets there and he's working out a part and I said, "Well, we should record this." Eddie Kramer wasn't there that day, so Eddie's assistant Frankie D'Augusta was engineering. Stevie's out there working on the part and I'm saying, "Record it, just record everything he's doing." And Mick's going, "But he's only working out the part right now." I said, "Yeah, him working out a part is like gold dust—I don't want to miss anything." So he gets it and of course it's phenomenal, and then he says his goodbyes. Calvin, Stevie's brother, was there and they left together and I thought that was the last time I'd ever see Stevie, but it wasn't.

April 22, 1977, was my twenty-seventh birthday and we're still recording, and the door opens and in comes Stevie Wonder holding a big box. He walked in with a brand-new Nakamichi cassette player, a huge thing, and its travel case, and these great headphones that had microphones in each ear too. It was kind of mind-blowing at the time. I wanted him to sing, but they had already opened the champagne and he was drinking it. I said, "So what do you think about singing?" He said, "You got me too drunk!" That's one of my best birthdays ever.

Stevie had this phone number and when you called it, the voice mail answered and it was him saying, "I'm going to play you something now, and when I've finished, leave your message but leave me some music."

At first my father hadn't been keen on the Beatles. But by the time they released *A Hard Day's Night*, he was a big fan. They were okay then; clean-cut, wearing suits, and he got used to their hair being a little over their ears. The Stones, Dad would say, "look so filthy!" My parents arrived at the studio later that evening and missed seeing Stevie, but they walked right into Mick Jagger.

I was watching through the glass as Dad arrived, and then Mick and my dad were standing in the studio talking to each other. I was just smiling and thinking of things my dad had said about the Stones. I have no idea what they were talking about, but Dad loved it. He really liked Mick. He said, "He's a wonderful chap. I never realized! What a nice man!"

I said, "Would you sing on a chorus for me, Mick? I let you listen to Stevie." He said okay, but he didn't feel in great voice. After, he said, "Maybe I'll do that again, on another day"—but I knew he would never come back, so I kept it and I used it. I probably shouldn't have, but I did. But when I asked if I could put his name on the album, he said no. Stevie said yes, but I wasn't allowed to use a picture of him. This was in the days when the record companies were so weird about all that stuff. Maybe because we all bought a lot of albums back then.

It was one of the worst periods of my life, doing *I'm In You*. Chris Kimsey left, said he had to go off and work on another project. But I was throwing tantrums in the studio because I was scared stiff that I didn't have the goods. Honestly, I'm surprised it came out as good as it did. It's definitely not my favorite, and the only decent track on there was the single, which went to number two, but all of a sudden I'm now a teenybopper artist.

And the outfit on the album cover is ridiculous—again. Didn't I learn? Stick with jeans and a T-shirt. Another very famous photographer, Irving Penn, was booked to take the cover shot. He came in and I'm sitting with the satin pants and the Little Lord Fauntleroy shirt and the puffed-up hair, again, and he sat me down and he goes click, click; "All right, that's it." It was so stupid of me to let that happen. But I think I'd given up at that point. I think I'd just said uncle. I didn't want to do the record, so I just kind of went along with it. And the combination of that cover and "I'm In You" being a ballad was a disaster for me the musician.

I was in this bubble, and time was standing still. That's what happens. I was so separated from everything that I didn't move on. I stagnated at that point. What should've happened is that I should've found a great producer, and before we went anywhere near the studio, we should've worked together for a long time—go away, write some more, come back and "Yeah, I like this, this is good." Work as a team. But I'd never worked with just a producer, and I should have cowritten with different great songwriters.

There was no time for input; it was all output. I needed at least two years off the road, not making a record, just to come to terms with what had happened, instead of pushing on. Taking the time to recuperate from what no one had done before. That was the mistake, and I wasn't strong enough at that time to say anything.

I remember Jerry Moss (who I have the utmost respect for, and he has always been a great friend) said, "The longer you take to make the next record, the worse it's going to be." And I agreed with him at that point, but I actually think he was wrong. I know what he was saying. The more time you take, the more the pressure's going to build and build and build. But no one came to me and said, "Why don't you work with so-and-so, this great producer?" I could have had my pick. Or maybe they did and I said, "No, I'll do it my way"—the control freak. It's very easy to look back and see what I should've done, but since then I have spent many years learning how to get out of my own way!

I'm In You came out in '77. Which is ridiculous—*Comes Alive!* was still on the charts. People get greedy. It's almost like we doused the success of *Comes Alive!* by releasing *I'm In You*. Yes, I was pushed into doing it, but I went along with it all, I have to take responsibility. It was my fault, too.

Dee didn't want anyone near me. Remember, he only got to keep a little of the money because he had to give most of it to the Mafia. He was running out of cash, and there was so much going on that I didn't know about. I would just pick up little hints, the bagman going back to New York and all that stuff.

But I believe that's another reason why I was pushed into the studio, because of someone pushing him.

At the American Music Awards, I was sitting in the front row, because they expected me to have to walk up. When I didn't get the award for best rock/pop album, during a commercial Dick Clark said something along the lines of "I'm sure there's a very surprised person in the audience, and a lot of other people, too, who thought this wasn't going to go this way." It was like a foregone conclusion, but I think *Frampton Comes Alive!* had sold too many and the Eagles' *Hotel California* deserved to win anyway—and I also didn't get a Grammy; I got the People's Choice Award, for Favorite Male Performer of the Year, and the *Rolling Stone* readers' awards.

We did some dates with Fleetwood Mac, whose *Rumours* came out in early 1977. I remember speaking to Lindsey Buckingham and saying that we should do more shows together. I was thrilled with their success. It wasn't a competition. The Eagles, I couldn't believe we kept them at number two. Again, "Am I good enough? I'm above the Eagles?" Then I'd be number two and they'd go to number one—and we both toggled back and forth between the two top spots that whole summer. I was selling a million records a week at one point. I was the first person to sell a million cassettes. Horrible quality, but I was the guy.

A kind of numbness from the success set in. The I'm In You tour was very successful, but I didn't feel that the pitch of the audience was quite the same, and that's my job, to read the audience. The I'm In You tour was all girls. The Comes Alive! tour was much more of a fifty-fifty mix, a general crowd. And then as it went along, it was more girls. Girls come to the front, the guys go to the back. Now the guys hate me because all the girls are at the front, so I've lost my male audience. *I'm In You* did not have anything like the energy of the live record. So I don't blame them.

I was hating every moment, not really caring anymore. We were starting to get bad reviews because the show was suffering. Our first gig for the I'm In You tour was JFK Stadium again. What I found out about JFK the first time was that the capacity was 115,000. That's the number of tickets they told everybody were sold—but Dee and a promoter had printed up another ten or fifteen thousand tickets and sold those and kept all that money themselves. There were actually 125,000 people there, but I was only paid on 115,000. It was all too much money, and they knew exactly what they were doing and at the time I had not a clue.

When we were recording *I'm In You*, after the tracks were done, John Siomos's brother came to the studio and said, "John's in a really bad way." I said, "What do you mean?" He said, "Well, he needs to get off heroin. There's a way we can do it so that he doesn't have to go through withdrawal—I've got this doctor that'll put him out for three to four days and then he'll wake up and he'll be over the worst of it."

I loved John. As big of a problem as he was, he was still my friend. So I said, "What are your plans?" "Well, we'll just take him down to the islands and get him out of the way, put him to sleep for a week, baby him back, and then come back." Well, guess who's paying the bill? So three of them fly down privately—anything to save John. It saved his life, but they kept on calling me and saying they needed more money. Now I felt like I was being ripped off by the doctor. Everybody wanted a piece.

John started the I'm In You tour, but he just left one day when he got in bad shape again. We were basically playing the exact same show, but John was there one day, then he wasn't there another day. The first night he left we had no drummer, so Bob played most of the night and I played drums for his piano solo. We had to start flying drummers in. We were doing these mammoth stadiums with pick-up drummers for the night. We tried them all, and of course no one fit like John. They could be the best drummer in the world, but they weren't John, so it didn't work. So now the band didn't even sound like the band anymore. It was all falling apart. The saving grace was dear Joe Vitale, who we finally asked to come play with us, and suddenly all was good again and I felt safe.

My brother had graduated from college and came out to be with me on the I'm In You tour; he was in charge of getting the bags off the plane. After six weeks or so Dee could see that Clive was having too much of a humanizing effect on me, and I was getting a family reality check. Dee felt threatened by this and made the excuse that his daughter Marla needed to leave the tour, and could Clive chaperone her to Washington, where her sister Michele was staying. My brother tells me; nobody else tells me. *The emperor has no clothes.*

Everywhere we go, I'm in a suite of a hotel. It's like the scene at the end of *2001*, when he's old and sitting in the all-white room. His little capsule is over in the corner. He's got what looks like a room service table and all you hear is the knife and the fork on the plate. No music, just very severe. Everything is so intense at that point and you're trying to work out what the hell's going on. Well, every day, I'm sitting at this room service table, alone, with the noise of the plate and the knife and the fork.

When my brother came, he must've stayed a couple of weeks, and we'd sit at this same room service table and I'd say, "Clive, I hate this. I want to go home. It's all going to hell." And he said, "Well, you should." I went to everybody, Dee and all the powers that be—because that's the way I felt, that they were the power, they had me convinced of that—and they all said, "You can't do that! Do you not understand how much money that would cost you? They'd sue you. All these shows have been booked; they're all sold out." I said, "Well, I don't feel like doing it, this isn't what I want to do."

Still, after the mammoth success of *Comes Alive!* I wanted to sign with Dee for life, literally. Vince Morrow came to me and said, "You can't do that," because he knew. But I was thinking, "Look how great everything's going—I want Frank, I want Dee, I want Jerry, I want everybody as my team," not realizing at all what was going on behind the scenes. In the end, I signed with him for ten years. Which is not a normal contract; the normal contract would be three or four.

I bought a house in Nassau, Bahamas, next to Frank's, right on the ocean. In New York I had my own driver/body guard now, Kevin Moran, and we're now driving a Mercedes. Kevin also looked after the property in Westchester, and I'm hidden away up this long driveway pretty cut off from everything. I had a camera at the gate, one of the very first. The camera was tied into TV Channel 3, which was always an unused channel in New York. Whenever commercials would come on, we'd switch to Channel 3 to have a look and see what was going on at the gate.

We had a guard at the gate, in a guard box. There were all these people outside the gate having their photo taken and we're watching and laughing—until we found out that the guards were letting people come up to the house if they gave the guards a blowjob. Martha Quinn, one of the original VJs on MTV, was one of the "girls at the gate." She told me that she used to come there because she lived close by.

It was forty acres of trees, a huge driveway; it was actually a house that had been a hunting lodge, and Martin Luther King, Jr. had used it for meetings. We turned the hunting lodge into a big house, with a studio and everything.

The beauty of the record deal was that Dee had nothing to do with it—unfortunately for him, fortunately for me. A&M paid me directly, because he wasn't around when I signed that deal. But everything was going good. I thought you needed a tough manager, and at that point I did. I hadn't been able to think about anything long enough to realize I was probably being screwed.

I didn't really go to accountant meetings. I didn't want to know. It was one of those things—"You take care of it, that's your job." And of course, Dee was meddling with all of it. My accountant was his accountant; his lawyer was my lawyer. It was all bullshit, and it was my own fault. But things were going well, so why change it? They (whoever "they" are) say you don't start making good adult decisions until your brain has reached its full potential when you're about thirty. That's my excuse and I'm sticking to it.

It wasn't until '79 when I said, "Where's my publishing money?" Originally, I was signed directly to Almo Irving, A&M's publishing company, with a songwriter's deal. I got my songwriting money, they got the publishing money. When Dee came in, he said, "We'll redo that," because he wanted to get some of that for himself.

"What we'll do," he said, "is we'll call it FramDee, and I'll co-publish with you." I said, "Oh, good"—not realizing that if there's a dollar, up until then I got all the writer's share; that's fifty cents, and the publishing company got the other fifty cents. Now Almo was going to take 20 percent of the publisher's share, and then the rest of it would be split between Dee and me. That's what he told me, and that's what the lawyer Elliott Hoffman told me. But in fact, I didn't get any of the publishing side; Dee took it all. I just got my writer's share again; he'd cut himself in for 30 percent, basically. Plus he took 20 percent of my entire gross income.

When I was touring, God alone knows who Penny was with, and I really didn't care what she did anymore. She was off with somebody else, so fuck you, then; I'm going to. Up until that point, I thought we had an exclusive relationship. I had signed on and as usual when I did sign on, no cheating. Why would you do that and affect the relationship forever? But Penny didn't care, so I finally didn't, either. She would just sort of turn up when she felt like it, probably when she needed more money.

There was a shop in New York called Jumpin' Jack Flash and they had every color of satin pants known to man. Her friend who worked there was basically a drug dealer. So Penny was going to Jumpin' Jack Flash to pick up clothes for me; meanwhile, she was using my money. He overcharged her for the pants and anything else she bought there, so then the "overage" would cover her drugs. "Wow! How many pairs did you get?" That's why I wore satin pants all the time, because of her drug habit.

Penny was cheating on me like crazy. I didn't know; I assumed, but didn't know, so it's okay if you don't know. It culminated at one of the Day on the Green shows in '77. She came back after we'd split up, and we're playing with Skynyrd—the bands with the two longest rock songs in history in one show! We had stayed up late the night before, but Dee had taught me this trick of his. If you're doing all daytime shows, it's fine. But when you've got a nighttime show, then you've got to travel. And if you've then got an afternoon show the next day, like all the stadium shows were, this is what you do: set your alarm for two hours before you have to get ready; wake up and take one of these pills—it's green and clear, a time-release upper; go back to sleep and then when you wake up, you wake up like *b-dang!* The other option was the black beauty, which was all instant, it wasn't time release. I hated those; those were horrible.

So I hadn't slept, I was high as a kite, and I was drinking toward the end of the set. People started walking out because "Do You Feel" was about an hour long; it's the only time in my entire career that I went on stage out of it, completely gone. It was then that I found out somebody else she'd slept with or whatever. We were going back to the hotel, and on the way in the limo we're arguing. She's high, I'm high on the uppers, we're going at it hammer and tongs. They put us in separate rooms that were next to each other, but no connecting door, so we're screaming at each other through the walls. That's how bad it was, and that was kind of the end of our relationship, I think. It was on again, off again, on again, off again from then on, but that was that.

In '77, we'd gone to all daytime shows, festivals, and stadiums, so we hadn't needed massive stage lighting, just maybe some fill light. We'd changed the stage floor color from black to white, the equipment is white, everything's white, so as long as you didn't wear white you would stand out. Our first nighttime show was in Hartford, Connecticut, at the racetrack in front of 40,000 people. Back then, how the show started was I would get announced and then run on stage, wave, say hello, sit down, pick up an acoustic, and play three songs solo. Then the guys would join me and we'd build the show from there.

So this night I ran on—but no one had put a line on the front of the stage floor, which is imperative. The super trooper spotlights hit me, blinded me, and I ran right off the front of the stage. I landed on the wooden crash barrier, which ended up under my arms. It was insane. As I disappeared off the stage into the pit, the crowd all went, "Ohhhh, noooo!"

I turned around and I managed to get my foot on the front of the stage and Bill Anthony, Dee's brother, ran to pull me up. So one foot is up on the stage and he's pulling and I'm wearing my satin pants with no underwear, and he finally gave me this huge last-ditch-effort pull and as I rose up my pants split from seam to seam, so my ass is out there for forty thousand people to see and they all go, "Ahhhhh!"

They got me back on the stage, but I'm grazed, there's blood everywhere, and I'm kind of numb. I said, "Get me a new pair of pants!" We traveled with our own grand piano. At the back of the stage, they made the piano case, which is huge, into a dressing room right on the stage. I said, "Go get Penny's pants—we wear the same size."

Lucky for me that her pants were already off, because she was in the limo with the drummer of the opening band. Apparently, this was a normal occurrence on that tour. I didn't realize until later why they were able to come back with those pants so quickly. I do remember they were white pants that had a black stripe that went all the way around. I'll never forget those. I did the rest of the show in agony, but the show must go on—and it was a great show and everybody loved it.

Everyone knew about her except me. The band and crew knew. Nobody wants to be the messenger and tell the king that his girlfriend is not actually wearing any clothes right now. That's a horrible feeling, being played for a fool, you know? But maybe I was the fool to be with her.

Chapter Ten

Toward the end of 1976, Dee came to me and said, "I've got you a million dollars to star in a movie." I said, "You're kidding me—what kind of movie?" He said, "Well, it's a musical based around songs of the Beatles . . ." I said, "Stop. No. I'm not going to sing Beatles' songs, I'm sorry. It's not going to happen." I still call it, to this day, sacrilege. Unless you can do "With a Little Help from My Friends" like Joe Cocker, which is such a valid version. I feel my version of "While My Guitar Gently Weeps" is a valid version, because it was a tribute to George; we'd just lost him when I started doing that. But there are only a very few Beatle songs I might have the balls to sing. So I just said no; I didn't want to do that.

He said, "Oh, the other thing, the Bee Gees are in it. And you're all in a band together." I loved the Bee Gees; they're great. "New York Mining Disaster 1941" was one of my all-time favorites. I met them on *Top of the Pops* with the Herd, so we knew each other. I had been good friends with Maurice way before the film, but as a band I didn't feel they were thrilled with my name above theirs in the credits. I had been in two really successful UK bands already; neither was as big as the

Bee Gees, but the seemingly overnight *Frampton Comes Alive!* success took everyone by surprise . . . mostly me! So, to start with, it was a bit of a sensitive situation with these lads. I'm sure they would have preferred Andy Gibb to play my part, and in retrospect I really wish he had. But the producers obviously thought my name value would be better for the film.

Dee said, "Look, I can get you a million dollars, and I've got your first American Express card." So I said, "Oh, wow! Thanks, Dee!" I don't know how he talked me into doing this movie, but he did. It was like, "Aerosmith's in it and Earth, Wind & Fire's in it, and Billy Preston's in it. . . ."

Dee must've put me on the phone with Robert Stigwood (a larger-than-life character who had worked with Brian Epstein, had managed Cream and the Bee Gees, ran his own RSO record label, and would go on to produce *Saturday Night Fever* and *Grease*). "Peter, how are you? You're very, very loved here. And we've got all the credibility in the world, Peter, because Paul's gonna be in the movie. He's going to be the savior in the end." I said, "Really? Paul McCartney's gonna be in it? Okay, that's it; I'm in."

It was all a big lie. I assumed, when I got to LA to make the movie, that Paul was in the movie, at least in that last scene saving Heartland. But the Beatles ran for the hills, and I don't blame them. Dear Pattie Harrison and her sister Jenny came to the set to see me—both good friends, and I told them how awful the whole thing was.

The very first day wasn't a shooting day; it was a press day. There was a bandstand that we all played on in the movie, and they had that in the middle of the square. It was a huge set, a set where Elvis had once filmed. They introduced everybody to the press and then they brought me up to say a few words. On my way up onto the stage, as I went past Maurice, he tripped me up. I didn't fall over, but it was embarrassing, and I heard them all giggling behind me. This was like school, and I wasn't thrilled.

It all came to a screeching halt for me—there's no Paul Mc-Cartney and the Bee Gees don't like me. Oh, this is gonna be fun for six months. In the end, though, they were the saving grace. They were all really nice people, and Maurice became my closest friend on the set, and we were close until he passed away.

The movie was to be the story of the Sgt. Pepper's Band from the town of Heartland and it was a bit like *It's a Wonderful Life*, but no one was about to jump into the water—well, actually, I did jump off a building. The bad guy, Mean Mr. Mustard, wanted to corrupt the town, make lots of money, open XXX movie theatres, bring in hookers, and *we*—the Sgt. Pepper's Band—were the good guys trying to protect and save our town.

Mr. Mustard was played by a phenomenal English comedian named Frankie Howerd. My parents were staying for a few weeks at this huge mansion the film company had rented for me and all they wanted to do was meet Frankie Howerd. So I said, "Why don't I invite him over for dinner?" The behind-the-scenes things were the most enjoyable, to see my mother and father falling over laughing with this legendary British comedian. He was such a lovable character and I'm honored that he joined us for an evening at the Stone Canyon mansion.

George Martin was producing the soundtrack, and he came over for lunch one day and we sat out by the pool and you can imagine all my questions. I got to know George, and what an amazing person he was. I often wondered if George himself thought this was the right project for him. It must've been so frustrating for him, those songs and no Beatles on the other side of the glass. The great Geoff Emerick there, the Beatles' engineer, and all these top session guys—Max Middleton on keyboards, Bernard "Pretty" Purdie on drums, Marcus Miller on bass, so it's ultra-clean, perfect. They're all phenomenal players, but to me, it didn't sound like it should. It wasn't a band sound; it wasn't dirty enough.

I was so bored and fed up with working on the movie, I said to George, "Anytime you want me to come in and play guitar . . ." So he took me at my word and I played on two or three tracks with all those guys, and then I overdubbed guitar parts on most of the record. I'd be filming during the day and I'd go to the studio at night. Guess which one I enjoyed more?

There was a script, but the way I remember it was you opened it up, and it was as if every page was blank. It said "Walk in here, someone will yell 'Playback' and then you lip-sync." There was no story. Everyone thought we were too big to fail. We had the director who directed *Car Wash*, Michael Schultz. Very nice man, but I don't think he'd heard the Beatles much; I don't think he was the right guy for the job.

We had Owen Roizman, the fantastic Academy Award–winning cinematographer, wonderful man. I hung out with the camera crew more than I did the actors—"Oh, what lens? Okay, here you go!" I was really into all that. I had my own little sound movie thing going; I was making a documentary of what was going on. It was just like a long Monkees video to me. "We're doing this song today." It was all based around the songs, linked by this really weak story.

Meeting George Burns was a thrill. We started to get to know him, and we had a dance scene with him, which was horrible for me. I hated it, kind of a soft shoe thing. But then his dear friend Bing Crosby passed away while we were filming, and George disappeared into his trailer. He was a very nice man, but we didn't get too much time with him.

I knew immediately; I knew before I walked on the set. I knew from Day One that it wasn't good. After I'd said yes, I saw the script, and I thought, "We don't say anything? This is ridiculous." Even when I got to read a telegram, George Burns's voice came out of my mouth. It was just a horrible, horrible experience. Should I tell you how I really feel?

At that point, I didn't realize that I could've walked out. It would've cost a fortune, I'm sure, but I could have done it. And I wasn't the only one; the Bee Gees felt exactly the same way. They were worried about what I was going to sing and what they were going to sing, and they should sing this and I'm . . . whatever. We've got a lot more to worry about, you know?

We were about to do a full day's filming of the whole town, lots of extras, all the dancers, and us. We're on the top of a double-decker bus with no top, sitting open air, and we're supposedly going around the town—"We've saved the town!" kind of thing. I don't think that's even in the movie. It was a Monday. Maurice and I had both been up late, not together, but we'd both only had about two or three hours' sleep after a long late weekend, and one of us had these little white-cross dexies and we both popped one at about nine in the morning.

As soon as we did that, I looked over and saw Owen Roizman looking through his lens thingy at the sky and shaking his head. Finally, I saw him going over to Michael Schultz. I said, "Maurice, I think I know what's coming and we're not going to know what to do with ourselves." Owen said, "We cannot shoot today; the sun is not right." Maurice and I looked at each other; what are we going to do? I don't remember what we did, but we didn't go to sleep, put it that way.

I was living in this lovely mansion. It's just me and the dog, and a housekeeper, a lovely lady. It's Sunday night and I've pushed myself to go to bed because I've got to get up at five or whatever it was. I was asleep and Stephen Stills shows up—in those days it wasn't texting, "I'll be right over." He just arrived. Talked his way through the housekeeper and navigated around my dog Rocky then came upstairs. He saw that I was asleep, took out a straw, filled it with coke, and blew it up my nose while I was sleeping!

That's the quickest I've ever woken up in my life—"What the hell is going on?" He said, "Well, we're going out." I said, "I'm asleep." "Well, you aren't now!" So we went out, and then of course I didn't get back until probably three in the morning. When Stephen wants someone to play with, he's going to wake you up.

When you're in the middle of making a movie like this, once you get over the shock of how bad it's going to be, you just get on with it. And there were good things. This is when I first met Alice Cooper. He didn't have a trailer, so we said to come share ours, and we got to know him really well. There was the night shoot with Earth, Wind & Fire, and the big fight scene with Aerosmith. Those were the two best parts of the movie and the two best songs. And guess what? Those sounded like a band was playing them.

So some of it was fun—I wouldn't want people to see it, but it was fun to do. There were some very good-looking dancers. I made do with a bad situation. That's really all you could do.

There was always the hope that they would edit it and pull it together and it would be okay. But I didn't have much hope. I was so frustrated at the end of the six months—if it wasn't six months, it sure felt like six months.

During or just after the filming of *Sgt. Pepper*, Dee got me a meeting with Dino De Laurentiis; Dee had suggested to Dino that he might want to see me about a part in his next film. I said, "I'm not doing another movie right now." But we went in and there's Dino De Laurentiis, and he said, "Do you think you can do a New York accent?" I said yeah, probably. He said, "Would you be interested in this part?" The film was *King of the Gypsies* and I said no.

I could feel the anger from Dee—I'm turning down Dino De Laurentiis. And this was my first major stand. I'm saying no. I did want to do some acting, but on my own terms. I wanted to choose what I would do.

I wanted to learn to act. I got the bug. Orion Studios had just formed, with Mike Medavoy at the helm. I went to a meeting at Orion while we were filming *Sgt. Pepper*, and I sat down. I'm at one end of the table, Mike Medavoy's at the other—and it's a big, big table, a lot of people. They offered me a three-film deal, and I thought that was great because now I could get involved; I could hopefully choose what I could get my teeth into. I was so nervous at that meeting because this was a big deal. Well, that deal I would've taken, but it disappeared as soon as *Sgt. Pepper* came out.

I was still in LA doing reshoots, and I walked into a restaurant, and James Garner was in the entrance. He came running at me and says, "Oh, Peter, Peter, it's so nice to meet you. I gotta get your autograph for my granddaughter." I said no problem, no problem. And he says, "Oh, thanks so much—good kid, good kid," that kind of thing. I'm going wow! He's one of my favorite actors. He was the nicest guy. You hoped he would be, and he was.

We sat down at a booth. I look over and there's Robert Conrad. I was a huge fan of *Baa Baa Black Sheep*—which was later retitled *Black Sheep Squadron*, because no one knew what "baa baa black sheep" meant. It's about war planes, not about sheep. I loved it; it was just a great show. So I went over and said, "Excuse me, I'm a huge fan—my favorite TV show is *Baa Baa Black Sheep*." He said, "You're kidding me!"

He said to sit down, so I did, and I said, "Do you think there's any chance that I could have just a walk-on part, play some bit part on the show?" And he said, "You want to do that?" I said, "Absolutely! It's my favorite show." So he said, "Let me see what we can do; I'll talk to the producer."

I went home; I was finally home from shooting the movie, and a script arrived from *Black Sheep Squadron*. I opened it and it said your character is so and so. I read through it, and there's me, there's me—the whole bloody show is me! I didn't realize it, but it was the last episode of *Black Sheep Squadron* ever. I often say, "Hire me; I can end your series in one episode."

My road manager, Brian Stanley Coles, and I went to LA and rented a car. Before we went out, I learned not just my part—I learned everybody's part. We would read it through and read it through—I thought you had to learn the whole thing, in one go. First scene, I go up to the actor I'm with and I say, "You know when I say to you . . ." "What? I haven't read that yet." "What? You haven't learned it?" "No, I just learn it before we shoot it." You're kidding me!

But when we shot the very first scene, I blanked, because I was so nervous. That was the only time. I was petrified! This is my first actual speaking role onscreen—after having had the starring role in a big budget movie. Now I actually had to learn some lines.

The first day they had me do the most physical scenes, like water stuff, pushing an outrigger into the water and jumping on it, and looking like I've been doing this all my life. I've got my fatigues on, my hat, and everything, and I'm running into the water holding this outrigger. I trip, fall, and go right under the water, and everyone's laughing behind their hands. "Somebody get a hairdryer!"

Red West, who was Elvis's main man, played the part of the pilot of the big rescue seaplane that comes in and saves the downed pilots from the ocean. There's a scene at the end where I'm in the outrigger waving to Red at the end of the show and I'm supposed to laugh, but I couldn't laugh. I couldn't even muster a snicker. I actually wanted to cry at that point. I was so exhausted; it was so tiring doing all this stuff on the first day. I became good friends with Red, heard a bunch of great Elvis stories, and that was wonderful. (He actually came to a show on my Finale Tour and it was so great to see him again.)

There was a young actor in the show, and since "My Country 'Tis of Thee" has the same melody as "God Save the King," they had him singing "My Country 'Tis of Thee" and me singing "God Save the King" at the same time. We're pulling up the flag in the morning, having a spot of tea. I was supposed to be an eccentric English earl, so I had long hair. But I had streaks in it—in 1943! I don't think so. I said, "I'll cut my hair for this," and everyone said, "Oh, no! Don't do that!" They wanted me to look like me. I couldn't even get that right!

It came out and we beat everybody's ratings for the first thirty minutes, which was wonderful to know. Then I got a call from Barry Gibb. He asked, "What are you doing?" I said, "I'm doing some acting that I didn't do for the last six months." He said, "But it's coming out before the film!" I said, "Yes, it is"—I didn't really care. I enjoyed that one week of shooting more than any one day in six months of *Sgt. Pepper*. I knew I had so much to learn, but I was acting, and by the second day, I was excited to do more and enjoyed every minute.

Barry was not pleased that I had done it. I think probably now he would think differently, he would understand why I did it, because we all hated the damn movie. They went to the premiere in New York; I didn't. I was in the hospital.

We'd finished the movie, and I was estranged from Penny. She was down in the Bahamas, and she was obviously with somebody. So I went to St. Maarten—I'm going to go down to the Caribbean and do some writing. I took a guitar and just went on my own. I took some tennis lessons; there was a tennis pro there, and I developed quite a wicked backhand. I'd never had tennis lessons before.

But then I thought, "I need to go and see Penny and sort out where the hell we are." I try to call, no answer. So I got myself from St. Maarten to Nassau and went to Dee's place; Val, his wife, was there, and I said, "Can I borrow your car?" I went over to our house and there was a motorbike outside. I went inside and there were two guys sleeping in two of the bedrooms, so I threw them out.

The dining room table still had food on it. Someone had finished a meal and there was this stuff lying out called rush, sort of like a poor man's popper, like a speed thing, whatever. I saw all these Polaroids of Penny with various different people, so I took those with me and instead of going back to Dee and Val's place, I turned left and went to the bar, which was called Traveller's Rest. I must've had three or four double brandies, and, so I hear, I got raucous, and I phoned someone who knew Penny and said, "I need to find her."

It was late in the afternoon and I'm driving back to Val's and I'm loaded and tired; I hadn't slept. There's this one house that's on the ocean side that has a big white wall that bends around the corner—it's the house they used in the James Bond film with the sharks or alligators in the pool. I fell asleep at the wheel, woke up as I hit the wall, and then the car jerked over to the other side of the road and I saw this tree coming at me and that was it. That's all I remember.

Luckily, a kid, John Georges, whose parents had rented the James Bond house, he and his buddy heard the crash. They came out and they took me out of the car and called the ambulance.

I woke up in the Nassau hospital with a curtain around my arm, and I'm obviously feeling no pain at this point, but I knew I was in bad shape. I said to the nurse, "Is it compound?" And she said yeah, so I thought, "Oh, God, compound fracture." The doctor came in and told me everything, and then I went back to sleep.

Dee found out about all this from Val. Vince Morrow got his doctor, Dr. Tallury, and rented a Learjet. They flew down to Nassau, and came to the hospital. The last thing I feel like being is moved, so Vince is going, "We need to take you to New York"—because they didn't want me operated on down there. I went, "Oh, no, I'm very comfortable." "No, you want to go now." And the doctor's going, "Yeah, he don't want to go; he want to stay here." Dr. Banes wanted to fix me up, I guess. Even the doctor wanted a piece of me!

Well, it was good that I did go to New York, because afterward I went back to Nassau one more time to sell my house and I met someone who said, "Oh, I know you. Butcher Banes was working on you." Butcher Banes? "Yeah, Dr. Banes—Butcher Banes. My brother's arms aren't the same length anymore thanks to him." So he obviously wasn't known for his accuracy.

Penny had been found and was asked to bring pillows to the plane. Well, she was late, of course, and both my feet were broken, both hands were broken, my arm was broken, my ribs were broken. I've got a cut from my eyebrow to the center of my head. I'm a mess. Dr. Tallury, who became my New York doctor, purchased some morphine from Dr. Banes, and also the drug that stops you from getting nauseous.

They took me to the airport and one side of the walkway is commercial flights—like American, United, Delta. The other side is for the private planes. I'm in a hospital gown with the back open, and it's flapping. They bring me out of the ambulance on a stretcher and they try to get the stretcher in the door of the Lear, and it's not going to work. They've taken a couple of seats out and put an airbed in the plane for me, right in the middle. I said, "Stop, stop, let me get off," so I got off the stretcher and I walked on broken feet and got in the plane myself. Meanwhile, all these people are getting off the

Eastern flight as I'm flapping away in the breeze showing all to all. When I got on the plane, I was still thinking, "Did they all see my rear end?" It's so surreal, the things you think about at times like these.

They finally got me to lie down on the mattress, and I apparently started singing. I was so high from the morphine. That got me to Manhattan and then they took me straight to Lenox Hill Hospital, where it seemed I had every doctor and nurse known to man and woman look at me.

News of my accident had reached my family in England, so Mum, Dad, and Clive immediately flew into New York; it was the same day I arrived at Lenox Hill. Clive stayed with me at night sleeping on a mattress on the floor. He took care of the night duties and Mum and Dad were with me during the day. People were dressing up as medical staff just to get in my room, so I had to have guards outside my door to keep everyone out except my family and my *real* doctors.

I wonder how many people still have a vial of my blood they've kept somewhere. I had more blood taken while I was in Lenox Hill than I think I possessed. I have no idea how many of these "nurses" or "doctors" were just fans with plans but no medical degree! Clive recently reminded me that when I was trying to delay taking the next morphine shot to wean off it, the doctor suggested that smoking a joint would definitely help. I thought this was a terrific idea and then had to teach Mum how to roll a decent joint. She was very much into detail and became one of the very best joint rollers I have ever known. She would use that Ozium spray after I'd had a few puffs just in case anyone could smell what I was doing. Well, they *all* knew what I was doing!!! My right arm was in a cast, making it impossible for me to play guitar. But I looked at the position of my arm and thought, "I could play a saxophone!"

Frank Vicari, who played with Tom Waits, was a good friend and an incredible sax player. I asked him to find me a nice old vintage Selmer Alto sax. I did actually play some very painful beginner's notes while in my hospital room, so they moved me to another floor. Apparently, people were really dying because my playing was just killing them.

It was an awakening for me—it was like "Put the brakes on, buddy." Something had to give. I was living an explosive life at that point. On the surface, it seemed like I was handing everything really well. But going from barely being able to make ends meet after Humble Pie, and slowly building back up, and then becoming the biggest-selling artist in the world, and then going back to nothing again over a short space of time obviously is going to leave its mark mentally. It's going to mess with you a little bit. It takes some getting used to, and every artist's music career is different; there's no default template of what to do next. If I didn't have such a strong core, I probably wouldn't still be here.

Our very first time going to South America was in 1980. We played Argentina first, then we went to Brazil, and these were sold-out arenas; it was a big deal for me. We actually went back to Buenos Aires to add another sold-out show, but before moving up to Central America we played the last two shows in Caracas, Venezuela.

The first time we went to Argentina, we stayed in an international hotel—fantastic hotel, just like in New York or London. When we came back, because it was an unplanned, quick return trip to Buenos Aires, the only availability we had was rooms in a national hotel. I didn't quite understand why there was such a disparity between national hotels and international hotels. As we went to check in, there were a lot of local Argentinians at the front desk, all looking at us like they wanted to kill us. The Argentinian economy was in bad shape during the 1980s, and there was a tinder-box vibe; it was just eighteen months before the Falkland Islands war with the UK.

We went up to the rooms and within ten minutes or less, everyone in the band and crew was back in the lobby—"I'm not staying in that room!" It was filthy, smelly, and just horrible. At one point the rooms had nice grayish rugs, but now they were all black with cigarettes stubbed out all over them. The bedding hadn't been changed since the Spanish-American war. We've all stayed in some really bad hotels but this really was remarkably awful! It was sad but interesting, how they put on a fanfare for the international travelers, but for their own, not so good!

The first night we played in Caracas, it was a very full arena, around twenty thousand, like Madison Square Garden. In front of the stage, they had the little wooden posts that they have at a movie theater or club with a red rope to keep you at bay.

There was no crash barrier, nothing. Our production manager, Steve Lawler, had asked many times that day for a wooden or metal barrier to be erected. He was denied, but he told them this wasn't going to work for the safety of the crowd and the band. They said no.

And then behind the rope, standing facing the audience, were all these—I don't know whether they were military police or they were regular police, or army; they just looked like bad dudes to me, loads of them all standing in a line in front of the stage. There was unrest outside, people were trying to get in because the shows were sold out. After the first show we found out that someone had hurt a policeman or a security person outside, who then radioed whoever was in charge of these bad dudes in front of our stage.

Toward the end of the show, word of the outside fracas had obviously reached these guys in front. To my amazement, they all took out their machetes and started waving them high in the air, and then they stomped the entire distance of the hall from the front to the back using a chopping motion with their weapons. Everybody was climbing over each other to get off the floor. I saw chairs coming down on people's heads. The audience was getting hurt, so I threw down the mic and walked off because I won't play in that situation. I've never seen violence like that. It scared us—not a good feeling.

We had one more night booked to play there, and after what happened the first night, I had no intention of playing the second show. As you can imagine, there were a lot of heated discussions going on between my team and the venue and promoter's teams. The guards would be gone, but still no crash barrier, just the damn red rope. We played the second show and it was incident-free and the crowd was very respectful—there was no crashing the stage. Who knew how close the machete men might be!

After the Caracas shows, we had one day off, so we flew ahead on a commercial jet to Panama—Noriega's Panama at the time. Usually we were flying on a big enough plane that the gear would go on the same plane. But this time, we didn't fly with the equipment because we had time, so we used a cargo plane, a Convair 880, for all our gear.

Venezuela had just discovered massive amounts of oil, so it was cheaper to fill the cargo plane in Caracas with enough gas to make the return trip. Of course, we don't really know, but it was most likely a loading problem; they loaded all the gear up front to have the correct balance to fly safely. Well, as it took off, it's thought that one of the straps or chains securing the equipment must have broken or come loose. The plane jerked to one side, then a wing touched the ground, and the plane exploded. It never got off the runway. There were six people on the plane—pilot, copilot, loading inspector, and others to help with the loading and unloading—who all lost their lives.

The picture of the plane on the runway on fire was on the front pages of all the South and Central America papers. It was like an H-bomb had gone off, because it had so much gas. No one could get near it for five or six hours, it was such a huge blaze.

I was just about to eat lunch in the hotel restaurant in Panama, and my road manager, Rodney Eckerman, came to me and said, "I've got some bad news." He told me that the cargo plane with all our gear had crashed on takeoff. I said, "Oh, my God." I wasn't carrying my Gibson, I was carrying another guitar because it was smaller, easier to carry onto a commercial plane. I said, "My guitar, as well?" And he said, "Well, yes, but we think everyone was killed on the plane." This was devastating news. All of a sudden, the loss of our gear didn't mean much anymore. Rodney pointed to the bar and as I looked over, he told me that was the pilot's wife, waiting for her husband. She didn't know yet.

Sidney Frampton. My grandfather was a submariner. He served in both WWI and WWII.

Owen Gordon Frampton. My father in Africa during WWII.

Peggy Grace Frampton. My mother while working for the US Army in London.

Mum and Dad getting married at the beginning of WWII.

Me, my brother, Clive, and Dad playing in our back garden on one of the infrequent hot British summer days, 1957.

Bandad, me, and Clive on an outing in the boat, Koala, that Dad built for our family.

Me and Mum
at the beach.
I am wearing
her shades.

The beginnings
of a gadget freak,
and a love of
photography.

Eight years old.
My first decent guitar.
A Hofner Club 60
that cost £25.

The very first performance of the Trubeats in 1962. Me, Dave Roffe, and Terry Nicholson. Clive is in the front row.

A Preachers' rehearsal session in 1964.

The Herd in 1968. Andrew Bown, Andrew Steele, me, and Gary Taylor.
(Pictorial Press Ltd/ Alamy Stock Photo)

The beginnings of Humble Pie, 1968. Steve Marriott, Jerry Shirley, me, and Greg Ridley.
(© Barrie Wentzell)

Steve Marriott and me tuning up backstage before a show.

Pete Drake, George Harrison, Ringo Starr, Billy Preston, and me at George's sessions for *All Things Must Pass.*

Frampton's Camel in 1972. Me, Mick Gallagher, Rick Wills, and John Siomos rehearsing for the second US tour.
(Photograph by Michael Putland/Getty Images)

My band in 1974: Rick Wills, John Siomos, me, and Andrew Bown.

Bob Mayo backstage warming up.
(Photograph by Michael Zagaris)

Bill Anthony, Bill Graham,
and Dee Anthony side stage
at Day on the Green.
(Photograph by Michael Zagaris)

Performing "Show Me the Way"
at Day on the Green in 1976.
(Photograph by Michael Zagaris)

Rough day!
After Day on the Green.
(Photograph by Michael Zagaris)

The enormity of an empty JFK Stadium in Philadelphia at sound check.
(Photograph by Ken Regan/Camera 5)

Cameron Crowe and me hanging out in Los Angeles in 1977.

Les Paul's birthday party in New York City in 1981. (Photograph by Adam Scull/ PHOTOlink.net)

My day at the White House, with Penny McCall, President Gerald Ford, and his son Steve. (Courtesy Gerald R. Ford Presidential Library)

Caracas 1980. (Photograph by JD Dworkow)

Me and David backstage on the Glass Spider Tour, 1987. (Photograph by Denis O'Regan)

David, Dad, and me at the Glass Spider Tour press conference/gig in London.
(Photograph by Denis O'Regan)

Ringo presents my son, Julian, with his very first drum kit at age seven, in 1995.

The Shadows at the *Fingerprints* session at Mark Knopfler's studio, British Grove, in London in 2005. Hank Marvin, Brian Bennett, me, and Mark Griffiths.
(Photograph by Denis O'Regan)

Me, Bill Wyman, and Charlie Watts. The Rolling Stones rhythm section at the session for "Cornerstones" on the *Fingerprints* album. (Photograph by Denis O'Regan)

Matt Cameron, Mike McCready, me, Adam Kasper, and Gary Westlake in Seattle for the *Fingerprints* session for "Black Hole Sun" and "Blowin' Smoke."

Jade and Julian Frampton, 2019, backstage at Madison Square Garden.
(Photograph by Austin Lord)

Tiffany Wiest and
Mia Frampton.

Clive and me at his home.

On vacation in Mustique.

A couple of my favorite guitars at
Phenix Studios in Nashville.

The Phenix rises. (Photograph by Gregg Roth)

The Finale Tour. Dan Wojciechowski, Rob Arthur, me, Adam Lester, and Steve Mackey. You gave us so much joy every night. (Photograph by Genevieve Neace)

Chapter **Eleven**

I remember lying in the hospital bed and having time to think. "Where's the money from my publishing? Where's this? Where's that?" I'm just coming to terms with everything that's happened to me over the last few years. Meanwhile, I could see the entrance of the hospital on the local TV news—"He's up there!" and they'd zoom into the window. "Here he is; he's over in this room here." There were thousands of people downstairs. I'm thinking, "Wow! This is just nuts."

After ten days, two weeks—I actually can't be sure how long it was because I was now enjoying my no-pain-with-morphine period—I'm still pressing a button for the nurse to come in and give me another shot of it. My bone doctor came in to check on me, took off the bandages, and said, "You're not still taking morphine, are you?" I said, yeah, I was. He said, "I think it's time you wean yourself off that." It's the afternoon, so he said, "Tell you what you should do. Don't take the shot tonight, just take a Valium, and then you'll have a shot in the morning, you'll be fine."

About three in the morning, I wake up in the fetal position and my stomach hurts and I'm shaking, I'm shivering, so I buzz the night nurse, and she comes in and says, "Well, there's nothing I can do." I said, "Can you get my clothes, my overcoat, everything?" I was so cold. So she got me a blanket and everything. I thought I had pneumonia or the like.

The personal nurse who I hired was very good, but a bit like Nurse Ratched—she was the only one who could deal with me. (I was not a particularly pleasant patient.) She came in very early in the morning, took one look at me and said, "Did you take your shot last night?" I said, "No, Dr. Crane, my bone doctor"—Ed Crane, wow, I amaze myself when I remember things—"he said to wean me off." She said, "Let me go and call Dr. Tallury." She came back in less than a minute, gave me a shot, and within thirty seconds, I felt normal again.

It made me realize that for all the things I've done in my life, this kind of drug is something I will never do, because I saw how powerful it was. And that wasn't even intravenous. It was just intra-muscle. I thought of all the guys I knew who would kill for my pure morphine, and it made me realize that I could never go down that road.

It was three in the morning and I was asleep, but the nurse came to the door and said, "You have a phone call." I said, "Who's it from?" She said it was a Mr. Wonder. I said, "Oh, my God! Yes, put him through! Put him through!"

Stevie said, "How are you, Peter?" I said, "I'm fine; much better hearing from you." He said, "I just wanted to call you, and I'm going to play you some songs." What? He said, "Yeah, I've been doing some recording, and I've got the tracks; I'm just going to sing live for you." I'm listening to a Stevie Wonder song that to this day has never been released. It was something about the sun, and he was singing full voice. No one will believe this, but it happened.

We often spoke on the phone after that, and he would play songs with buttons on the touchtone phone—if you push number two, it gives you one note; number three gives you another note. They're all different tones and he would play tunes on the phone buttons. I said, "Okay, let me try that." So we're playing songs to each other on the phone!

Stevie always made fun of his blindness. He would say, "Hey, Peter, did you see that movie last night?" Yeah, I did. "Oh, I heard it was good." Shit like that. "What was it like? I heard it, but I couldn't see it." When his brother Calvin wasn't around, if he needed to go somewhere, I saw how he did it—you just hold your arm out and he holds on. So I'd walk him around wherever he wanted to go at the studio.

The premiere of the *Sgt. Pepper* movie happened while I was in the hospital. I swear I was so thrilled that I didn't have to go! My mother went; she was staying at the Carlyle Hotel there in New York, which is just a short walk to the hospital. So I'm watching the red carpet on TV and there goes Mum! In the movie, there's a scene where I'm so upset about losing Strawberry Fields that I go to jump off the roof—and people in the audience were shouting, "Jump!"

But Mum said, "Oh, yeah, it went really well. Everything was good." I knew that it was a dud, though. It had to be. I realize now—and I knew then—that there were so many things that were wrong. It was all wrong. With Stigwood at the helm and all the great acts we had, everyone involved felt it couldn't fail. That, of course, was before we started filming!

I saw *Across the Universe*, the musical that came out in 2007 with all the Beatles music, and it was fantastic! It was a really great movie, because everybody knew what they were doing. They had a plan, they had a storyline, and the sound and arrangements were different from the Beatles versions. *Sgt. Pepper* had none of that.

Which reminds me of another project that no one thought could fail: the Philadelphia Fury. I bought into that North American Soccer League franchise along with Paul Simon, Mick Jagger, Rick Wakeman, Jerry Moss, Dee Anthony, Frank Barsalona, and others. So here we have our whole team buying a team. The New York Cosmos were owned by Ahmet Ertegun and his group of investors. They were lucky enough to have Pelé on their team. We had some great players, too, including Alan Ball from the UK. But it was just a tad early for soccer in the US. As the league was failing, we had all signed promissory notes, so we had to reinvest sometime later. That was the most painful check I have ever had to write. Another $500k was still due.

I was in the hospital for quite some time. It seemed like months, but it was probably three or four weeks. Before I was discharged, I did a *Good Morning America* interview with David Hartman, the show's anchor. I was supposed to have left the hospital, but they said, "Can you stay one more day so we can film in there?" And then the day of the shoot, Dr. Crane came and said, "I've got to take the stitches out from your arm surgery and I need to give you a shot." Of morphine? I'm just about to do an interview. "Well, yeah, otherwise, you'll be in pain." Needless to say the interview was very relaxed and totally enjoyable.

When I left Lenox Hill, my mother and father arrived to take me to the hotel. As I descended from my room, the elevator doors opened to the ground floor and the whole lobby of the hospital was just a sea of people. I was waving, thanking everybody. It was like I was doing a campaign rally—without a single cell phone present! I know the hospital staff must have been happy I was leaving. I remember on the TV news the spokeswoman for the hospital was asking people not to come hoping to see me, because it was interfering with the daily running of the hospital.

My stay was as good as it could be under the circumstances, and even though I met a lot of people who pretended to be a doctor or a nurse, the real ones put me back together again and I am eternally grateful.

In the fall of '78, we went to Japan, Australia, and New Zealand. I thought it was a good idea at the time, to have something to look forward to while I was recuperating. When we were in Australia, David Bowie happened to be there as well, so he came over with Coco, his manager/assistant, and we hung out for a day in Sydney and he said, "You shouldn't be on the road yet." He was always so protective.

He said, "Are you sure you should be doing this right now, so soon after your accident?" He was definitely concerned that they were working me to death. But I thought it was the right move, because I enjoy playing live so much, and I was still able to play. Thank God I didn't lose an arm, because when the doctors first looked me over they thought it was a possibility. When my arm broke, it had pushed out some muscle to be lost forever, and a bone will only survive if it has enough muscle to cover it. Thankfully, I had just enough left.

While I was on the Far East tour, I had to go around to different premieres of the *Sgt. Pepper* movie in each country. They were releasing it down there to coincide with my tour dates. I would go up on the stage at the beginning, before the movie, say hello to the audience, introduce the film, and then I'd leave. It was incredibly frustrating, having to go and flog a dead horse, knowing it was a piece of crap. I realize now it's become a sort of cult movie, but not in the *Rocky Horror Picture Show* league. Instead I could have been taking time off to reflect on the craziness of my recent success or, more importantly, writing songs for the follow-up album.

I wasn't doing very well, personally or mentally. I was at my worst as far as drinking and taking drugs. The thought of having to compete with myself and follow up *Comes Alive!* had made me feel as if I had lost before I even started. Everything was starting to hit the fan for me right then, and I could feel that my spotlight was destined to fade. And I realized that money was missing—a lot of money was missing. I'd already started talking to my lawyer. No, it wasn't a good period for me. I was going down to clubs in Manhattan and getting loaded, carried out, and sent back to Westchester. It was getting old hat and embarrassing.

I initially moved from the hospital to the Carlyle Hotel, because the doctors still wanted to check on me and it was close to Lenox Hill. It was suggested that I talk to someone and I remember a psychiatrist coming to see me in my hotel room. After we had been talking for a while, he told me he believed I'd tried to kill myself the day of the crash in Nassau, but I still don't agree with him to this day. I don't believe him—by downing shots of Rémy Martin during the day of the car accident, I definitely put myself in a position where I could possibly get hurt, but I don't believe that I drank specifically to off myself.

Whether he was right or not, I don't know. But that doesn't sound like me. I'm a survivor. None of us are looking forward to not being upright one day, and the last thing I would do is hurt myself, because I want and need to be here for my children.

But I'm sure that to this doctor, not caring about yourself to that extent is in fact putting yourself in danger. I was going to Studio 54 and Xenon and all these other clubs. I was pretty much on my own. Penny was gone, that was over. Finally, through a mutual friend, Phil de Havilland, who owned the club Trax, I met Barbara Gold, who became my girlfriend and then my wife and the mother of my first two children, Jade and Julian. And I believe she saved me from worse things that I don't care to think about. I definitely needed looking after at that point. My confidence had left, and so had my career.

I heard somehow that Penny was going to be on New York's local ABC Channel 7 news right after *Good Morning America*, and so I called David Hartman, and I asked if he knew anything about this. He said he didn't. I thought it was so strange that they were interviewing her. I watched her interview, which was pitiful. She tried suing me for palimony, but it thankfully got laughed out of court.

In a word, I now believe the success and fallout from *Frampton Comes Alive!* had completely blown my mind. There was some mental repair needed at that time in my life. Barbara and I definitely had our fun times. We had our clubbing, and then more clubbing, till it was light out the next day. But as our relationship grew, we started to calm down.

When we had our first child, Jade, we stayed home for the first month or so. Eventually, we thought we deserved our first "date night" and decided we'd just go out for a meal locally.

Nervous already about leaving baby Jade for the first time, we asked the nurse from the hospital to babysit. As soon as we sat down in the restaurant we noticed that the doctor who had delivered Jade was waving from another table. Is this a test? We felt it was an omen we shouldn't stay long, and instantly started feeling guilty we had gone out at all. We ate fast and left, because really we were both missing being with Jade. Our second night was much longer; we went into Manhattan just for the evening. We went to a club, and even came back relatively late. At about four in the morning, I paid the nurse for babysitting again, and we were just starting to say, "Okay, good night," and as we closed our eyes, Jade starts to cry. Welcome to reality. Things were about to change. We can't do this anymore.

We did the Far East tour in the fall and came back and started working on the *Where I Should Be* record. There were a lot of people involved in that one. I started doing it on my own, but I didn't really have enough material. I brought Andy Johns in and he listened, and I went back and called Chris Kimsey, and we sort of wrangled it into something. I was still competing with myself, and that was a high benchmark, but I just wasn't inspired.

I'd lost the itch—the itch that made me care. It had backfired on me, as far as I was concerned. I'd had huge success, but it had a huge backlash. It was like I got myself into trouble by being successful. I was responsible and hadn't taken care of business. And it took a while to unwrap all that. I had to take the reins back.

I had met Elton John a few times and he was at a party at the house of my longtime friend, the amazing guitarist Steve

Lukather. When Barbara and I arrived, I was ushered into the powder room where Elton was, and we chatted for quite a while. I remember him saying that it was such a shame that after all the touring and years of working I had done, my career had petered out.

Toward the end of my time with A&M, Dee was managing Peter Allen, and Peter Allen wanted to do a Broadway show, so Dee needed money to put into the show. They say never use your own money to start up a new venture, so Dee used mine. Instead of getting a loan for Peter, he went to Jerry Moss or Gil Friesen and said, "Peter needs money." And he didn't mean Peter Allen.

So A&M wrote out two checks to me and, in that green pen that he used to use, Dee endorsed both over to himself. The total was over a quarter of a million dollars, and I didn't know a thing about it. Neither Jerry nor Gil mentioned anything to me because they assumed, rightly so, that Dee must have given the checks to me.

I went to my lawyer, Elliott Hoffman, who happened to work for Dee as well, and I said, "Where's my publishing money?" My record royalties came straight from A&M to me, thank God, but my publishing money came from Almo Irving to Dee and then to me. I found out he owed me almost a million dollars, and that was only my publishing royalties. In 2020 dollars that's nearly four million.

Elliott and I went to see Dee and I remember what Dee always used to say—when someone asks you for money, you just say, "I don't have it; I just don't have that money." So Dee was doing "I just don't have it" to *me*. I said, "I've heard that before.

You say that to other people. Where's the money? You're going to have to find some, buddy."

I wanted out of all our deals, but I wanted him to pay me first. So I got Dee to come up to my house, and I said, "Bring your co-op papers. Until you pay me back, I want to hold your house." Well, I didn't realize at the time there was no equity in it—he owed on it, he was behind on his mortgage for this block-square apartment on Park Avenue in Manhattan. And here he is, the big tipper. The more he could tip someone, the better: a bell boy, a room service person, valet car parker—the big roll of hundreds and fifties would come out of his pocket.

Before Dee arrived at my house. I had microphones hidden all around the room and I'm recording our conversation downstairs in my studio. And he comes in and he starts talking in a whisper. He knows; he's talking very quietly.

He gives me the deed to the house, but I realized later that a deed's no good; you need the mortgage, the paper—you need much more than what he gave me. So he says he'll pay me back, then leaves, and basically that's it, I'm done with him. He came to one more gig that we did in Long Island with his wife, Val, and we didn't let him in the dressing room after the show. We just got in the car and drove away; it was too late for talking.

As we were getting ready for court, my lawyers said, "Okay, it's time for your skeletons-in-the-closet meeting." I said, "What?" They said, "Well, we have to know everything that you've done that could be used against you." I thought, "This is actually good, because the guy who supplied me with drugs was Dee." He kept me high, and for good reason, from his point of view. "Don't you worry, just leave the business side to me."

We got a forensic accountant at Price Waterhouse, and found out that Dee actually had no money. He'd spent it all or had to pay it out to "you know who." So we were preparing to go to court and Price Waterhouse said, "Hold it, because this man has no money." My lawyers told me that if we went to court, I would most likely win hands down, but the judge would say at the end, "Okay, Mr. Anthony, you owe him x-million dollars; how do you propose to pay this?" And he'd go, "Your Honor, I can afford to pay one dollar fifty a week," and I'd have to accept it. And in the meantime, every time I wanted to go do a tour, he'd depose me. He could mess with me to stop me from working.

They said a trial would cost me $500,000 with all the lawyers and everything. I didn't know where my next buck was coming from at this point, because things weren't going well. So rather than not be able to work, and be tied up in litigation for four to five years, I settled. I actually had to pay *him* to get out of my contract, because it was a legal, binding contract. It wasn't much, but I did pay him to get out of it. But I got my publishing back, and my self-respect, which was the main thing.

In the mid-'80s, when I was managed for a short time by Tony Smith—who was the manager for Genesis—I told him that Dee had handled all the money. He said, "Let me just do a quickie for you and tell you that if that's how much he took from your publishing, he'd been skimming you all the time." He put it at around eight million that he could have taken from me—that's $31 million in 2020 dollars.

As you can see, money had never really been an important issue for me. But now I didn't have the money to sustain the lifestyle I had attained. Houses were sold, and it was back to renting apartments. Meanwhile, Dee sold his block-square co-op, sold the place in the Bahamas, and Michele, his daughter, bought Dee and Val a cottage up in Connecticut and looked after them.

I had known Michele a long time, and when she found out what had happened she took my side and helped me by making sure any of my personal stuff her father had came back to me.

I don't think Dee saw it coming when I left him, but he'd spent all his money and a lot of mine. Yes, I made a lot of money, and I spent a lot myself, but I believe he spent more of mine than I did.

As far as my music career was going, I realized that, no matter what I did, it was kind of over. That was what I felt at that time. It was like my career had been totally front-loaded. Now it was over, I'm done for, that's it. My career is over. I can't do this all over again. That's what I was feeling.

I did *Where I Should Be* in Los Angeles. We went to LA just to be out of town, go somewhere else, and do it. We had great musicians, and did my songs and a couple of covers. We had Steve Cropper and Duck Dunn play on a couple of Sam & Dave numbers. They had already played on the originals.

Then on *Breaking All the Rules*, I worked with David Kershenbaum, and that was an enjoyable record to make. We had Jeff Porcaro and Steve Lukather from Toto, and my keyboard player, Arthur Stead. John Regan was now the bass player in my band. During the 1979 tour, Carl Radle had been playing bass, but he had to leave abruptly because of health issues. Bob Mayo had told me that John was a great player, and he came in with no rehearsal and saved the day. After his very first show, I asked him to join the band. Since then, we've played together on tons of tours and albums and written a lot of music together. We each only have a handful of real friends, and John is one of mine.

That was the best album that I made during that period; it would have been great if that had been the one after *Frampton Comes Alive!* and I believe it would have been much better received than *I'm In You* was. It would've been a hit. It was very good, but I still felt as if I was swimming against the tide.

David was so into it, and I really enjoyed working with him, and he was always very encouraging. But it was still a heavy drug period in those days. It was just crazy. Everyone was still doing coke, including me. So that record could have been even better.

There are actually three versions of the *Breaking All the Rules* album. The first two versions were only for South America, *Frampton Especial* in Brazil and *Rise Up* in Argentina; different title but same album. David had come to New York to work on the demos and preproduction at my home studio in Croton-on-Hudson. I had wanted to go to South America, as I had never been before, so a short tour was booked down there before we cut the master recordings in LA. The special album was released in South America before we went down so that there was something to promote the tour.

To our surprise, the song "Breaking All the Rules" became the music for one of the biggest cigarette commercials. Hollywood cigarettes! It was a red and white pack similar to Marlboro Reds'. So when we got to Brazil, we couldn't work out why everyone was holding up their ciggies to show us. We were treated like the "Cigarette Gods" because the commercial was all over TV. Whenever we played that number in the act, it went down better than "Do You Feel."

After the *Art of Control* album was released, A&M dropped me. It had gone from bad to worse. I'd love to get the master tapes of *The Art of Control* so I could remix it, because I had nothing to do with the mixing at all. Eddie Kramer's mixes were good, but it wasn't the same as if I had been involved.

But I really didn't care. That's awful to say. I'm this fastidious person, a perfectionist all my life, and now I just don't really care. I had lost my mojo, baby! It was a period of "What do I do now, and how do I get my mojo working again?"

I decided to take a break. Meanwhile, Ahmet Ertegun knew that I was being dropped by A&M, and he called me himself and signed me to Atlantic for two records. I was signed by Atlantic in '83, but I didn't give them anything until '86 with *Premonition*.

It was time to not tour, to stay home and to enjoy being home. After Barbara and I had our first child, I said, "Well, this is like a natural break here." Things weren't happening, and we'd moved houses from Croton over to Pound Ridge. Later, we sold it, and then those people sold it to Tim Robbins and Susan Sarandon.

In '96, Pearl Jam invited me to play in Ohio for a Rock the Vote event, and Tim Robbins was there. Tim said, "We bought your house, the one on Honey Hollow Road." I said, "Oh, wow, that's great, it's a great house." He said, "Yeah, we love it, and we've often been in the pool late at night in the summer and said to each other, 'I wonder what this was like in the seventies when Frampton owned it. Must've been wild parties with chicks everywhere.'" But it wasn't like that at all; by that time, and after having our baby, we had to be grown-ups!

So I decided not to launch into another album, and I was just writing and spending time with family. But it wasn't a particularly enjoyable time, because I had no idea what was going on.

My career was in the toilet, basically. I can't afford the mortgage; it's not looking good. I was in the kitchen one day and I got a phone call from Pete Townshend.

I love Pete. We've known each other for a long time. I wouldn't say we're close friends, but we have a mutual respect. So I get this call from England. "Hey, Pete, it's Townshend here, Pete Townshend." Oh, blimey, how are you? Long time. He said, "Yeah, so I've made this decision that I'm not going to tour with the Who anymore. I'll still write the songs, but I want you to take my place, and . . ." Wait, what? I remember the first thing that I said—when he paused—I said, "That's an enormous pair of shoes to fill! I can't do that." He said, "Yes, you can, and I'll be there with you."

I said, "Wait a second, Pete. Have you spoken to Roger or the others about this?" And he said, "Not yet, I'm going down to talk to him tomorrow." I said, "Okay, why don't you call me back when you've had a chat with them about this. They don't know you're not going to tour anymore?" "No, not yet; they'll know tomorrow."

So I hung up and I told Barbara, and I freaked out. I said, "This doesn't sound right. This is off. This doesn't make sense at all." I would be laying myself open to scrutiny and the fury of every Who fan. But on the other hand, what a wonderful offer, an honor to say the least that Pete considered me that serious of a candidate. I would love to have played with the Who, but only with Pete in the band, no way on my own. I couldn't do that! But, well, maybe I could have. Half of me was saying, "I got nothing going on, and maybe this could work." But I'm just grasping at straws; realistically, I knew this would not be good for the Who or me. No one would accept the band without

"Towser." And my windmill needed a lot of work, as well as my ten-foot jumps into the air. No way was this a good idea.

So a week goes by, nothing. Two weeks go by and I'm losing it. I kind of knew he must have thought about the offer he made to me, but I wasn't going to let him off the hook. Three weeks go by and my wife says, "For Christ's sake, call him!" Because I was total hell to live with at that point.

I find him in a studio somewhere in London; it took me four or five calls to get him and all I let him get out was, "Oh, hi, Pete." And I said, "You haven't called me back in three weeks! I got nothing going on in my career and the inventor of the Who—the songwriter, and the major player in the Who—calls me up and offers me his position in the band and then doesn't call me back! You've left me hanging." He said, "Oh, I'm so sorry." I'd never heard Townshend like that before. I had to make him understand, hey, you fucked me up for three weeks here; it's not been a good three weeks for me. He apologized profusely saying, "I'm so sorry, I should never have done. . . ."

A few months later, Bruce Springsteen was playing the Garden, so Barbara and I went to see the show and go backstage at the halftime intermission. We were standing right behind the stage and guess who I see talking to Bruce? I looked at Barbara and said, "Wait here."

I went over, and Pete's talking to Bruce, and I just stood there with a smile on my face. He's taller than me, so he just looks at me, gives me this big hug, and leans over and kisses me on the top of my head. 'Nuff said—it was over. We moved on.

I love Pete dearly, but I have no idea what was going on in his life at that time. I don't even know if he remembers calling me.

I would run into the Stones every now and again. I remember I was at one studio session, and of course only Bill and Charlie were there. They would always turn up on time. I was messing around, playing Charlie's drums. In the studio at Olympic, the door is behind you, so I couldn't see him. He was listening and said, "That's good; you play well, Peter." He said, "All you guitar players are good drummers!" I'll never forget that. I mean, thanks very much, but I prefer your playing! Charlie, he's the nicest man.

When they were recording the *Undercover* album at the Hit Factory in New York, Chris Kimsey was engineering and producing. Chris called me up and said, "You want to come down tonight? Mick and Keith are doing some overdubs." I said, "Oh, I'd love to see them again." So I came down and Mick's there waiting for Keith, and Keith arrives a little later and he brings his guitar because he's got a solo and a vocal to do. He opened up the guitar case, and he said, "Oh, I didn't have time"—there's only like two strings on there. There was no guitar tech or anything, so I said, "I'll do it for you if you like." I restrung Keith's guitar and I went out into the studio and as I'm just playing along with the track, making sure the guitar's in tune, all of sudden Mick's standing there right next to me listening to me playing. I kind of froze—it was a weird situation.

Once I've given Keith the guitar, we're in the control room, and Keith comes over to the desk and he gets a little vial out and puts some coke on the console and Mick says, "No, you know we agreed no coke before a vocal, Keith." And Keith said, "Well, it's too fucking late then innit!" We all laughed. So I think I did some and Keith did some, and then he went out to play the solo, and Mick came over to me and said, after each take, "Was it in tune?" I wanted to say, "Shouldn't he be a little out of tune? 'Cause otherwise, it wouldn't be the Stones. It's got to be on the edge a little bit." But I said, "Okay, all right. Yeah, it's in tune."

Apparently, they weren't really getting on that well at that time, and it's none of my business, but we were leaning on a Leslie cabinet in the middle of the live room, Keith and me, and then Mick comes out of the control room and there's the three of us around the Leslie and then all of a sudden there's a great conversation, they're getting along, and I thought, "Wow, maybe I helped just a tiny bit by being there." But it was really interesting, it was just great to see how they were together. They're like brothers: some days they're on, some days they're off. But it was a privilege to be around them working together.

I had no money after Dee and then two more questionable business managers. I was left with debts and a lien due to the mishandling of my affairs. I wasn't touring and record sales weren't good. And so, yes, I was broke! So I went to Ahmet. It's the most awful feeling, but Ahmet and I had a great relationship and he was a dear friend of mine. He was always my champion, he really was, since he thought he had signed Humble Pie, and he knew me for what I was—a musician.

I went into his office and I said, "I don't know how to ask you for this. I know I'm signed to Atlantic, and you've given me an advance and everything, but I need some money to live." And he said, "How much do you want?" I said a hundred thousand. By the time I left the office, I had a check.

I was upside-down and could've used that million dollars from my publishing from Dee, or the other five or six million he took from me.

I'd never been in this position before, and I guess I could've gone completely to the dogs at that point, but that's not my makeup. *Premonition* finally came out in '86, my first album with Atlantic, and out of the blue, I got a call from Bowie and he said, "I love your playing on *Premonition*, I just listened to it. Would you come to Switzerland and play on my new record?"

Chapter **Twelve**

I had just finished touring, opening for Stevie Nicks, when David called. It had been a great tour, my first since 1982, and now I was getting songs ready to do *When All the Pieces Fit*. But I put all that on hold, even though I couldn't wait to get back to it. Now Dave and I were actually going to play together; we hadn't done that since the art block stairs in '62.

The fact was that he could have any guitar player in the world come out and play with him and he chose me. He knew that the world was confused as to what I was—I'd first arrived in the US as this guitar player with Humble Pie, but then I had this huge record where, yes, there is great guitar playing on it, but there was this perception out there due to my looks and choice of wardrobe that I had slipped back into the teenybopper mode.

Dave saw how the perception of who I really was had changed and knew I was not happy. He gave me a huge gift by taking me around the world, reintroducing me as a guitar player. I could not and can never thank him enough. That was a huge leg up he gave me, and from that moment on, I started to get my confidence back, and it made a huge difference to me and what was to come.

I went to his house when I arrived in Switzerland and the next day I went to the studio with the engineer. Dave came down and gave me all the lyrics, and we played through the tracks on what would become *Never Let Me Down*. He said, "See what you can do here and here," and then he basically left me alone to do whatever I thought would work.

He seemed like he was really into the album. He'd come down to the studio every day after he'd gone to the gym and have a listen, and he was excited. I thought the whole album was great. After *Never Let Me Down* came out, I now understand, he felt the album should have been different. His next project was Tin Machine, so he certainly did change it up after that—and then many years later, they remixed and redid the whole album!

While we were there, we would go out for dinner and one night Dave said, "I know you're probably going to go back and do your own album now, but I'm doing this big tour, called the Glass Spider Tour—would you come and play guitar on the tour?" And I said yes in about a nanosecond. I said I would put everything else on hold; this is an opportunity that I can't miss, it's wonderful, thank you.

It was the biggest production I've ever toured with in my entire life. In Europe, the trucks are a little smaller, but I was told there were forty trucks, 240 people in the crew, and three giant spiders. You had to leapfrog two separate stages, because it took days to put one up. You would perform on one stage and the other would travel, so the next spider would be ready to go. We had yet another one in Australia, which was left there and burned—which is what you do to spiders, don't you?

When we were in rehearsals, it was all choreographed and I'm not used to that. There was a stepladder to simulate my entrance at the beginning of the show because they didn't have "Pete's Plinth," as it was called, made at that point. So instead I had to get up on the stepladder. I did it the first time and then said, "I'm not going to do that." Dave said, "You didn't get up on the stepladder!" I said, "Well, it'll be all right on the night—I'll wait for my plinth."

Every part of the show had to be staged properly—because there was not only the band and Dave, we also had dancers. It was a great team, great people to work with, except they did sometimes get in the way on stage. At one point in "Let's Dance," the dancer, Melissa Hurley, walked backward and stepped on my pedal board and turned me off in the middle of the solo. Another time, during a quiet part my loud button got stepped on.

David couldn't have given me a grander entrance. Carlos Alomar would do this great shredding guitar intro, and then there was all this taped stuff with controlled chaos going on. Then we start the opening song. Just before it got to the guitar solo, I went up these steps up on the back of this gold plinth with room on the top for me to stand. By the end of the number, the light's off me and I climb back and come down to the front.

As the tour went on, and people were relaxing a little bit more, they taped a couple of pages out of *Playboy* on the plinth first, and then it got more and more pornographic each show. Each night the crew were all snickering and pointing at me and I was laughing, too. Every day it's just getting worse and worse; the last show was over-the-top disgusting, but still funny. When Dave was in *The Elephant Man* on Broadway, he invited me to see the show and I went backstage after and we were chatting about it. At one point in the show he was in a bath on stage, and he told me, "You wouldn't believe what the production crew place in that bath some nights—rubber duckies, brushes . . ." Anything really uncomfortable to sit on, I guess.

It was a very enjoyable tour; we had a private plane. A bus or large van would pick everybody up, all the dancers and the band, to go to the airport. If we had a bad review, Dave would travel in the car behind, but if we had a good review, he'd travel on the bus. I totally get that! Even for the reviews in a foreign language, we would get a translation from Dave's publicist.

Playing some of those super iconic guitar parts, like "Heroes"—it was phenomenal that I was getting to play these things that all these great guitarists had played. Obviously I'm not Stevie Ray Vaughan or Robert Fripp, so I'm not going to play like either, but I played my version of their parts. It's pretty much written as to what you play, so it was a challenge; but I love a challenge. I knew that I was going to be compared to a lot of incredible guitar players, and luckily I believe I came out of it pretty well.

I've always said, from when I started, that I just wanted to be the guitar player in a band. Dave wanted me to do more backing vocals, but I said that I just wanted to play guitar. I didn't really want to sing. But every night was a forum for me to come out there and do my best on these legendary songs. The only time I played any hint of my own music was in "Jean Genie." In the solo, I slipped in the intro from "Do You Feel" and the crowd went nuts. David smiled; he liked it. It was my way of reaching out and saying, "Hey, it's me."

We'd go out to dinner on the tour. One night right before the first date in the EU, he and I got shit-faced together and then they kind of started keeping us apart for a while. He was like me, same thing. There was always the possibility of becoming addicted to anything. I know he became sober in later years, but we definitely tore it up that one night, just the two of us.

People would ask me to go talk to Dave about stuff, because they knew that he'd listen to me. But we had a personal relationship and a business one; he was the boss and I played guitar for him. When we were together, it was the same as usual. I never called him David; I always called him Dave, because I knew him as Dave from school. He was a very caring person. After he'd passed, I sent Iman an email saying what a great older brother he was to me, always there to help when needed.

Dave was a regular kind of guy. The persona portrayed on different albums and tours was an act. It was all carefully worked out. He'd reinvent himself all the time and he knew what he was going to be—it was a new character each time. He was a great actor. Meanwhile, he still had this amazing ability, lyrically, musically, and vocally, to write all those legendary, thought-provoking songs.

But that tour set me up for what was to come. On my farewell tour, we had a great video opening: all these pictures of me, bands, and people I've known start to appear, first slowly then really fast, building up into a crescendo and ending on a video of David pointing and saying, "Peter Frampton on guitar"—it's film from the Glass Spider Tour—and then I walk on stage. He brought me on, which is so cool. I thought because it was the last tour, it would be great to have Dave introduce me. Thank you, Dave.

While we were on the Glass Spider Tour, I found out Dave was really frightened of flying—though I shouldn't laugh. After about my millionth flight, I'd reached a point where I started getting bad, too, so I decided I would learn to fly. For my tour in '79 we had our own plane, and both our pilots were also flight instructors. So Rodney Eckerman and I would go back to the airport on days off and take lessons. I ended up with a whopping fifteen hours, but learned that you have to almost force a plane not to fly unless there is a mechanical problem or pilot error. (Oh, and it's always advisable to make sure you have enough fuel before you take off. You'd be amazed at how many accidents happen by pilots running out of juice.)

So by taking a few lessons, I'd exorcised my fear. I still have my logbook, but I never continued flying after the tour. One day, our pilots hadn't been available and I had an instructor who really wanted me to do my first solo flight. I already had over ten hours in a Cessna 152 and had been landing and taking off with no help from the pilot sitting next to me. I would have liked to solo, too, but this was a new airport for me. It was a little rural airport with a narrow runway with major power lines crossing the start of the runway. So you couldn't do a normal approach, but had to stay higher than usual to get over the power lines and then drop down quickly to land. Needless to say, I didn't think that should be the first and last landing I ever made, especially at this airport.

Anyway, Dave was not a fan of flying at all, but we always had great planes. Once, we had to use a different one; it was a 727, like our regular one. We're on the runway and it starts to move, and you know how sometimes when the air conditioners come on, they kind of put out a fog, which is actually condensation? Well, there was an awful lot of condensation this time, and it did look a bit like smoke. So Coco, who was David's right-hand lady, and David start yelling "Smoke! Smoke!" Coco starts running to the back—we're already taxiing to the runway, and she goes to open the back door and the flight attendant runs back shouting, "Stop, stop, don't do that!" I don't believe the door would have opened due to the plane already having been pressurized. But if you did open it at altitude, you would be sucked out of the plane.

So the pilot pulls off the runway, and we stop. The flight attendant opened the door at the back and a chute came out, which inflated for everyone to slide down away from the plane. As Dave came down the aisle, he grabbed me, and put me in front of him, and then pushed me down the slide. He made sure he got me off the plane before himself. Another thing I thanked him for. He was always there looking out for me.

There was a bedroom suite on the plane, with gold faucets and the whole thing, but Dave would never go in. He and Coco would take turns sitting on the jump seat right at the back of the plane, as close to the exit as possible, rather than be relaxed and comfortable in his private space.

Barbara and Jade came on the plane a couple of times. Jade would hang out in David's room, watching videos on his TV, and come up to him and—she was three or four—say things like, "David, you promised me you'd come and play with me." And he was great with her. She got on his case a couple of times. She called him Davin Bowie—"Davin, you haven't played with me yet."

We didn't spend that much time together over the years, but it was almost a brotherly relationship. He was protective of me, and I think it also had to do with the relationship he had with my dad. He was family.

When I started the Bowie tour, Barbara and I had already moved from New York to Florida, to an apartment in Fort Lauderdale on the beach, on Galt Ocean Drive. We had to sell the house in New York, so we went down and rented two apartments that had been joined together, and it was a great place. By the time I finished the tour, we'd moved to Los Angeles. And that's when I started to find my spirit again. Unfortunately, or fortunately for me, I always seemed to be on tour when the house moving happened. Barbara did this at least twice without me. And yes, I did feel a lot of guilt!

Her sister Carole was in Florida on vacation. She called me up and said she had just heard a version of "Baby, I Love Your Way" on the radio, and it was on all the time. And also it was joined with another song. I said, "That's bizarre; I don't know about that. Maybe you think it's somebody else, but it's really me?" I started to do some homework and got my team to investigate, and we found out that a band called Will to Power had released their recording of the song as a medley combined with "Free Bird."

They were a duo—a girl singer and a DJ who had apparently always put those two songs together in his set and it worked well, from slow dance to rocking out. So he thought: "Well, let's do it as a record." They made a little mistake, though. When you want to record a song written by someone else, you don't need to ask the writer for permission, but you do have to speak with the publisher of the song and agree on a publishing rate. Well, neither Will to Power nor their label had called my or Lynyrd Skynyrd's publishing company, and their record company should have taken care of this before it came out.

Lynyrd Skynyrd's publisher and my publisher got together and agreed that if they had been approached before the release by the artist's record company, it would have been regarded as a medley and Skynyrd and I would have each received 50 percent of the publishing and songwriting royalties. But with no one contacting either publisher before the release, both publishers decided they could charge 100 percent of the normal rate for each song. So Will to Power, unfortunately, had to pay twice the amount that a two-song medley would normally have cost them.

I wasn't a fan of their version, but it was a big hit. It was actually number one for a week. "Baby, I Love Your Way" with "Free Bird," who would've thunk? It definitely made people think about me and Skynyrd, though, so I guess as much as I didn't like the Will to Power record, I was still honored that someone wanted to cover my song. I would've preferred they hadn't, but it was on the radio everywhere. I was even on MTV for forty-five seconds, talking to Kurt Loder about it, and for a while radio stations were doing Tuesday twofers, so they'd play the two originals, and it all helps.

The bottom line is that when my next publishing statement came, the first "Medley" sales had earned me $500,000 as writer of my half of the track. So Will to Power actually helped more than they'll ever know. I really needed the money then, so it got me out of a hole. It couldn't have been better timing, and it was responsible for getting my and Barbara's heads above water financially.

I was just sort of living a normal family life now. I didn't have any touring or anything lined up after the Bowie dates, so it was time to finish writing and recording *When All the Pieces Fit*. "Dad" was off the road and home with the family. If you think about it, I started playing professionally when I was sixteen, so it had been album/tour, album/tour, album/tour for exactly twenty years, so I think I was way overdue for a break. Even if the reason wasn't my choice—the fact that the bottom had fallen out of my career—now we had our wonderful firstborn,

Jade, and when your first one arrives, it's all-consuming. The best thing was that I had time to be there to enjoy our growing family.

Before Jade was born, when we were still living in Westchester, I actually did two or three dummy runs from the house to the hospital alone in the car, because I'm that kind of guy—I wanted to know exactly how long it took at different times in the day. That's me. Then Barbara's getting ready, we drive to the hospital, and it's quite a long birth. As Jade is arriving, Barbara has a firm grip on my arm. Her grip gets stronger and stronger and then voila, we have a baby! As soon as we had all calmed down a bit, I did finally ask if Barbara could let go of my arm now.

When we moved to LA, Barbara was pregnant with Julian. When the day came, she said, "Oh, I've done this before, no big deal." We had a nanny who was trying to get Barbara to leave and get in the car. "Miss, you got to go! You're going to have the baby here!" I was getting a little worried. Barbara said, "I have to eat," so she's eating this huge cheeseburger in the kitchen. Finally, we get her in the car, and of course I'm speeding now because she's started moaning. Just please don't have the baby in the car! Let's get to the hospital. I go my planned shortcut way—because, of course, I've done a dummy run for this route as well.

I'm honking and honking. People are getting out of my way, and then a police car pulls me over, and I wind down the window and he asks, "Sir, do you know why I stopped you?" I said I had no idea. He said, "Excessive honking." I said, "You're kidding me! Well, this is my wife; she's just about to have a baby. Would you like her to have it in the car or at Cedars-Sinai?" He said, "Follow me, sir." So I'm driving with one trooper in front, and I see there's also one behind us, and now we're really honking in addition to two sirens. So Julian literally had horns and sirens trumpet his arrival, his own royal fanfare.

We pull into Cedars, and she's going to have this baby literally any second. The nurse comes out and hurries her in. Meanwhile, the cop goes, "Could I get your autograph?" Er, okay, so I signed for both cops, but now I haven't a clue where Barbara went, so I'm running in shouting, "Maternity?!" "Oh, second floor." I don't know where she is, because they've rushed her in, and I'm putting on the scrubs, which you had to wear back then. As I'm walking down the hallway, I hear screaming, so I open the door—it's not my wife! It's somebody else having a baby. I'm in the wrong room.

I shut that door quickly and finally find her, and Julian was born within two seconds of me walking in the room. Our pediatrician wasn't there at that point, but there was this giant male nurse in with Barbara, he had the full set of silver braces on his teeth, so he looked scary, like something out of a James Bond movie. Our pediatrician, Peter Waldstein, arrived then and checked things out, only to find all was well with our lovely little son Julian.

After the Glass Spider Tour, I'd gone home to our new place in the Hollywood Hills. Yes, I missed helping with the move, this time because I was on tour with David. Barbara had to do it on her own, again, moving us into the new house near the top of Outpost Canyon. There was only one room upstairs, which had been an office before we bought it. It had a separate entrance, too—perfect, I could immediately see this space being my new home studio. I put a nice area rug down and started to move in all my gear: 3M M79 24 track analog machine, Studer 2-track, Amek Angela console, and all the outboard gear and microphones I had collected since the '70s. I bought a Mac SE and Performer Midi software as my Christmas presents to myself, and after Christmas dinner, as the tryptophan started to put everyone to sleep, I made my way upstairs and opened a Mac manual for the very first time.

One dear friend I met around this time was Richard Landers, a recording engineer who was working for Steve Vai as his studio manager/engineer. I really needed help wiring up my new studio and Richard said that Art Kelm, who was managing a big studio called The Complex, would be perfect. So he called Art and next thing I knew, I was all set up and ready to rock. After I had recorded a few tracks done with programmed drums, synth bass, and guitars, I could see it was time to record real drums and bass, and some really loud guitar solos, in a nice-sounding room.

Richard had a wealth of info about LA people, so we started to discuss engineers. He mentioned Chris Lord-Alge, who's one of the top mix engineers, and very soon Chris came over and I played him what I had. He seemed to really like the new stuff, and he loves great-sounding loud guitars. So it sounded like this partnership could be just what was needed.

Chris and I were working on the tracks during '88 and then *When All the Pieces Fit* came out in '89. I was very happy with it—didn't do that well, but I was very hands-on again; it was nearly all done at home. Chris then recorded the drums, with Denny Fongheiser, John "JR" Robinson, and Steve Ferrone each on different tracks, and Nathan East came in to play bass. It doesn't get better than these players, and I was so pleased with how the record turned out.

We were also doing sessions at Allen Sides's Ocean Way Recording studios on Sunset Boulevard. It has a legendary history; it used to be called United Western Studios and everyone from Frank Sinatra and Ray Charles to the Beach Boys and Phil Spector has recorded there. Bill Putnam Sr. was the founder and chief engineer, and he pretty much invented the recording console and so much of the outboard equipment we still use today. I would record my vocals at home using my Neumann U47 modified by Stephen Paul that I've had since 1980. Chris had made me what we call twenty-four-track save reels on two-inch tape to take home to do the vocals. After I had the vocals finished, I would bring back the save reels and then he would add the vocals on to the master digital thirty-two-track in time to mix. Chris is a phenomenal mix engineer and so I was always thrilled with the results.

After *When All the Pieces Fit* came out, I met up with John Kalodner, the famous A&R executive, at a party. He had worked with Aerosmith and Sammy Hagar, and had just put Damn Yankees together. The first thing he says to me after "hello" is, "Your solo career is over. You need to form a band." I believe there was moment or two of silence as I was melting down inside, with smoke coming out of my ears. After I had processed his words, though, I actually thought, that's not a bad idea, let me try to put a band together. So I asked Denny Fongheiser if he would join me on drums—fantastic, I got a yes. I found a bass player called Vito San Filippo, and the three of us sounded really great and did a few demos. I wanted to find another guitar player or keyboard player who was a great singer and writer and could be another front man. That should be easy . . . so I started asking different players to come in and jam with us, but I wasn't getting that special feeling like I did the first time Humble Pie played together.

Meantime, Barbara and I had split up. It had just run its course, I guess. Barbara wanted out, so that was it. Divorce is horrible, but time heals and we are all very close now, which is great for the children and just makes life easier. Life's too short, in many, many ways. As an older person, I have to try to drill that into younger people—the grudge that you hold isn't worth the time that you lose.

When people stop communicating and don't talk to each other, for whatever reason, it all just festers and you feel it's never going to end. Then an olive branch can sometimes reinstate communication, which is the key to being in a better place than you were before. Looking back, it's such a waste of time!

For many, many years, I just hated what Dee Anthony had done. I didn't hate him, but I hated what he did, how shortsighted he was. How greedy he was. But would I be sitting here now, today, if I hadn't met Dee Anthony, or had him manage me? No. My life could've been drastically different. He had some great points, so I've learned to put that behind me—it takes a while sometimes to understand, and this helps me every time: "God grant me the serenity to accept the things I cannot change, courage to change the things I can, and the wisdom to know the difference."

I'm still trying to get a band sorted out, and Barbara said to me, "The trouble is, you know who you're looking for, so why don't you call him up?" I said "Who?" And she said Steve Marriott. I said, "Oh, my God, yes! That *is* who I'm looking for, obviously." I knew the power of that combo—of the four of us together in Humble Pie, but especially the interplay between Steve Marriott and me.

It took a while, but I found him. We hadn't spoken in years. I said, "What would you think about seeing if we can write together again, and maybe do some recording?" And after a while he said, "All right, why not?" I said I would fly over and see him.

So I went over to England, and the first day I went to his cottage, we wrote a song. It was bing, bang, boom—it was instant. There was something about the two of us together when we were alone in a room, when his ego disappeared and mine did, too, and we were on the same footing. He had a riff, and I had something else, and so we wrote a song called "Out of the Blue," which later came out on the *Peter Frampton* album. Then I played on something he'd already recorded on his little Portastudio thing. And I thought, "Wow, this is great."

He said, "I've got a couple of gigs left to do in Germany. After I finish those I'll come over." When Steve came over, he rented a place in Santa Monica with his wife, Toni. I had this make-do studio in Le Mobile's Warehouse in North Hollywood. Steve would drive in every day during the week and we'd work on something. One of the songs I had started writing needed words for the verses, so Steve helped me finish those. I already had the chorus, "I won't let you down." We started by singing the chorus, the two of us on my U47 mic and we were singing together again, and it was classic. Chills. It took me right back to when we first sang together and now we're both laughing and looking at each other like, wow! It was the best.

So we set up a day for the band to play together for the first time. We got together at my studio in North Hollywood—Vito, Denny, Steve, and I—and we started jamming on some of the things we had been writing, and it was sounding amazing. No doubt this would have been another great band. We needed a record deal, and I had already met John Branca (who was, among other things, Michael Jackson's lawyer) socially, so I spoke with him and told him what we wanted to do. He said, "Well, you've got to call it Humble Pie." I said no, don't push that, because Steve and I don't want that. It's not Humble Pie. It's Marriott/Frampton—or Frampton/Marriott, depending on who you talk to.

We had a meeting set up with John to talk about a deal and everything, but Steve got lost coming from Santa Monica and he never made it. He turned around and went home, and so I'm sitting there and I thought, "This isn't good." I called him up and said, "What happened, man?" He said, "I fucking got lost," and just kind of grumbled. He just went off, and I was getting a feeling from him, like I did in the old days. I believe that Steve didn't want to go to that meeting because it could mean that things go really well and we might get a great record and publishing deal—it's like he wanted to short circuit everything in case we were successful.

I suddenly felt that we weren't on the same wavelength anymore. He was drinking from a Perrier bottle in the studio, and dumbass me didn't realize at first that he's got wine in there. I would drive him to a restaurant at the end of each day, his wife would pick him up, and they'd go back to Santa Monica. I started saying, "Steve, if we're going to do this, we agreed at the beginning that we would work straight." So that's when it got into "Well, fuck you, then" . . . *The wheels on the bus go round and round.*

I went down to Santa Monica and talked to him one more time and he was being silly—"Honey, bring me the heroin! I need to do some heroin." He was joking. So I could see we weren't getting anywhere and I said, "I don't care what you do on the weekend, but if we can't work straight, I can't do this."

It was very upsetting to me. He flew home ten days after we had stopped working together. It was winter, so it was cold back in England. They decided to stay with friends for the night and go home in the morning—"We don't want to have to start the furnace up and everything, let's go and stay with our friends."

But in the middle of the night, the friends caught Steve going to get another bottle of wine and put him back to bed, and when they woke up, he'd gone. Toni, his wife, said that he left while she was sleeping. He went back to their house and got into bed and passed out with a cigarette in his hand, and it caught fire to the mattress, and that was it. He was only forty-four. That was April 20, 1991. It was two days before my birthday.

I was on the phone with my brother, Clive, in London and I was telling him how things had not gone as I had hoped and Steve had now gone home. Then call waiting beeps in that I had another call and I said, "Hold on a minute, Clive." Normally I would've ignored it, but I wondered if it was family or something, so I clicked over and it was a journalist from a paper in England and the guy goes, "Uh, Peter?" "Yes?" And he said, "I have some disturbing news; I'd like your reaction to it. Steve Marriott was found dead this morning. His house burnt down." I said, "I'm sorry, I can't say anything right now, no comment." So I clicked back, I said, "Clive, Steve's dead—I've gotta go. I've got to find out what happened."

After we stopped working together, before he went back to England, Steve had called me up one day, out of it, and just said, "Hey, how you . . . oh, didn't mean to call you," whatever. I said, "How you doing?" "All right." "How are you, Steve?"

"Oh, I'm fine. All right mate, bye." I think he might've been calling to get things going again, but he was just in no shape.

Maybe it was a cry for help. But he got off the phone, I didn't. Could I have done more, and would it have been worth dealing with his drinking? But the answer I get every time I think about it is no! I'm sure it was devastating for him, too, that it didn't work. The time we had together, when we were on the same level, same plane, was unbelievable. Steve would always make my jaw drop, no matter what he did—harp playing, his great bluesy guitar—but his voice, oh, my God.

On that tape, when we're singing the chorus together in "I Won't Let You Down," if you solo those tracks, you can hear us giggling in between each line. It's so great! So we had those moments; we had another time together when we were creative, and I wish we'd done more, but obviously it wasn't to be.

E ither the Caracas airport or the insurance company or both had to guard the debris until a search was done by Venezuela's version of the FAA. And as it turned out, though everyone on board was killed, there were about four or five guitars that apparently weren't destroyed by the crash, and most likely a guard grabbed them. He thought that they would be a little safer elsewhere, so he took them home. But then I guess he thought, "Well, they're very safe here now, but I could be a lot richer if I sold these." There were two of my Gibson Les Pauls, the black one and a white one—it was like the negative version—plus my '55 Fender Strat, and I had a '63 Precision bass that I always brought as a backup for John, plus a couple more. All these wonderful instruments.

The black Gibson was sold to a musician in Caracas, who apparently—and this is where it becomes a gray area—played it for about fifteen years, until it got too hot for him, because everyone was going, "That looks an awful lot like Peter Frampton's guitar, the one that he was playing before the crash." It got worse and worse, and he finally left Caracas and moved to the island of Curaçao. I guess when you retire in Venezuela, you build your mansion on Curaçao and you go live there.

Chapter Thirteen

From when I was sixteen to when I was forty-two, I had cluster headaches. Each cluster would last for a period of about three months. The headaches would go on for about forty minutes and then crescendo with what one doctor, who also had them, described as "the ice-pick ending." That's when it got to its worst, and it's literally like there's hammering just behind your eye, like there's an ice pick going in your head. I had no idea what these were when I was sixteen, I just thought I had migraines. But toward the end of the three-month period, one would finish and I'd go straight into another one, finish that one, go straight into another. Then all of a sudden they would go *pfft*—"Oh, well, they're gone now, thank God." Gone for another nine months anyway.

One thing that brings them on is alcohol and pot, or anything that dilates your blood vessels. Before we left Westchester for Florida, I went to a headache treatment center and I found out what these painful episodes were all about. When I had my accident in the '70s, my GP came in to check on me at the hospital and he said, "How're you doing?" I said I was fine, but I was having these bad headaches, and it was blistering right then. He said, "That can't be—you're on so much morphine right now, there's no way that you can have a headache." I said, "Okay, well, I *do* have a headache and it's killing me."

He said he needed to do some research. When he came back, he said that the only thing that will cause severe head pain after using morphine is a cluster headache. So he prescribed me ergotamine, but you had to put this pill under your tongue as soon as you felt one coming on, otherwise I'm not sure if it worked that well. But he found what they were; it's the only headache pain that an opioid like morphine can't help. So I started taking this pill whenever I would feel one come on.

When we moved to LA, I found a doctor who, it turns out, is Lisa Kudrow's father—not that I knew that at the time. He was a cutting-edge doctor and because he also suffered from the same headaches, he was on a quest trying different therapies to stop people's pain. Up until meeting Dr. Kudrow, there didn't seem to be anything that would stop them. "Let me explain to you what cluster headaches are," he said. "The brain tells your blood vessels to open up, because it thinks it needs more oxygen up there." In a study, he told me, a patient came in while they were actually having one of these headaches, and at its peak of pain, they took an x-ray. The incoming blood vessel inside the brain was eight times its normal size at the peak of the headache. Ouch!

So then he told me that the easiest way to get relief during a three-month cluster was oxygen! *What?!* Yes, you trick the brain into believing it now has plenty of oxygen because you're now breathing pure O_2 at a high rate. In five to ten minutes, the pain would leave. Hallelujah!

He gave me a prescription to go and get an oxygen tank and instructions to call him in the morning. This was incredible and it changed my life for those three months every year. They also call them the "alarm clock headache," because you could set your watch by them; always at the exact same time. Wake you up with one, stop you from sleeping with one.

I did a light treatment study for him because, even though at that time they didn't know for sure, we all have something called a circadian pacemaker, which sets the time we wake up and go to sleep. Jet lag plays havoc with it because it's trying to reset and doesn't understand why it isn't dark yet! I'm not a doctor (though I'd like to play one on TV), but being blessed with something special like cluster headaches to deal with, I wanted to find out everything I could, so I knew what I was talking about and could give the doctor good feedback. So I got a tank of oxygen delivered to the house and the first time I got the headache, he told me how to set it, and it went away in ten minutes. Ten minutes! Because it told the brain, "Close down vessels; we have enough oxygen here." "10-4!"

I couldn't believe it was this simple. No pills, no nothing—oxygen. So on tour, I started to travel with an oxygen tank, and if we would fly, I'd have to open it, let the O_2 go, and have my tech go and get it refilled when we arrived at the other end.

It was just something that I lived with. And when you haven't got a clue what it is, and people are saying, "Oh, go take some aspirin," and nothing works, it's frustrating and you feel hopeless. Barbara would come into the bathroom in the middle of the night, and I would be lying on the floor with my head on the cold tile, because that made me feel better. Physically banging my head against the floor would help, too. The headaches finally went away when I was forty-two, so the whole nightmare was a twenty-four-year cycle.

When we lost Steve, it was devastating. It was a tragedy not only because he died so young, but also because we were all deprived of his talent way too early. In the back of my mind was always the thought that we would try again, after having time to come to our senses. The bar for a worthy and inspiring partner for a new band was set so high. So I decided I would put my solo band back together. I needed to go out and play live again.

I first called up a dear friend, the great bass player John Regan, and told him what I wanted to do. It had been about five years since I had toured and I could no longer fill arenas, so we booked six weeks of clubs—and we were tearing it up. We're sold out everywhere, people want more dates. Six weeks turns into six months, and we kept touring, going into bigger rooms, until we were back in amphitheaters. Co-headlining or being a major support in an amphitheater was fantastic. We did some headline dates, too, but they were in smaller venues like the Ritz in New York.

It made me realize, wow, there *is* an audience still out there for me, so we just kept going and touring more. I enjoyed it so much. All right, so it wasn't Madison Square Garden, but I've never cared about the money as long as I have enough to pay the rent.

There's one thing that Dee Anthony said to me the last time I saw him. This was the final settlement, to get my publishing back, and we were tearing up the management contract. Obviously things weren't great for me at that point. And he said, "You'll be fine." I said, "What do you mean?" He said, "Well, you know how to do it now." And I knew exactly what he meant—"Play in front of as many people as you can in the shortest space of time." If you're a great live act, people want to see you. And he was right.

Now we're doing amphitheaters supporting Foreigner, Sky-nyrd, REO Speedwagon. We're back in front of tons of people again. My audience was growing and we built it back, and then I got the urge to do another album. I was living in a furnished apartment on Hollywood Boulevard, which Barbara had found for me. Very soon after, I met Kevin Savigar, who had written hits for Rod Stewart as well as played keyboards in his band. Dear friend and a wonderful musician. We really hit it off, person-ally and musically, and we produced the new album together. I also wrote two songs with Jonathan Cain from Journey—"Can't Take That Away" and "Waiting for Your Love." They're both great songs, in my humble opinion.

I decided I wouldn't turn on my computer until I had written a song on acoustic, electric, or piano. So many times, being too techy for my own good, I had spent hours and hours program-ming an incredible drum loop, but then had incredible difficulty coming up with the song part—the most important part!

The whole Seattle grunge scene was now a huge influence on what was on the radio. A big part of having a long, successful career is not trying to be a carbon copy of the last band who topped the charts, but to be unique, which is very hard to do, especially when the suits say they love your band but at the same time ask you to sound more like this new current hit act. So I was writing on acoustic like I used to—a little bit on piano, a little bit on electric, but mainly acoustic.

I thought the *Peter Frampton* album was good, there are some strong tracks on there: "Day in the Sun," "Can't Take That Away," "You Can Be Sure," and the instrumental "Off the

Hook." But it just wasn't strong enough to break through, and it was out of sync with what was on the radio right then.

But this "six-week club tour" kept getting longer and bigger the more we stayed out there. We started on Valentine's Day 1992 at the club Hammerjacks in Baltimore, and by June we were headlining at the Pine Knob amphitheater outside Detroit. It was a great sense of accomplishment, and I could finally start to feel my stomach telling me that all the touring was paying off. My audience was still there, and we were making new fans at every show.

In March, we were playing Cincinnati and I was in a shop next to the Pfister Hotel that had lots of great photos of the city. A girl came up to me and said, "Hi, Peter, do you remember Tina?" Back in '79, on the Where I Should Be tour, I met Tina Elfers in Cincinnati after my show there at Riverfront Coliseum. I'd asked her if she would come with me on the plane and I took her all around, and then she had to go home because a friend of hers was in a car wreck and we lost touch. Now it was thirteen years later.

I asked the girl who approached me, "Is Tina in town?" And she said, "Yes, she's going to a Bryan Adams concert." I said, "Well, that's no good—ask her to come to my concert," and she did. It was great to see Tina again after all those years, and I could feel that this might be something to get serious about.

We started talking on the phone, and then after the tour I invited her out to LA to visit. She and Tiffany, her daughter, came out and met my children, Jade and Julian. In fact, we all had Thanksgiving together at my Hollywood apartment. I remember there was a very small earthquake as we started to eat dinner. When the visit was over, Tina and Tif flew back to

Cincinnati and pretty soon after, I rented a townhouse in Bel Air that was big enough to house this new and blending family.

I found the house, but I had no furniture and no money. I literally had the beds and that was it. It was like going back to the very beginning again. I owed more than I had coming in, and I hadn't been aware that my business manager had let me down, too. Which unfortunately left me with a lien from the government and all sorts of crazy stuff. I was minus flat broke.

I've never been great with figures, and I became lazy because someone else was looking after my finances. There lies a potential problem; you hire them because you think you can trust them and they're supposed to know how to save and make your money grow. But there are so many cases of fraud in this area—Bernie Madoff being one, if not the worst.

So I had to change business managers. I went to a chichi Beverly Hills firm. They were all dressed in suits and they were awful. I didn't have any money, so they said, "Well, what are you going to do?" I said, "Aren't you supposed to figure that out—what can you do for me?"

Luckily, I met Gary Haber, who was to play a huge part in my life, and my family's. This is the person who literally saved my bacon. I think he took me on at first because he could see I was going to be a huge challenge; I was a financial mess. So, thank God, he took the challenge. When I first went to his office in Encino, he was wearing jeans and a shirt. He said, "I don't wear suits like they do in Beverly Hills, but I'll find every penny you are owed, wherever it is."

Gary was unbelievable. Tina and I became close friends with him and his wife, Sherri. He was a really great managerial advisor as well as my business manager. Gary recommended managers for me to try, and we definitely tried a few until he introduced me to my current manager, Ken Levitan, who has been the architect behind my career path since 2005. I was already aware of how many successful acts Ken had worked with and is still managing, from Emmylou Harris to Kings of Leon, Kid Rock to Richard Thompson.

By this time, downloading (and, soon, streaming) music meant that record sales had sunk down to almost nothing, so there was a need for alternative marketing. Touring became the only way of compensating for the lack of royalties from record sales. Before we started working together, Ken said, "I will raise your worth as a live act and it will pay for my percentage." He was right! After fifteen years working with Ken, my awareness is at a level I thought I would never reach again.

On my father's teaching salary, my family got by . . . just. My dad would do some wallpaper and fabric designs for a European company to pay for our summer holidays and any extra luxuries. So I should have known better and paid more attention to detail. When I picked up my first check for the first wave of sales for *Frampton Comes Alive!*, it was for a million dollars. I was twenty-six and, all of a sudden, I thought I had arrived and didn't have to worry because this was never going to stop. Oh, boy, was I wrong! It's wonderful to have a nice nest egg, it alleviates some obvious problems and worry, but money won't buy you love or happiness.

I was probably meant to be shown a lesson by being successful, with millions in the bank, and then go down to zero—and minus—so that I would appreciate and respect money, if I ever got another chance. I have a great deal of respect for it, but I'm not a hound for it, either. Never have been. I have never based any of my career decisions on money. It's always been because of what I feel I need to do creatively.

In America and Canada, I commanded a very nice figure for a show, especially on the Finale Tour, but in Europe not so much. Jerry Moss came to see me at my last show at the Forum in LA, and he said, "You know, I always thought that Dee would manage you to be an international act." But he was so shortsighted—he could get instant cash right here in America. To build an audience, you have to take care of it and tour everywhere and then go back. We should've toured the rest of the world as much as we did America, but we kept on going 'round and 'round and the act got tired. It got to the point that you couldn't get any more blood out of this stone.

There was another manager in the mix in the '90s, and after the first tour we did with him at the helm, I realized that once he took his percentage, I was in the hole for something like forty grand. Then I heard that his wife got a brand-new BMW. So that was the end of him. Then there was another manager, and he didn't last long, either. But I just kept working my way back up touring.

The artist has his agenda, which is to write great material, record, and perform great live shows. The management's agenda can be very different from the artist's; the more money there is coming in, the more blinded by the wealth they can become and start to believe it's all theirs.

I actually don't remember too much of this down period because when I met Tina, she said, having seen how my moods would change, "I think you need to go see a doctor about an antidepressant." I've suffered with depression all my life, but I also think it's the nature of what performers do. It's that high from the show and adulation from the crowd. Then you come home and it's almost like you expect a round of applause when you get up.

I heard that when U2 finish a tour, Bono's wife has him check into a local hotel for a few days before he's allowed home, just so he can assimilate back into being a regular guy, husband, father, and person. It can be hard after playing to all those adoring fans to come home and go right back into taking the garbage out and changing the cat litter.

Tina suggested getting help, some medication for the depression. The first one was Prozac, so I tried that and started feeling better. I went through a couple more prescriptions until I got to the one that I've been on for years now.

I used to describe depression as feeling like you're in a pit. You feel yourself going into the pit, climbing down the ladder. Then someone takes the ladder away and you can't get out. It's that helpless, hopeless feeling of not being able to get out of bed, not wanting to do anything, and this would go on for weeks.

People who just have bad days don't really understand depression—they think, "Well, I'd better start taking those pills." It won't work for those people. An antidepressant isn't a pick-me-up, it's something for long-term clinical depression. So instead of months of not feeling good, it's now only a few days. The ladder now gets left in the pit, and so I'm able to climb back out relatively quickly.

Thankfully, I no longer suffer anywhere near as much with my depression. I still have bad days, like we all do, but I'm one of the people who those pills are meant for. The difference is incredible, and I'm very lucky.

Meantime, oddly enough, another version of "Baby, I Love Your Way," a reggae version, had come out and exploded. My original single got to about number fifteen, I don't think it was top ten. This recording, by a group called Big Mountain, went number one—around the world!

The producer Ron Fair had asked me if I would want to redo the song for the movie soundtrack of *Reality Bites*. In the movie, there's a scene when my live version of "Baby, I Love Your Way" comes on the car radio. Ron asked me what I thought about doing a reggae version of the song. I said, "No, I've done that song for years; I've done it so many different ways of my own choosing, I think it would be best if you have somebody else have a crack at it." He said, "Okay, well, I did have someone in mind if you weren't interested—a band called Big Mountain." I said, "You have my blessing." When I heard it, I actually thought it was an incredible version. It definitely worked. So, yeah, that was a nice surprise.

The *Peter Frampton* record had just come out, so I flew on a Sunday night to New York for a week of promo. I'm on the radio at seven-something on the Monday morning and one of the DJs says, "You live in LA, don't you?" I thought he was going to start in with the New York/LA rivalry, but he said, "There's just been a 6.9 earthquake in Los Angeles." I said, "I think I have to leave!"

It was freezing in New York. Everything was frozen. Every plane I got booked on was canceled. I finally got a flight and arrived back late that night. I had a car pick me up, and we're driving through an obstacle course from the airport. It's insane. We drive down Ventura Boulevard by Van Nuys, and I'm looking down Ventura, it's on fire. The shops are all on fire. The road's all split and we make our way to Bel Air and no one's in their house. Everyone's sitting in their cars, out on the street, because they don't want the garage to collapse on them. It's midnight and everyone's trying to sleep in their cars.

Tina rolls down the window and looks out. Before she can say anything, I said, "I know, we're moving." We didn't have too much furniture, so it didn't matter, but everything in the kitchen closets flew out and smashed on the floor. Thankfully, no one was hurt; it was Jade, Tina, Tif, and a hamster that was thrown out of his cage and caught midair by Tina. Unfortunately, she went back in to get one last thing from the kitchen with no shoes on and cut her foot on some of the broken glass.

We moved to Arizona first, because we wanted to be close to my children, who were still with Barbara in Los Angeles. So we went to Scottsdale and rented a townhouse on a golf course. I loved the sunsets, but we couldn't stand the heat. The owner of the house was also British and when we met him, he asked what we thought of the weather. I said, as you do when living there, "It's okay because it's a dry heat!" To which he quickly replied, "Yes, like a blow torch in your face!" We laughed because he was right.

Jade and Julian would fly up every other weekend, but in the summer, they would fall off their bikes and burn themselves on the sidewalk. They'd have heat stroke—it could be 117 degrees out there. The day we moved in, it was 120, and the day we moved out, it was 120. I remember the day the moving truck arrived from LA and the guys were unloading all our stuff. Oh, and the air conditioning had iced up and stopped working because the front door had to be open. And there are my guitars all on the front lawn, in their cases, but in that unbearable heat.

I had to rush them all in and find the coolest room inside to store them.

It was a really nice place, but the kids hated flying so often and I don't blame them at all. You really need a summer home if you live in Scottsdale, because the rest of the year is so beautiful—especially the sunsets by Claude Monet every night. Frank Lloyd Wright's amazing winter home, Taliesin West, is there and it's now the headquarters for the Taliesin Foundation. He obviously had this whole summer-versus-winter living thing down pat.

Around then my music publisher had called up and asked, "Have you ever thought about going to Nashville and doing some writing sessions for a week, ten days, something like that?" I said I hadn't, but that I'd love to. That sounded great. So as Tina said goodbye to me at the airport, she said, "Hope you love Nashville!" Which I did, very much, instantly.

I met all these great people, many different writers, and got the feel of the place and just loved it. We decided to move and got a house in Brentwood that was almost finished—a brand-new house in a cul-de-sac, and I had the contractor build on a little music room, for all my recording gear and instruments.

Before we moved we had been hoping Tina would be pregnant, but it had been a while and we decided to try in vitro fertilization. Unfortunately, after doing that, we also thought it hadn't worked. So we packed up and flew off to Tennessee. After we were settled in Nashville, Tina went to the doctor because she was very upset, thinking she'd had a miscarriage. When she came back, she came into the house crying, and I thought the worst, "Oh, my God, what happened?" I was thinking the doctor had confirmed that she had lost the child. Then, to my surprise she said, "I'm pregnant." We were ecstatic—laughing, crying, and in shock all at the same time! We were all extremely happy. There's a possibility she had actually been pregnant with twins, but if she was, one sadly didn't make it.

Mia was born on March 4, 1996—same day as Tina's mother, Bette. We had a new baby girl for us and a birthday cake for Grandma!

When Tina gave birth, it was an amazing experience welcoming little Mia into the world. After all the excitement, I could see that Tina needed to rest, so Bette, Tif, and I left to get some sleep ourselves. I went back the next morning early to find that Mia was not in Tina's room. I said, "Where's the baby?" She said, "They haven't brought her to me yet, I think the pediatrician is doing the newborn exam." So I said, "Okay, let me go and check on that."

I went to the nurse's station to ask where the doctor was examining Mia. They said, "Oh, she just left here to go talk to you guys in your room." I must have passed her on the way. Our regular pediatrician, who came very highly recommended, had sent another doctor from her practice to do the exam. Yes, I get it—she was probably very busy, but really?

I turn around to walk back to the room and halfway back, I hear Tina's voice crying out, which I will never forget, so I started to run. The doctor, who we're meeting for the very first time, has already gone in and spoken to Tina, and told her that she has some bad news. Tina said, "If you've got something to tell me about the baby, please wait until my husband gets here," but she wouldn't wait, and said, "I think your child has Down syndrome." But it wasn't true. Unfortunately, this woman had her own Down syndrome child, which is very sad, but every time she examined a newborn, she would look for it even if it wasn't there. She was overly sensitized to it. You'd think she would be the last doctor on the planet to be examining newborn babies. We stopped going to that doctor altogether.

Obviously, we were devastated by the incorrect diagnosis, and went immediately to see two specialists to have her tested for anything and everything. There was a two- to three-week waiting period for some of the tests, and Tina and I were both numb with worry. Two weeks is a long time to wait.

When we got the results, they were sure it wasn't Down syndrome, but told us that Mia had a little hole in her heart that would most likely close up as she grew. She was born a little prematurely, so her lungs weren't fully developed. By a month later, the hole had closed and everything else was now normal, and we were so relieved. The only lasting thing Mia suffers from a little is asthma, which she has pretty much grown out of now. We're so very thankful that Mia is a very healthy girl.

The first I heard about the *Wayne's World* sequel was that they had requested the use of the *Frampton Comes Alive!* album cover. In the scene, Mike Myers is flipping through some albums and finds *Comes Alive!* and says, "If you lived in the suburbs, it came in the mail like samples of Tide." When I first saw the movie, I had no idea this was coming. I just thought I was going to have an album on a wall or something, but then they actually bring me into the context of the piece. So that was a lovely surprise.

Mike invited me to be in a crowd scene with him and Dana Carvey, but it was mainly ad-lib and I don't think I added enough ad or lib, because it never made it into the film. It was great meeting everyone and we had a chance to chat. Believe it or not, Mike Myers told me he was actually at the *Frampton Comes Alive!* concert—and so was Woody Harrelson, who I met when I went to Cuba for a writing trip with Cuban writers. They were apparently both at the Winterland Ballroom show the night we recorded *Frampton Comes Alive!*, but of course neither one of them knew the other. I found that unbelievable. I don't think Kevin Bacon was there, but who knows with his six degrees of separation!

For *The Simpsons*, this lovely lady, Bonnie Pietila, called me up. I was living in LA and she said, "I'm the casting director for *The Simpsons*. Have you seen *The Simpsons*?" I said, "Uh, yeah, I love *The Simpsons*." She said, "Oh, good—well, we would like to know if you would be available to be in one of the shows." I'm thinking they must have the wrong number, because nothing's happening for me at this point, at all.

I was in total shock, wondering why on earth they would want me in an episode. I asked what the story line was for this particular one. She said, "You would be the headline act on a Lollapalooza-like concert, called Homerpalooza." I said, "But, Bonnie, I wouldn't be headlining that kind of a show." She said nothing, there was a pause, and then I started to laugh and I said, "Got it. That's the joke."

She told me that Smashing Pumpkins and Sonic Youth were already on board. After I heard who was on the show, I said to her, "Okay, I think I know what you want from me now. You want me to be the old, crusty, been-there, done-that, rock star." She said, in a nutshell, yeah.

It was one of the most enjoyable things I've ever done, something that was completely out of my orbit. I went to the studio and I got all my lines down. Great people to work with, they really knew what they were doing and what they wanted, which gives you so much confidence. I've been involved in many other things where it hasn't quite been that way. . . .

They said, "As you're walking off the stage, we don't have anything written, but can you come up with something—you've been through all this hell, the talk box didn't work, you lost your Pink Floyd pig. Can you just say something as you walk past the mic, as Homer's coming back on stage?" I thought for a minute and I said, "Okay, roll it." So I walked past the mic and muttered, "Twenty-five years in this business, I've never seen anything like this," and they animated my line. I'm so proud of that—I actually wrote a line of *The Simpsons* and they used it! That was a huge thing for me.

Later, I was asked to appear in *Family Guy*. Death comes to my door and I open it and go, "No, no, I'm too young to die, shouldn't you be at Keith Richards's house?" So that was another great experience. All different stuff for me, and so much fun to do. These opportunities came my way when there wasn't that much going on for me with new music or touring, but it kept my name out there, which was wonderful. Can't thank those people enough.

I could be pissed off because they're making fun of me, but it was the ultimate form of flattery to be the punch line of, say, a Johnny Carson joke. I remember the first time Johnny Carson said my name on his show. "Did you hear that? Johnny Carson just said my name!" That was the very first time I heard my name on TV when I wasn't actually on the show. So all these little vignettes and name-checks made me realize that all was not lost.

Bill Wyman and I have been friends since I was fourteen, and one day he called me up and said, "Jeff Beck played on this track for my band, the Rhythm Kings, and then I got the bill—can you come over and do the solo?" I said, "What, the one that Jeff Beck just did?" He said yeah. So I said, "Oh, dear—well, okay," my stomach turned hearing this, but I said, "Yes, but do me a favor, please? Don't play me what Jeff played before I do my solo."

I set up my amp in the overdub room of the small studio, and at the exact moment I opened the control room door to go in and listen to the track, what do you think I hear? Jeff's solo, at a hundred thousand watts. Perfect! You always know when listening to a new Jeff Beck solo that it's going to be amazing and at the same time very humbling. After a few deep breaths, a valium, a joint, and a shot of brandy, I played the solo. (By the way, the only part that is true in the last sentence is the deep breathing!)

Bill must've liked what I played, because he asked if I would play on a couple of other tracks. Then he said, "We're going to do a UK and European tour. Would you like to play with the Rhythm Kings?" I said, "Who's in the band?" He said Gary Brooker from Procol Harum, and, to my delight, the incomparable Albert Lee and Georgie Fame; I've always been a huge fan of both. When I was still at school, I would go see them play in London, Georgie Fame with his Blue Flames and Albert with Chris Farlowe and the Thunderbirds. These were two of the earliest bands I went to watch, which would have been around the time of the Preachers, pre-Herd.

The tour was about three weeks long and we played dates in Europe and the UK. Sometime after that tour Bill called to ask me if I would come back over to play the Royal Albert Hall, which was a great show, and I sang one of the songs off my *Now* record, "Flying Without Wings." Mark Knopfler also joined us for that show. During this period, I was still sort of in limbo. I was touring, but nothing was happening with my albums, so it was a great opportunity to play live with Bill for the very first time ever. Bill is great. He never changes, nothing ever seems to faze him. I have a lot to thank him for.

I also played with the Ultimate Rock Symphony that went to Australia with Alice Cooper, Roger Daltrey, Paul Rodgers, and Gary Brooker, with Zak Starkey on drums and Simon Townshend on guitar. We had to pick up different orchestras in the different cities, so some nights were better than others. But as well as doing a couple of my songs each night, I got to sing "Norwegian Wood" with Paul Rodgers, which was a dream for me. I came in singing the harmony with him, just a 12-string guitar and the two of us, which was always great and was my favorite part of the night. Paul is another singer like Steve Marriott who has this legendary voice that always gives me goose bumps when he sings. Lovely man and we had some great hang time together during the tour.

I'd known Alice for quite a while; in fact, I first got to know him during our earlier stint making movies. But this tour of Australia was when I really got to know him and we became good friends. I found out that he would watch old black-and-white horror movies before he would go on stage. But he would make fun of me ironing, which was part of my pre-show meditation. Alice would have a video player and a monitor— and I would have an iron and an ironing board. Each to their own, I guess. That's how differently we mentally prepared for the show.

Of course, Roger and I had known each other for a long time, too, and I love Roger. One time we were backstage, and he said, "Here, let's have a laugh and freak everybody out a bit.

I've got these Tic Tacs. Put some in your mouth, and then we'll fake an argument and I'll hit you in the face and you'll spit out all the Tic Tacs." So we started to fake argue in the green room backstage and it worked really well—everyone was screaming, "You've knocked his teeth out!" Very much a Who thing, and of course I went right along with it.

Then I did two tours of duty with Ringo's All-Starr Band—an American tour and a European tour. It was Gary Brooker (again), Simon Kirke with Ringo on drums, Jack Bruce, me, and Dave Mason. Everyone got along great, except for Dave Mason, unfortunately. The deal was, each person in the band does three of their songs and Ringo does six of his. So we all had to learn everyone else's songs as well as doing our own. Well, Dave couldn't seem to learn our songs, but at rehearsals, every time we made a mistake on one of his, he would give whoever the stink eye.

No one said anything, but we were all feeling the same way and I could see that Ringo was, too. The last day of rehearsals was the dress rehearsal—without actually dressing, we were going to go through the whole act in the morning, have lunch, and then go through the show one more time in the afternoon. Then it would be off to the first show.

That day, Dave Mason came in with two women who we hadn't met before, and Barbara Bach, Ringo's wife, was there, too. The women sat and talked while we played the set through in the morning. When we broke for lunch, Dave said goodbye and left with the two lovely ladies. Ringo called a band meeting on the rehearsal stage. He said, "Dave can't make the last run-through." We were all very surprised to hear this because, to be honest, we needed to run it through again with Dave because it wasn't right yet. Ringo asked us how we all felt about this and the consensus was thumbs down for Dave.

I think Ringo said Dave told him he had a doctor's appointment. But these two women who were sitting next to Barbara were telling her, "Oh, we've been trying to get Dave to take us shopping for a while, and he's finally said this afternoon we can." And apparently, he also had his own show booked somewhere that night.

Ringo called Dave and said, "It's not going to work for us." Sometime later Dave apparently called him back, and he said, "Can I talk to you?" Ringo said, "As long as it's nothing to do with you being back in the band, you can talk about anything."

Ringo turned to me and said, "Can you handle it, just you on guitar?" Absolutely! That would give me a little bit more control over my area in general. After lunch, we did the last rehearsal without Dave and it sounded great. I had to get another couple of guitars for different parts that I was now going to have to play—instead of playing one part, I had to put two parts together—but I loved it. So things obviously didn't work out with Dave on that tour, but we all remain friends and there are no hard feelings.

Jack Bruce and I got on like a house on fire. I couldn't believe it, because you hear all these stories about him. Back in the '60s, I'd watched him play from the front row with the Graham Bond Organisation, with Ginger Baker on drums and Dick Heckstall-Smith on sax, just like I would go and watch John Mayall's Blues Breakers. So I was nervous at first because I'd heard how Jack could be difficult if he didn't like somebody. Most of all, I was very nervous about playing the Cream stuff. But we hit it off and he liked my playing—thank God. The feeling of playing with Jack was elevating and it always pushed me to try to play something better each day.

"Do You Feel" was interesting, because I never in a million years would've thought that Jack Bruce would be playing the bass part, and even playing a solo, which was phenomenal every night. He would always play something completely different. He never ever played the same thing twice, which I just loved.

When we went to Europe, I finally got to play Russia, and it was only five years after the Berlin Wall had come down. I remember getting to Moscow and quickly throwing my bags in my room because we were right off Red Square and I couldn't wait to go walk around. I had already bought some rubles in the hotel and I wanted to get a bunch of postcards to send to people from Moscow's Red Square.

There was a little mobile gift shop on the edge of the square, and I asked the woman how many rubles for the postcards and she says, "No ruble, no ruble; only dollar, dollar." We had arrived on the day that the ruble crashed. The country was in a mess, but just to be in Moscow and walk around, to take it all in and get a tour of the Kremlin, was unbelievable. Now here was something else I thought I would never get a chance to do—to visit Russia . . . and actually play music there!

In Humble Pie and the Herd, I'd been through the East German corridor to get to West Berlin many times. Back then you had to drive through East Germany to get to the US sector of Berlin. East German guards stood with machine guns at the checkpoints, and you had to get out of your vehicle and be checked. Pretty scary stuff for me at sixteen. As you drove along the very narrow corridor, there were warnings in English and German about the electric fences on either side of the road, and also land mines.

But now here we were in Russia. The next city was St. Petersburg and we were taking the train. We were told it was the presidential train, the Soviet number one train. Barbara and Ringo had the presidential suite, and we all got these little tiny cell-type cabins, three of us to a sleeper cabin. There was so little room that the sink folded up into the wall. These cabins were bad enough, but then Ringo and Barbara told us that they had to sleep on the couch because they didn't even want to touch the bedding, everything was filthy. So they slept sitting up; at least we could lie down.

Everyone had asked, "Should we eat before we get on the train?" "No, no, no, they've got a wonderful restaurant car, beautiful, first class and everything." Then we got on that train and it was a piece of shit! The only good thing was that it went really slowly, so we could sleep. The overnight sleeper trains take eight hours to get to St. Petersberg from Moscow, as opposed to the high-speed trains that do the trip in four. We woke up and still had a bit to go and we hadn't had anything to eat or drink, not even water. We hadn't taken anything with us, no food, nothing.

So after an interesting night of nap and wake, come morning, we get a knock on the door and it's a waiter and he said, "You like tea or coffee?" And we go, "Oh, yes, yes, yes! Coffee, tea, coffee, please." He pours all our drinks. "You want milk or cream?" Yes, yes, either please! The waiter paused briefly and then said, "We don't have." Totally straight-faced, too. So on top of everything, we had a jokester waiter. We were laughing about that for the rest of the tour.

When we played Monaco, Ringo had a residence there, so he wasn't staying in our hotel. Tina and Mia had come out to visit me there, so he said, "Why don't you take my suite in the hotel?" Which was very nice of him, so we did. It was great because I now had my family with me and we had much more space.

I had no idea, but in Monaco, they don't clap. They wave their white serviettes—it reminded me of the John Lennon line, "People at the back clap your hands, and people at the front, just rattle your jewelry." So that was strange; never witnessed that before.

It's the same everywhere, playing with a Beatle; the audience gets the same feeling as when you meet a Beatle for the first time. I just saw it recently when my band met Ringo at the Forum on the last tour. He and Barbara came an hour early just to hang—I didn't know when they would be coming into my dressing room; I was playing with my back to the door and all I hear is the door come open and he goes, "Shut that bloody racket!" He's arrived!

It was great to talk and relax. We were just catching up and I said, "You want to come meet the band?" They said yeah, so I took them in to meet the band and I saw the looks on their faces—the "I'm meeting a Beatle" face. And you never really get over that. I've met Paul a couple of times and it's the same thing. Meeting the musicians who changed the world, it's a heady experience. But Ringo hung out, took pictures with everybody, and he's just lovely—he's Ringo, you know.

When the All-Starrs were on the plane, the band preferred that I sit next to Ringo, so that I might get him telling stories for us all—because Beatle stories are pretty cool, right? So I would be wracking my brains . . . "So on, uh, 'Day Tripper,' what snare did you . . . ?" "I don't remember that!"—but then he would take the conversation somewhere else just as mind-blowing. When Ringo talks, everyone listens, because you're getting the inside scoop on being one of the Fab Four.

When we first started rehearsing, Paul had just recently given Ringo back his drum kit that he'd played on *Sgt. Pepper*. (If you need to pause here to reread the last sentence and go, "Holy crap!" I will totally understand.) He played that kit one day at rehearsals, but it didn't make it on tour with us. Ringo took only one of the cymbals, which has written on it, "Thanks for the loan of the kit, love, Paul." Jeff Chonis—a great drum tech and good friend in LA who looks after Ringo's drums—said to me during rehearsals, "Have you looked at the floor tom?" There was the arrangement written out, in Ringo's handwriting, for "A Day in the Life." Written right on the drum, on the skin. And it was still on there. Now I'll say it again—"Holy crap!"

So all the skins were still the same. Paul hadn't removed them; he kept it exactly the same as it was. I guess that drum kit could be the one on "Maybe I'm Amazed," because Paul played the drums on that whole first solo album. Whenever McCartney played drums on his own stuff prior to those rehearsals, I'm guessing it could've been that kit.

Another moment like that came when I wrote a song with Ringo in 2016 called "Laughable." I'd brought over a couple of riffs that I'd played using a looper pedal, and I played him about six. He said, "Oh, you choose, because I like them all." So we picked one to work on finishing the music, using my loop as the main bed of the song, and then sat and wrote lyrics together. So there we are with paper and pencil, I mean MacBook and Word, and we are writing the lyrics to our first song together. I already had a chorus line, "It would be laughable if it wasn't so sad." I thought of it because I was somewhat despondent that the US had just elected a very different kind of president. After we were happy with the lyrics Ringo said, "You better do a guide vocal for me, so I know what to sing."

I noticed this beautiful, original Neumann M49 micro-phone, and I was just about to start to sing and the engineer said, "Has Ringo told you about the mic?" I said no, what's the story? "Well, when John gave Ringo Tittenhurst, his great place in England out in the country, he left everything, including the studio, and this mic was John's mic. Can you guess what songs he sang on it?" And I said no. He said, "Well, 'Imagine,' for one. Ready to sing this?" I said, "No, no, I'm not ready. Give me a second, would you?" Luckily, I sang it in one take, before it all sunk in.

Actually, that kind of thing spurs me on. I get nervous, yes, but you've got to rise to the occasion here, buddy. That was a huge deal to spend the day together writing a song that ended up on Ringo's *Give More Love* album. I'll never forget that day. I can't tell you how great an experience that was, to write with my longtime friend—who happens to be a Beatle, too.

All these tours that I was asked to do with other artists were very enjoyable, especially musically. I can look back on it now, though, and see that it was also buying time. But whatever my next project is, it always becomes all-consuming and I give it my all. I didn't know where I was going, but I've never really known where I'm going. There's never been a master plan. It's always just been about the music and how I can change it up, write new songs that turn me on, and improve my guitar playing.

I was always hoping that I would be able to reinvigorate my solo career, but I kind of thought, "Well, this is it, I'm the hired gun now." I've always enjoyed that, but there was still something else gnawing at me to do more myself. But I definitely thought at that point that the Frampton solo career wasn't going to take off anymore. I didn't really have a lot of hope in the '90s.

One bright spot, which eventually helped turn things around, was that around this time, Lisa Jenkins came on board as my day-to-day manager, which she remains more than twenty years later. Come to think of it, that's longer than any of my marriages lasted! People love working with Lisa, and for me she's family, such a great friend as well as always taking care of me and making sure that I handle all the things on my list—from doing interviews to finishing this book!

I was drinking on and off, but mainly off. It did get to the point where I couldn't trust myself anymore, but not in those work situations. Since the '70s, I never drank anything before I went on stage. To me, being on stage and playing is holy ground. That's something to be respected. But I was still a time bomb, a binge drinker, so I never knew which was the wrong night to have a drink. Most nights, I could have a glass or two of wine, and that's it. But then there would be those other nights when one was too many and a thousand wasn't enough.

Chapter
Fourteen

Cameron Crowe called me up and said, "I'm doing this movie—it's a rock movie." And I said, "No, you're not. We've always talked about how you and I hate rock movies." He said, "I know, but I'm going to do it right." I said, "Well, if anybody can, you can. You've been there, done it." He asked if I would come out to LA so we could talk about it.

I flew out and he told me all about *Almost Famous*, and he gave me a script and said, "There's a little part for you I put in there." I'm looking at all the big parts and I said, "Oh, I'd like to play this part." He said, "No, that's already cast. Look deeper." So Reg, Humble Pie's road manager at the card game—oh, that's me. Which was great, but that wasn't my main job. Cameron needed another song for Stillwater, the band in the movie. But I ended up writing two songs, with Gordon Kennedy and Wayne Kirkpatrick, who were part of the team, with Tommy Sims, that wrote "Change the World" for Eric Clapton.

Cameron already had all the Stillwater album titles, with the track titles, so we just had to choose a title and write to that. "Hour of Need" was the first one we wrote; we did a demo of it and I took it out to him. I wanted to physically give it to him. I played it and he loved it. "This is perfect, this is perfect!"

I said, "I'll tell you what"—this is the pushy Frampton—"you don't have what I call an encore song; they're all very Free- or Bad Company–style slow songs." So he said to go write one. We picked "You Had to Be There" from the titles and wrote that one too, and it's one of the songs that Stillwater performs in the live scene when they're supporting Black Sabbath.

I was touring, so I couldn't be on the set all the time, but I was there for all six weeks of preproduction, and I worked with Billy Crudup on how to play guitar well enough to look like a guitar god. He had to be convincing. Whatever part Billy plays, he's always totally convincing. He only had a couple of weeks of guitar lessons before we met. It amazed me how quickly he picked it all up. The playing and the stance were all important. So I was an on-set library of band information to help Billy and Jason Lee create their characters.

Jason would say, "So when I go out there as the front man of the band, what is my motivation?" I said, "Well, what you're trying to do is, you just got the cover of *Rolling Stone*, you're opening for Black Sabbath, and—just like we did in Humble Pie—you want to burn from the second you get on till the second you get off, and steal as many of their fans as you can. That's your job, to pull people in and make them remember you. That's what you're going for."

Four of the solos in the movie are played by another great player and friend, Mike McCready from Pearl Jam, and two of them are mine. I would learn Mike's solos so I could show Billy, and when I couldn't be there, he would film me before I left so he could keep working on them while I was away. Whenever I was on the set, I was with Billy playing. Cameron asked, "When will you know, what sign will you get that will make everyone think Billy looks legitimate?" I said, "That's easy—when he's playing and his fingers are on the right notes, and he's looking up with his head back and his eyes closed. That's when we'll know he's got it."

So we come to the big day. Usually we're just shooting using one camera. This day, we've got like four Panavisions and a Steadicam; they're all over the place. We were in the arena in San Diego, with John Toll, the Academy Award–winning cinematographer—he taught me so much, because I'm a camera freak. I would always hang with the cinematographers when I could. We're sitting by the screens, looking at all the camera angles, and John comes up behind me and puts a headphone set with a mic on me. I said, "What's this for?" He said, "You know the music better than I do—call the shots." I thought, "Oh, wow! The power!"

My job was to explain to the camera operators where we were musically. "Drum fill—three, two, one, drum; guitar solo, second verse, come back to Jason. Okay, back to the drum." It was a madhouse, but it was very exciting. And then the moment came, mid-solo, when Billy threw his head back and closed his eyes, and Cameron and I were standing together. *Big high five! There it is!*

There were other things with the props I would notice. "Those mics weren't invented yet," stuff like that. That's why I've hated all the rock movies; it's supposed to be the fifties and there's a microphone that wasn't invented until the eighties. So I was the perfect guy for that. I was the "authenticity advisor"— that was my name for it, anyway.

During the big live shoot in San Diego, I couldn't remember whether we used wooden barricades back then or metal barricades. So I called my old stage manager, Steve Lawler, and he said, "Metal—what else you want to know?" They said, "Okay, we've set the stage. Black Sabbath's gear is going to be behind them, right?" And I said, "Yeah, you'd have black drop cloths over everything, you'd cover it so you wouldn't see anything except the band in front." The right amps, the right guitars, I love all that stuff. That's the fun part.

When we did the ballroom scene, the Steadicam guy asked if I wanted to try it. I said, "Yes, please!" Back then, Steadicams were so heavy, I could barely walk with the thing. I have a great picture of me beaming, wearing this huge Steadicam.

That was how to make a movie. Cameron commanded such respect; he's great with actors. In the director's cut, I'm in another scene besides the card game, right at the very beginning. I'm in the lobby of the Hyatt and I see Penny—Kate Hudson—and I haven't seen her in a while. My character's with another couple of friends and we come over and we're talking to her, and one of the actors had a line he kept blowing.

Cameron took me aside, he said, "Can you do that line for me?" I said sure. I didn't know it, so I studied it, but I kept saying one wrong word—I was ad-libbing and I don't remember what it was now, but it seemed inconsequential. But it was not the word Cameron had written. He was very good; he wouldn't correct me in front of other people. He took me aside and whispered the line in the script. I realized, okay, he wants it exactly as written, and rightly so. It's his script. He labored over every word. And he's Cameron Crowe!

Almost Famous was a phenomenal experience for me. It almost made up for *Sgt. Pepper*.

We moved to Cincinnati in 2000 or so. We'd been visiting there quite a bit from Nashville because Tina's father had been diagnosed with esophageal cancer. Unfortunately, it wasn't long before he lost his battle and passed away. Tina didn't have to say anything; I could see that she wanted to move closer to home. I thought it would be the best thing for the family, especially for Mia to be close to her grandmother.

So we left Nashville and moved up. Found a great place, a spec house, brand-new, and it was perfect because underneath the three-car garage was this huge tomb-like area with fourteen-foot ceilings—because it was on the side of a hill, it had to be built that way, and it had a window too. So I said, "Control room!"

I brought someone up from Nashville, studio designer Dave Mattingly, to build the studio, and he turned the space into a phenomenal creative space. The whole house was wired so you could record in any room. The living room had a great sound and the piano was in there. Acoustic guitars and virtually any instrument sounded really great. It had to be the shape and all the wood and stone that gave it such a special sound.

Being in Cincinnati was okay, because I was nearly always on the road at this point and I had this wonderful studio, with all the equipment that I'd been collecting since the mid-'70s. So I could make records there and it wouldn't cost me anything except the players and the crew. Gordon Kennedy would come up to write with me; later on Chris Stapleton came up and we wrote a few songs. I'm pretty much of an isolated character anyway, and I really loved Cincinnati and the people I met there, it was home.

That's where I was on September 11. As horrible as this was, the interesting thing to me was that this was the first time, apart from Pearl Harbor, that someone had physically come to attack America on this scale.

As I watched the second plane hit, I knew America would never be the same. An enemy had violated the US feeling of isolated safety for the first time. This was going to shock a lot of people, especially people here who lived through the Second World War. Now they might understand a little bit of what Europe had been through.

As a child who played in bombed-out buildings, and who realized as I got older what had just gone on five years before I was born, I definitely connected the two. I didn't realize as a child what had happened and what it really meant. I didn't see it firsthand, thank God. I wasn't born yet. But seeing it happen in New York on September 11 made me think about what England, Europe, and the rest of the world had gone through. Most cities in England were obliterated. Not just bombed but obliterated—leveled.

It really did make me feel patriotic about the fact that, yes, I'm English. I was born there and I'm very glad I was born there. But I've been living here and paying US taxes since 1975. I was virtually an American, and I really did feel like I should have formalized that earlier. As soon as I could reach my lawyer, I said, "I've got my green card, but I'd like to become an American citizen." That process started immediately and within a year or two, I'd become a US citizen.

We were also in Cincinnati for what became my second first birthday: November 5, 2002. Paavo Järvi, the maestro with the Cincinnati Symphony Orchestra, was Estonian, and very famous. He'd actually started off as a pop drummer. The local newspaper, the *Cincinnati Enquirer*, did a competition for a "rock meets classical" meal, so one couple would meet him, one couple would meet me, and then we'd all have dinner together. Just before I left the house, Tina looked at me and said, "Don't drink." Now, I had already got that in my mind, but when someone tells you not to drink, what do you do? You drink.

I didn't really want to get crazy, but soon I'm under the table and he's just sitting there going, "I don't know what's wrong with him, he is lightweight." I was sozzled and I drove myself home—my wife's car. This is before GPS, and I got lost in a not-so-good part of town. At the light, I realized, "Oh, I better go right here," so I changed lanes. And there was a police car right over there.

They flash me and stop me and they get me out. I do a Breathalyzer; I'm over, and they put me in handcuffs and put me in the back of the police car, which is not a place I ever wanted to be. It's the most humiliating thing I've ever experienced in my life. I went to the police station and they took a blood test, too. I let them do everything—it's a fair cop, guv'nor.

My wife had to come pick me up from a jail cell and wanted to take me to a hotel. I said, "I'm not going to a hotel; I'll sleep in another room. Just let's go home." And the following morning, I got up, I went straight to our bedroom, and I said, "I'm going to AA. That's it. I could've killed someone."

Two good friends who were already sober took me to my first AA meeting. There are people who have had multiple arrests, multiple DUIs, which I don't quite understand. I guess there's a bottom for everybody and mine was my first and last DUI. I'd caused enough damage in my drinking career, but it wasn't as if I'd lost my job or lost my wife—although I was very close to losing my wife over this.

I went to meetings every day for a year, even when we were touring. It didn't matter where in the world I was; I was amongst "us." It's a brother/sisterhood, whatever you want to call it . . . it works for me.

I usually went to the noon meeting at a church hall in Indian Hill, near where I lived in Cincy. One day I missed it. I was working, and I looked at my watch and said, "Oh, God!" I looked in my little AA book—okay, the last meeting is in downtown Cincinnati at eight o'clock; I can make that. I was getting nervous that I was going to miss even one day, so I went down and I'm driving around the block, but I don't see the little flag, the little sign we put out for the meeting.

I see another car doing the same as me. So we both park our cars, and I'm looking at him and he's looking at me, and I'm going, "Are you looking for what I'm looking for?" One of us mentioned the name Bill W., who is one of the AA founders. It's code; for an example, if you're in an airport and you hear the name Bill W. over the PA, then you know someone needs help. They most likely need someone to talk them down from having that first drink.

So my new friend and I looked all around—this meeting had moved or had been canceled. We were going to miss a day, so I said, "Let's have our own meeting." Two people is considered an official AA meeting.

We went to a little sandwich and coffee shop close by with just a counter, no tables. We bought some coffee and stood up against the wall and spoke together for about thirty minutes. After telling our stories to each other, both of us realized we felt less stressed. Even though it wasn't the meeting we came for, we had one of the best meetings both of us ever had. Not a real meeting, but a *real* meeting.

I got in the car and I was beaming all the way home. I came in and I was so happy and Tina said, "You made his day, too." It was so great that he came and talked with me. I loved that. I never saw him again. But we both needed each other at that particular moment. I still wonder who he was, and hope he is still doing well and sober.

I firmly believe that if I hadn't hit bottom then, I wouldn't be here now. I realized that things weren't going to get better until I got better, until I stopped drinking. And within that first year, I started finding myself again, a little at a time. I started to feel safer knowing I would never drink again, and it gave me a new view of my life.

At AA we always say to take it "one day at a time" and I know a lot of people in AA would tell me, "You can't say you'll never drink again!" Yes, I am a recovering alcoholic and, yes, I do have an addictive personality. But when I make major decisions in my life, I seldom, if ever, go back on them. As I write this, I am in my eighteenth year of no alcohol. And for the last eighteen years, things have gone from worse to great for me. I can never thank the people in all the different AA rooms around the world enough, because without you and AA, my life would have been very different. Scary thought!

"Humility is not thinking less of yourself, but thinking of yourself less."

After I hit bottom in November 2002, we went to France. We were touring again and I went to meetings where I didn't understand the language, but I knew what they were saying, because the stories are the same, it's just that the details are different. That helped get me back into writing again—it was a time for rediscovery, I guess, and it felt like I was back on track.

Recording again was nerve-wracking, but I thought we had good material. Gordon Kennedy is such a great writer and has been a wonderful writing partner for twenty years now. If you look at all the songs he's written, it's a long list of amazing material. Our friendship and the ease with which we work really helped me get my confidence back. So it had been a long time between albums, but it felt so good when *Now* was released. As one of the tracks says loudly, "I'm Back!"

With the album out, it was time to get the band together again and hopefully bring Bob Mayo back, finally. He'd taken a hiatus and gone off to play with Foreigner and then with Hall & Oates, but I was thrilled he came back to join us again. One of the first things we did with that band was the *Live in Detroit* DVD at the Pine Knob amphitheater, before they changed the name to the DTE Energy Music Theatre. But it will always be Pine Knob to me. Last time Bob Seger played there, in his hometown, he wore a Pine Knob T-shirt. "Yeah!"—that's what the audience shouted, too!

Then we toured Europe. The last show in France was at the Bataclan in Paris—the place where the awful mass shooting happened in 2015. Despite that tragedy, I have a wonderful memory of the venue from that night in 2002. It was one of those shows when the band came off and we all agreed it was one of the best of the tour. My brother, Clive, came over to Paris to open for us with his duo Frampton and Weller. It was the only time Clive and I ever played on a show together. Needless to say, we had a blast being on the same show.

Next we were off to play this big club in Basel, Switzerland, and we had to travel by train to get there. We had to take two trains to get to Basel, and we had all our bags with us, and Bob's way behind. He always had this huge backpack with his whole life in it, and he keeps having to stop and he's panting. Bob had already seen my doctor in Nashville before we left because he had heart issues, and was all set for tests when he returned. We got on the second train, which had an upstairs level, so I went and sat up there and I heard this bang and it's Bob. He'd grabbed the railing to the stairs but he'd fallen backward and was lying on his backpack.

I started giving Bob mouth-to-mouth and then Shawn Fichter, our drummer, took over and I had a bad feeling—Bob was unconscious and his face was getting redder and redder. The ambulance arrived, drove up onto the platform, and they had him in there for half an hour trying to revive him. We went to the hospital and I knew that we'd lost him. The doctor came out and said, "He died the way I hope I die." He said Bob died from a massive heart attack. His heart just exploded, he didn't feel any pain. He was gone, just gone, straightaway.

I have that last Paris show recorded, and I treasure it. In fact, one of the pictures that we used in the montage before the Finale Tour is from that Paris gig. It looks like it could have been taken on any night of the tour, but it was our last night with Bob.

He had a serious drinking problem, and I'd told him, "Bob, you've got to sober up, because otherwise you can't be in the band." When Bob wasn't playing well, something was wrong. Bob always played well. MusiCares is such an amazing organization, and if it weren't for them, Bob would have never gotten sober. He was a little over a month sober when we went to Europe, and I would sit with him every night, and we'd have a little meeting together. The night before the Paris show, we sat in this beautiful old French hotel, in front of a lovely crackling fireplace, and we just talked, having one of the most in-depth conversations we'd ever had. He was so pleased to be starting his sober journey.

Bob was a special person, an incredible musician—my musical brother and my dearest friend. We had been through so much together. It's very hard to explain to someone who wasn't there what it was like for us in the '70s, but Bob and I were there, we lived it together. We both experienced the analogy of going to the moon and then coming back to Earth together. We were a team on stage; it was a four-piece band at that point, but wherever I would go in a solo, Bob would follow and change notes and chords to fit with what I was playing. He would listen intently and move with me. There are very few special musicians like that, and Bob was that person for me. We all miss him terribly and I think of him often. *Bob Mayo on keyboards, Bob Mayo!*

I was asked back by Universal Music to do a new record, after being without a label for a while—or, as we say, "independent." I went in to meet Bruce Resnikoff, who was the president and CEO of Universal Music Enterprises, and he said, "So what have you got planned for us?" I said that I wanted to do an instrumental record and it got a bit quiet. But because Bruce is such a big fan—thank goodness, a lovely man and a believer— he said, "I get it. I see it. It's time for you to do a guitar album." Thank you, Bruce!

My concept for *Fingerprints* was for Gordon Kennedy and me to write as many tunes as we could, maybe pick a cover or two, and then go ask my buddies out there if they would be up for playing. The first people I called were Mike McCready and Matt Cameron from Pearl Jam. We had initially connected through *Almost Famous*. Mike is a great player and I have always loved Pearl Jam. We met up while I was working on the movie and he asked, "Would you come and sit in with us for Rock the Vote?" I said, "You mean with Pearl Jam?" The concert was in Toledo, Ohio, on October 2, 1994, and I'm thinking what a treat this will be to play with these guys.

Neil Young was there. I'd met Neil years ago and it was great to see him again. He goes on, does a couple of numbers, and then Eddie Vedder goes to the mic to introduce me, but Neil goes straight into the next number. Eddie and Mike wave me to come on and after we finish, Eddie said, "If you didn't know, this is Peter Frampton!" We played a great guitar duel with Neil, Mike, and me.

So I went up to the guys in Pearl Jam—to Mike, Matt Cameron, and Jeff Ament—and I said, "Would you be willing to record a track with me for my next album?" They all said yes and then I told them I'd like to try an instrumental version of "Black Hole Sun." And then it hit me—I'm standing here talking to the drummer of Soundgarden! So I go, "Oh, my God, you probably don't want to cut this again." Matt said, "No, I'd love to do it again, especially an instrumental with you." Unfortunately, Jeff, the bass player, wasn't able to join us; he had a family event planned at that time. Both my amps got smashed on the way to Seattle, so their tech, George Webb, had to mend them before we started the session.

We went to their warehouse, which they'd turned into a studio, and we set up in a circle and ran "Black Hole Sun" and it sounded amazing straight away. I think we did it about three times and that was it. I had this other riff and asked if they wanted to hear it. So I played this kind of avant-garde, out-there riff and they loved it, and so we set about finishing it together. Mike came up with a great bridge chord sequence and now we had a second track, an original that became "Blowin'

Smoke." I had expected to just record "Black Hole Sun" with them, but we ended up recording the first two tracks together for what was to become the *Fingerprints* album.

I called up Warren Haynes from the Allman Brothers and asked him if he would join me on a track. I had a slow blues, just a backing track, and asked if he wanted to jam over that. He said, "Yeah, bring it up to New York—and come up a couple of nights early 'cause the Allmans are playing the Beacon Theatre for a thousand nights." I said, "Is that all right? Do you think Gregg will mind?" He said, "I'm the leader of the band." Warren was so well respected by Gregg and everybody—wonderful man, lovely guy, great friend, and incredible guitar player.

So, yeah, I sat in with the Allman Brothers, which I would never have thought in a million years would happen. They always had these seats at the Beacon on the side of the stage, taped off, so after I played, I sat back down in one of the seats on the side. Then Jaimoe, one of the two drummers, signaled to me from behind his drum kit. All of a sudden, in the middle of a song, he just stopped playing, got up from the drums. He came and sat with me and said, "Man, so you want to jam on another one?" I said yes! He said, "Are you ready for 'Statesboro Blues?'" I said, "Yeah, I think I can handle that!" They still hadn't finished the current song, so after he spoke to me, he just got back up and started playing again. It was wild!

Later on, I played with Gregg on some of his solo shows; we did some of his last dates together, and there was a real camaraderie there. Sitting in with him and his band was something else.

I think the day after the Beacon show, Warren and I recorded "Blooze." I had someone coming to take pictures of us playing, but by the time they got there, we were done! Literally two takes or something—it was as live as we could be on top of a track. Brilliant.

I'm a bit of a bull in a china shop and always jump straight into something and only then find out where to go, after I've landed. So *Fingerprints* was really guided by the guests, and that really determined what sort of music each session was going to bring. I called up Bill Wyman and asked if he had any ideas for songs. He must've misunderstood me about it being an instrumental album, because he kept sending me tracks with vocals on them.

Bill had a swing blues track, which we recorded first, but I also had another riff, kind of like the Pearl Jam sessions. We had Chris Stainton on piano, Bill on bass, Charlie Watts on drums. I've known them for years, but to be in the studio with them and to actually hear and watch them playing—that was the most enjoyable thing, hearing what everybody brought to the studio with their unique passionate styles. It was so good.

There was one more we recorded in England and it was with the Shadows. I had emailed Hank Marvin to ask him if he would join me on a track and he said, "Yes, I'd love to! Usually I'd have to ask you to come to Australia for this—but as it happens, I'm doing the last Cliff and the Shadows tour and we end up in London on this date and then I'm going back to Perth a day later." I said, "Could you put it off one day?" So he did—but instead of just Hank, I also got Brian Bennett on drums and Mark Griffiths on bass, so I nearly got the whole band! The Shadows minus Bruce Welch, a rhythm player few can touch.

Gordon and I had written a piece and Hank and Brian had written a piece, and we put our pieces together. Mark Knopfler was kind enough to let me use his studio, British Grove, which is fantastic, and to my delight, Hugh Padgham, who did a bunch of records with the Police and Phil Collins, came and engineered. The Shadows, Hugh Padgham, and a very excited me! Hank had to leave for Perth the next day, so we had to complete the track all in one day.

This was probably the most meaningful track of all to me. To actually play guitar with Hank Marvin . . . that's really hard to put into words for me. If it weren't for Hank, I don't think I would ever have started to play guitar. Yes, I was listening to Eddie Cochran, to Buddy Holly, Gene Vincent, and Scotty Moore with Elvis Presley. But there's something so incredible about the way Hank plays that red Fender Stratocaster, about that sound he gets through a Vox amp. His sound and playing have always been unique. Especially back then, when we were used to a solo singer with a session musician band. The Shadows were one of the earliest UK bands to have the three guitars and drums setup. Plus they were Cliff Richards's backup band, studio and live. Because the guitar bug bit me so young, I couldn't get enough of Hank's playing with the Shads. When I first saw them on TV . . . well, my future was pretty much set in stone.

Back to the session and when Hank's guitar tech surreptitiously asked me, "So what's your favorite Shadows song?" I said that it had to be "Wonderful Land." It's got the greatest melody, the most perfect guitar sounds, echoes with the big strings, and—the whole production. I didn't think any more about it, but after we had played the last guitar lick and I thought we'd finished the session, I noticed Brian was back at his drums, Mark Griffiths was next to him with his bass, and Hank was slipping on his red Strat next to me in the control room. I was wondering if I didn't get the memo.

To my absolute surprise and delight, they started playing "Wonderful Land" and Hank asks, "Where's my rhythm player?" Totally befuddled, I had to rush, get the acoustic, quickly tune it up. Of course, I was so nervous, I was playing all the wrong chords. But I played "Wonderful Land" with them, and there's just no words for that. I have goose bumps thinking back to how many times I must've listened to and played that track while wishing I had a red Strat in my hands.

A really important track to me is the one that's called "Oh When . . ." which, if you say it quickly, is Owen, my father's name. He passed away while we were making the album. They say there are many stages of grief, and the one I got stuck in was anger. I believe it was mainly because I couldn't physically fly home quickly enough to England to say goodbye; Tina and I arrived there the same day, only a few hours after he passed, and I know the sadness and frustration of the situation has stayed with me to this day.

I had let David Bowie's office know that Dad had passed, and we were all sitting in the living room deciding which picture we were going to use for Dad's funeral and all that horrible stuff you have to do, and the phone rang and it was David. Mum answered the phone and he talked on the phone with her for a while, and then she said, "Well, David, I know Peter wants to speak to you," and he was so compassionate. I know it was a loss for him, too. Dad meant a lot to David and vice versa.

It was one of the most awful times in my life. Losing a parent is devastating for us all because it closes a door you can't go through anymore. You can't pick up the phone and call, and it took me many years before I was able to delete my parents' phone number.

We flew back home to Cincinnati after the funeral, and a day later I was supposed to be back in my studio overdubbing on a *Fingerprints* track. I came in and said, "I've got to play something that I've been noodling with in England, but I really don't feel like playing anything else today." I was in pain with my grief. To keep me centered while in England, I had written a little acoustic piece while sitting in my mother and father's living room. It was just a little short idea that I kept building on. It was from my heart to my dad. My way of saying goodbye. I did three takes of it, all different versions, and then I said, "Guys, I'm done; I can't."

For the family to lose Dad right in the middle of the album slowed things down for a bit. I had asked John Jorgenson a few months before if he would join me on a track. He had also recently lost his father, so that's where the title—"Souvenirs de Nos Pères (Memories of Our Fathers)"—comes from. John is such a phenomenal gypsy jazz player—there are some incredible Django exponents, but he comes pretty damn close to actually being *Django*. So this was a huge challenge for me—I've listened to Django all my life, but to play that way is another thing altogether.

I learned so much from John during the process of writing and recording the piece, from the type of guitar to the special vintage RCA microphone Django would have used. I definitely had to woodshed quite a bit to be able to sound halfway decent on this track. Oh, I almost forgot, John plays every instrument in the world . . . and really well! In fact, just the other day he wished me a Happy Seventieth Birthday on a bassoon—you heard me, bassoon!

To flash forward a little bit, when I got the Grammy for Best Pop Instrumental Album, I wore a tie. I *never* wear a tie, but I wore a tie because my dad always wore a tie. So when I accepted the award, the last thing I said was, "I wore this tie for my dad today. He heard some of this album before we lost him, and I know he's smiling right now." I looked up and said, "Dad, I wore the tie!"

A Grammy shouldn't mean that much, really, should it? One should be confident about knowing how good you are at whatever you do. But the aftermath of *Comes Alive!* stripped me of my confidence as a player. I always go back to David—David saw it all unfold and he set in motion a reclamation for me, with his gift of reintroducing me in stadiums around the world as the guitar player. It reminded people of who I really was, and I felt my credibility coming back as a musician/guitar player. When *Fingerprints* came out, the reviews were phenomenal. It was a lovely surprise, and believe me, a nice change. "They think I'm a guitar player again—thank the Universe!"

But then when the public started to buy a few copies—still didn't sell a whole lot, but it sold plenty more than the last three records—I felt like I had finished my second apprenticeship. Isn't it weird? *You never stop paying your dues.*

Whenever we play the instrumentals from *Fingerprints*, I introduce them by saying they finally gave me a Grammy for not singing. I'd had no idea how the record would be accepted. You don't do an instrumental record for the money, but I've never done anything for the money. Maybe *I'm In You* was for the money—for everybody else, just not for me.

N ow it's another generation later. The man who bought the guitar in Curaçao has a son, and fifteen or so years later the son says, "Dad, this old guitar in the closet doesn't play very well; can I take it and get it fixed?" So he took it to a luthier in Curaçao named Donald Balentina, whose other job just happened to be immigrations officer at the Curaçao airport.

The kid brings the guitar in and says, "Can you make it playable?" And he said, "Yeah, sure." Donald opened it up and he apparently managed to save his gasp for after the boy left. He said, "Ummm, leave it with me overnight and I'll see what I can do. Come back tomorrow and I'll have it playable for you"—he needed to have time to take pictures of it and send them to a guitarist friend in Holland.

He took the pickups off, he took the knobs off, he took the strings off, everything. He did it forensically, a dozen or more shots, and he sent them to his friend, who could instantly tell what this guitar was. He emailed my website asking, "Is this yours?" When I saw the email and pictures of my old guitar, I involuntarily screamed out. This can't be happening, can it? Before the South American 1980 tour, I had just changed the black pickups (seen on the cover of *Comes Alive!*) to white ones from Seymour Duncan for something different, so I knew it was mine. But I wanted to be careful so I said, "I can't really tell till I play it . . ."

The son came back the next day. The guitar's all put back together, and Donald said to him, "I have to bring this up to you—you know what this is, right?" And the son said, "What do you mean?" Donald told him that it was Peter Frampton's guitar, from the Caracas plane crash years ago. And then the kid grabbed it, ran off, and just disappeared.

This is thirty years after the crash. Now my management gets involved, Lisa Jenkins is talking directly to Donald in Curaçao, and he said, "I don't know where the boy is now—I know who's got it, but I don't know where he lives." I thought oh, well, there you go, it's gone again. Close but no cigar.

Chapter Fifteen

We were still living in Cincinnati, but we bought a little house in Sherman Oaks, California, because Mia was going back and forth to LA with Tina for her acting auditions. While we were out there, I got a call from my son, Julian, and he said, "Dad, I need help." I said, "What? What's going on?" He said, "I can't go on like this, I'm scaring myself with drink and drugs." And apparently, he was doing everything—living in Hollywood in some horrible place that I didn't know about.

Being divorced from Jade and Julian's mother, Barbara, I didn't see my children as much as I should have—one reason was there was a lot of family friction at that time. I, wrongly, put my head in the sand and wished that everything would be okay. I let my children down. The blending of a family is probably one of the most difficult things I have ever tried to do. Bottom line is, we didn't blend too well.

I wish I could re-live that part of my life, because I see what it did to all of us, most of all my children. I used to say, "Oh, me? I don't have any regrets." Well, in hindsight and with a little wisdom, let's change that to "Yes, I have quite a few!"

After I hung up with Julian, I immediately called my business manager, Gary Haber, and let him know Julian's situation. He suggested Sierra Tucson and said he would call to get Julian in there, hopefully as soon as possible. Luckily, within forty-eight hours he was in Tucson and I knew he would finally be safe. Being in AA myself, recovery was something I understood well, and because Sierra Tucson is a twelve-step, AA-based recovery program, I had a very positive feeling about Julian's success.

After about two weeks, when patients are a little over halfway through the program, it's suggested that everyone visit and take part in "family week." If possible, both parents and any siblings come and stay close by and visit every day. Barbara, Jade, and I all met at the hotel and the following morning we traveled together to Sierra Tucson. Barbara and I started arguing in front of Jade before we even got in the door. It was awful. I'm surprised they didn't throw us out. We were moved to a private area because we were being so loud and upsetting other people.

Julian, seeing all this, said, "Please stop, don't you see this is exactly the reason I ended up here?" A moment of silence! Out of the mouth of my nineteen-year-old son came a bolt of reality that stopped me dead. He ran to find one of the doctors, who came in to calm the situation. This was one of the worst moments in my life, one of my biggest regrets, that I couldn't rise to the occasion to help our son. Instead, I was making things worse for this whole family.

What happened over the next week changed everything forever. We, as well as other families there, joined in a condensed version of what patients in the program go through on a daily basis. It was illuminating to experience the same routine and classes Julian had already been going to for two weeks.

By the second day, things were starting to ease between us all, and I really started to enjoy the lectures explaining so much about us humans and the "family unit." I was learning about first child syndrome, second child, third child. After about three or four days, something unbelievable happened. I had what can only be described as an epiphany. I'm sober, but I felt like I'd taken speed and I was speaking really fast and I had this incredible feeling in my stomach of . . . hopefulness.

What it really was, I'll never know; I can only hazard a guess. Until we arrived and started going through the family program, I was pretty much resigned to the fact that, after the divorce from Barbara and then my marriage to Tina, I wasn't going to have a close relationship with my son, and this was devastating. But now I could see that Julian's cry for help had led us both to Sierra Tucson and a total reboot of our relationship with each other, and with Jade and Barbara. It's the relationship I thought I was never going to have.

I was calling my friends after each day's lectures and they said my voice sounded at least half an octave higher. I was just so up and thankful, and I've never felt that way before or after. The feeling lasted for close to three months. *An epiphany! The moment when a character is suddenly struck with a life-changing realization, which changes the rest of the story.*

Between lectures one day, Jade, Julian, Barbara, and I were all outside, and I said, "This has obviously been fantastic for Julian and for the family, but for me, it's been something else." I couldn't quite explain what I was experiencing. I apologized for all the arguments and things I'd said and done to Barbara and the children. It was the strangest, most wonderful feeling I've ever had. We all hugged and cried. Life is too short to hold anger or a grudge. It'll make you sick. Playing a show in front of a hundred thousand people is one thing, but this feeling was a hundred times that, because it was so real and so important. Julian had brought us together through his plight.

Unfortunately, it also spelled the end of my relationship with Tina. When I apologized to Barbara, we all started to cry. It was one of those very powerful moments. She is a caretaker, she was always taking care of everyone around her, and I'd gone through the worst time of my life with her and I must've been hell to live with.

I imagine if I were Tina, I'd have thought, "Wow, maybe he's getting back with his former wife," but that wasn't it at all. Nothing could be further. It was just an indescribable feeling that I had. Mia and Tina didn't understand it. They couldn't understand why I felt so good; it was me realizing there was now the hope of a new beginning with Jade, Julian, and Barbara.

It was the strangest moment of my life so far. Wonderful, but still very strange. Eventually, my epiphany started to wear off, but I knew I was not going to let myself go back to where I had been before mentally. I can see how the two different Me's must've been hard to comprehend. One Peter leaves to go to Tucson dreading the unknown of what might happen there, and this other one comes home totally elated and extremely happy and optimistic.

Unfortunately, I could see my marriage to Tina was not going to work. My outlook on life had completely changed and it led to our divorce, which was so awful for all of us, but especially for Mia. We're doing so much better now, but back then I was walking out on her and her mom. I could see how painful this was for them and I still have terrible guilt about it.

But my life changed from that moment on, and I decided to live on my own. During my life there have been moments when all of a sudden I've realized that I can't stay somewhere that doesn't feel comfortable anymore. I make a decision and there's no going back. That family week at Sierra Tucson rehab set me off on a different course mentally, with my life, with everything. Everything changed at that point.

Thank You Mr Churchill was recorded again in my basement studio in Cincinnati. This was a really phenomenal working environment. It's unusual and very pleasing to be able to look out the window while recording and see sunshine, rain, hail, snow, or whatever is going on out there. Most commercial studios have no windows.

I had written a lot of new songs with Gordon Kennedy and the title track with John Regan and, for the first time ever, my son, Julian. Chris Kimsey co-produced the album with me and Don Gunn, and Chris engineered. Matt Cameron joined me again on drums. Also on drums was another great friend and amazing drummer, Shawn Fichter. So it was those two, with Craig Young and Stanley Sheldon on bass.

We went down to Nashville to record "Invisible Man," which was a tribute to the Motown house band who were known as the Funk Brothers. The best thing was that we asked guitarist Eddie Willis and bassist Bob Babbitt, who were part of that crew, if they would join us for this track we were dedicating to them. The answer was a resounding yes, and Eddie brought more Funk Brothers with him from Detroit. I had met them a year or two before in Nashville and had the privilege and honor to induct them into the Musicians Hall of Fame. I got to play Junior Walker's "(I'm a) Road Runner" with them that night.

I was asked to do the show *Duets* paired with Chris Jericho, the wrestler. This reality-type music show paired a known artist with a partner who wasn't known for singing. Then, one by one, each duet gets reviewed by the obligatory judges. Well, we obviously did such a great job we got voted off . . . first!

The memory etched in my mind from that show is standing side stage looking at the TV monitor and noticing that Smokey Robinson and Gladys Knight were standing in front of me watching the TV, too. I'd met both of them before. So I couldn't help myself. I went up and put my arms around them—which is tough, because Smokey is tall—and I said, "If it weren't for you guys, I wouldn't be doing what I'm doing." Motown is in my soul. Every time I go to Detroit, I go and stand in that room. I don't even talk; I just close my eyes and it's the Holy Grail for me.

I gave the album the Churchill title because from when I was very young, I heard my parents talk about Churchill's great leadership during WWII. Unfortunately, he was not a man who believed we are all born equal and his views on race are not acceptable today. But my parents told my brother and me we were very lucky to have had the perfect prime minister at the right time. After rewatching documentaries and reading books he's written, I believe that if it weren't for Churchill, I might not be here—especially when you know my father was in just about every major battle in Europe and Africa.

Getting older, thinking about how lucky I was to be here, I used *Churchill* to offer those thanks—it's not news that he liked a drink or two and he smoked big cigars. But the country had someone who the people felt they could trust and get behind. He was a champion for the British, the man who kept the UK going with hope, and the British people lived to hear his voice on the radio. "Okay, listen, Churchill's talking, we're going to be OK!"

Julian and I wrote "Road to the Sun," and we recorded it with him singing in the little vocal booth that we had in the basement. I was looking at him through the glass and at the same time looking at Matt Cameron and Craig Young, and I remember listening to my son in my 'phones and thinking, "What must be going through his head right now?" Because he's this super Soundgarden, Pearl Jam fan, and he's singing lead vocal on his dad's album. If I had my way, he would've sung the whole fucking album! It was so great for me to hear; I so enjoyed taking the back seat; the singer sings and I just play guitar. But especially to have it be my son, that was phenomenal.

"Road to the Sun" was the one song that got played on the radio, which I was so thrilled about. Julian and keyboard player Ben Sheridan opened for Gordon and me on the RAW: And Acoustic Tour, and then Julian would come out and sing with us in my set. I would tell the audience, "Out of all the songs on the *Churchill* album, the one that Julian sang is the one that got played on the radio." And he would add, "I guess I missed it that one time it got played, Dad."

After Tina and I separated and eventually got divorced, I thought I wanted to keep the house in Cincinnati, but then I realized that I was alone in this huge house—which was a great place, but now there was no reason for me to stay. I could be four and a half hours down the road, back in Nashville. I have so many muso friends in Nashville and you have everything at your fingertips: songwriters, incredible players, and phenomenal studios. So I made the decision to move back.

Selling my house in Cincinnati was difficult because it was now around the time of the big 2008 financial crash. Who needs a five thousand–plus square foot house with a full recording studio in the basement? Well, as amazing as it seems, there was the perfect person waiting patiently in the wings. Dudley Taft, who is a blues guitar player, is also part of the Taft family; his uncle is a descendant of President Taft. I believe he viewed the house when it first went on the market, but hung in there because the market was going from bad to worse. I had lowered the price a couple of times and then, just when I thought it was never going to sell, Mr. Taft came back into the picture and a deal was finally made.

Due to marriages and relationships ending and real estate being involved, I don't believe I have ever sold high. My motto had been "buy high and sell low!"—well, it seemed that way, anyway. While I had to sell the house on the lower side of what I would have preferred, the condominium building where I would end up in Nashville was now affordable. Luckily, prices were lower everywhere, and I actually got a place that would have been worth a lot more before the crash. (May it be known that this is the *only* time I have ever bought a property at a very good time.)

For a music studio, I thought I would find somewhere to put my gear and rent a little room like I did in LA. Gary Haber worked out the apartment deal for me, and then I started looking for a space to rent for storage and a place to work. It was recommended that I call up producer Richard Landis. He had a studio called Fool on the Hill in the Berry Hill area, and he wanted to sell it. I had just bought a condo that I could barely afford, but I knew Richard, so I thought I'd go see him and check out the studio.

I went over and it was amazing—five isolation rooms, lovely live room, big control room. He asked if I would be interested in buying the studio, and I told him I was only looking for a rental space now because I had just bought a condo. He said he would be willing to sell the studio just for the price of the building. I said, "What, you mean the console, outboard gear, everything?" He said yeah, everything you see here.

When I asked who his business manager was, I couldn't believe he said "Gary Haber." I started to laugh. "Oh, wow, we might be able to work something out." I called Gary and he said he would talk to Richard, and the next thing I knew, I became the proud owner of a fantastic, fully equipped commercial studio. And there was still all my studio equipment I'd been collecting since I got my first check for *Frampton Comes Alive!* record royalties in 1976 to add to the wall of outboard gear that was already there.

Meantime, I just kept on with more touring, co-headlining with the Doobie Brothers, Lynyrd Skynyrd, Foreigner, and Yes. Grinding it out, doing what Dee Anthony said I should do.

The great thing about playing with Skynyrd was that we had been the two top live acts of the mid-'70s, and we had played together a lot—me headlining sometimes, them headlining sometimes. I remember I had finished my tour in 1977 and gone out to Los Angeles to make the *Sgt. Pepper* movie. It was a Sunday and so I was home, just watching TV, sitting on the floor in the bedroom, and it comes on: "Lynyrd Skynyrd in air crash."

My road manager was Rodney Eckerman, who was the younger brother of Ronnie Eckerman, Lynyrd Skynyrd's road manager. We were all touring at the same time, but ours had ended sooner than theirs, and Ronnie and Rodney had both gone to rent planes for their respective bands. We got the four-turbo prop British Viscount; they rented a two-engine plane. So I'm watching this news, and half my crew had moved from our tour to Skynyrd's, because they were all from Houston, where Rodney and Ronnie came from. I knew them all really well, because we'd done so many shows together. My stage manager, Steve Lawler, was on that plane, sitting at the back—but the members of the band who were killed were sitting up front.

I remember managing to speak to Gary Rossington and helping them out some financially because I didn't think they had great medical insurance. Those guys were our dear friends and needed a lot of help. I think it was Artimus Pyle, the drummer, who said that as he was staggering through the swamp, wherever they had crashed, there were farmers shooting at them, thinking they were poachers. Imagine that—barely surviving an air crash and now you're being shot at! Unbelievable. So I have a soft spot for Skynyrd, they're part of the family for me, and to go back out and play with them is always so great.

Ken Levitan, my manager, had brought up the idea that other bands had started doing whole album shows for a tour, and that 2011 would be the thirty-fifth anniversary of *Comes Alive!* He asked if I had ever thought about doing a tour where I played the album from beginning to end. I said not really—I understood that it would be great for the fans and financially, of course, but I wasn't sure I could handle going back to just doing that old legendary set list. I was hesitant, to say the least.

If I were a great businessman, I would most likely be booking a residency in Vegas and playing the live album verbatim every night. Err—sorry, but it'll never happen.

So I came up with an idea that if we were going to do the whole of *Comes Alive!* for the anniversary, we would do the entire album, and then do another complete set. In the end, we played for three hours every night. We started off doing it with an intermission, but we all hated that, because when you come off after playing a whole album, your energy is way up and the last thing you want is an intermission. So we decided—and a lot of promoters didn't like it, because there was no bar time—that we would just keep going. I don't know how we did it! Sometimes it was three and a half hours! That was a lot of playing.

We did a whole summer, and then the spring of the next year, in the US and Canada, and then we went to Europe and did the same thing there. Frampton Comes Alive! 35 was a major success—and remember, I was the one who wasn't too sure about doing it. Ken is a fantastic ideas man, and ever since we started working together just before the *Fingerprints* time, he's been the major force in guiding my career.

The crowd went nuts. They knew the whole album, and even though the stage act was in a different order than the album—we did the original stage act as we recorded it: "Lines on My Face" isn't right before "Do You Feel"; it wouldn't work that way—they knew every number and they sang along. The very first date we did was in a theater in New Jersey, and we couldn't believe the reaction. It was like I'd put on a wig and pulled the satins back on! But I felt like it was a welcome back, as well. There were a lot of people who hadn't seen me for years and they'd come back, along with kids who had never seen me before, they came because we were playing that album.

I didn't think it was a great idea to start with, but seeing the excitement in the band made me excited about doing it. Then when we did that first show, it was sort of like the old days, with people screaming and hanging off the rafters. Some people left when we started into the new stuff, but most stayed till the very end. What I wanted to show the audience was, okay, here's why you know me, but also here's what you've been missing if this is the first time you've seen me in twenty years—or thirty-five years, actually. And it worked.

I was amazed at the reaction that it got so many years later, at the staying power of the record. And I enjoy performing it when the audience is enjoying it. As much as I admire Bob Dylan, I couldn't go out there and not talk to the audience. Introverted is me off stage, but there's a persona that comes out on stage that's developed—it's not an act, it's just me but on steroids. That version of me is the less inhibited me.

When I first started out as a solo artist, I was scrambling just to be heard. You're opening the show, hoping to appeal to some of the headliner's crowd. During that early period of solo touring, I was much more introverted on stage. People didn't know *Wind of Change* on that first tour. Then when *Frampton's Camel* came out, we had a few more really good pieces of music to add to the set. "Lines on My Face" is on that album, and it instantly became a staple in the act.

Gradually, as we were supporting all these amazing headliners, I was learning from them how to make my show better. When you're climbing up the ladder, you're grasping at straws every night—"Okay, good reaction there, great reaction that night, not so good here." And then as I became more accepted, I became more uninhibited, more open; I could finally feel they liked what I was doing. When we started headlining, now the audience was coming to see me. My name's on the ticket and there's no ZZ Top playing right after me. (Though I always loved opening for ZZ Top and I learned much from them, thank you.)

That acceptance adds to my creativity as well. There was one song on *Churchill* that was called "I Want It Back." It's just a rock and roll jam, and there's a section where it's obvious that you should sing along. People didn't know the song at all, but the first time they're hearing it, they're singing along. After we played it the first time, the band said, "You realize you got them singing along and they've never heard the damn song before?" I said, "Yeah, I know; that's pretty cool, right?"

In early 2013, Kerry Kennedy invited me on a nine-day volunteer trip she was leading to several Indigenous villages in Mexico. Kerry is the president of the Robert F. Kennedy Center for Justice and Human Rights, and they were one of the sponsors, along with Habitat for Humanity, the GO Campaign, and Tlachinollan Mountain Human Rights Center. I immediately accepted her invitation and flew into Mexico City with approximately twenty other volunteers from all over the world. I had no idea what to expect and was excited to be part of this special mission!

Our group helped build a school, and taught children art, basic math, English, and Spanish. I was part of the medical team and helped take children's temperatures, measured their height and weight, and recorded their medical history.

It was very rustic, as many of these communities did not have running water. We even stayed in tents a few nights.

One exciting incident happened on our way to an isolated village. Our convoy was pulled over in the middle of nowhere by *la policia* wanting to know what we were doing. I'm sure we stood out driving through the countryside in a line of nice SUVs. They were looking for a bribe and held us up for an hour or so. But, after much discussion, we did not give in and they finally let us on our way!

It was a heartwarming trip I'll never forget and it began my relationship with the RFK Center, which continues to this day. I'll always be grateful to Kerry for this, and for my becoming a member of their leadership council.

Ken Levitan and I were in Nashville watching the great guitar player Buddy Miller, who I love, and in between acts, Ken asked what I was thinking about for the next tour. I said I didn't really know, I didn't have any specific ideas. He said, "Have you ever thought about having other guitarists come and join you?" He had this idea of Frampton's Guitar Circus and I said, "I like it!" So we started thinking about different people—to have another major guitar player open up for us, then maybe jam with them, and also have one or two different guests at each show. Ken said we should call Brad.

Brad Goodman has been my friend and agent for twenty-one years. William Morris is my agency and that's where we first met. This time I was building my own team and Brad was there right from the beginning. I needed some really creative booking done to build my audience back. We've had a lot of tours together, with each one more successful than the last. Brad's been a huge part of my team and has always been a believer.

The Frampton's Guitar Circus tour kicked off in Nashville, and we were incredibly lucky to have Steve Cropper and Vince Gill as our first guests. It was such an honor that they both wanted to do it. When we put out feelers to agents and management, looking for someone who would be great to open for us, B. B. King was the first person who got back to me. I couldn't believe it!

B. B. asked me if I would come out and jam with him at the end of his set, which was always "The Thrill Is Gone." I was beside myself with the thought of playing guitar with the King. Every show B opened for us, I'd get the call from stage and would come out and we would sit together and play. Holy Moly!

He was a very generous man. When I first met him, I went on his bus; he didn't ever go to the dressing room, he always used his bus. I made my way through to the back room and there he was, and I'm now very nervous because . . . *it's B. B. King, for Christ's sake.*

I said, "It's so great to meet you, and thank you so much for doing this, I can't believe you're doing this with us . . ." I was now mumbling incoherently, trying to ask him if he might want to sit in during our show. And he said, "Peter, just tell me what you need me to do; I'm here for you. It's your show." So we just hung out and I realized this was one of the most humble people I'd ever met in the business. I was really taken aback by his openness, his friendship—immediately, you felt like you'd known him all your life. He did an interview right after the tour and they asked who he liked as a player. He said, "Well, I just played with Peter Frampton; you should listen to him. He's great." It was a phenomenal experience working with him.

The list of people who we got to join us was vast. In Los Angeles, we had Dean DeLeo from Stone Temple Pilots, who's a dear friend, and so is his brother Robert. We had Andy Summers from the Police, and Adam, my guitar player, does a perfect Sting vocal imitation. Andy and I were talking guitars, and Adam started singing "Message in a Bottle," and Andy's head snapped around and he just went, "What!?" He couldn't stop smiling, and couldn't believe how close to Sting Adam could sound.

It was such an enjoyable success that we did a second year of the Circus, with lots more great guitar players. By now people were aware of how B. B. King, Steve Cropper, Vince Gill, Larry Carlton, Don Felder, Sonny Landreth, and many more had joined the first time around and everyone would go, "Oh, really? Yeah, yeah, we're in."

One who really sticks out as being one of the most memorable is Roger McGuinn. Him joining us was very special for me because, apart from being a huge fan of his since he was called Jim in the Byrds, he had recorded "All Night Long," which I wrote with Mick Gallagher for the *Frampton's Camel* album. It was on his 1977 *Thunderbyrd* record. He chose it to be one of the songs we played together, so we're doing "Eight Miles High" and then "All Night Long," and I think we did four or five songs with him, we just didn't want to stop.

The second year, Buddy Guy was a big part of the Circus, and he is truly amazing. Lovely man. He came out and jammed on "While My Guitar Gently Weeps" and it was wonderful. We would always have this great musical conversation. It's what blues is about—your turn, my turn, let's do it together. I didn't get to spend as much time with Buddy as I did with B. B., but he was very mellow, very humble. Buddy's stage personality is dynamic. His face is a picture, his eyes are everywhere, and his *pièce de résistance*, of course—his playing—is pure Buddy Guy blues guitar. We so loved playing with both B. B. and Buddy, both legends who taught me how to approach the blues. I have to say thank you again.

It was a big kick up the ass to have all these different styles of players come along and jam with us. It was great that we were playing a lot every day, first learning the material of the two artists "du jour" in my hotel room, then running them through at sound check until everyone felt comfortable. It definitely pushed my and the band's playing to a higher level. People still ask if we're going to do it again.

Pattie Foster, a friend in Cincinnati, had introduced me to Victoria Morgan, the director of Cincinnati Ballet. Victoria first asked me if the company could use a couple of my songs for a *pas de deux*, a piece for two dancers, for an upcoming performance. I was away touring for their performance, but Victoria sent me an in-house DVD of the piece and I was just floored. I called Gordon Kennedy and said, "You've got to see this; it's phenomenal."

A year or two later, Victoria invited me to a Christmas ballet rehearsal; I believe they were doing *The Nutcracker*. Most of the area is dance space, with tiered seating at the back. I'm sitting in the first row, in front of all these dancers from all over the world, and they're leaping seventeen feet in the air—it felt as if they were going to jump right over me. Some were from Russia, from Korea, just about every country you could think of, and it was an eye-opening experience. I had always loved the ballet and admired and marveled at how they can do this. I'm watching up close, watching them put it together. It was very inspiring, knowing full well how many hours a day and years of pushing their bodies seemingly to the limit it had taken them to get to this room.

Victoria told me, "We're so glad that you liked what we did with the *pas de deux*, and we'd like to use some more of your music. Is that okay?" I said sure, just let me know what you need. And she said, "I don't think you understand—what we would like is to have you let us know what songs in your act you would like us to choreograph." I still didn't get it, so I'm still thinking she wants CDs of the tracks and then they'll use those for the performance and I'll be in the audience watching. Okay, great. But then she said, "No, let me explain—we would really like you and your band to be on stage, playing live behind the dancers!" I thought for a second and then saw how great this could be, so different from anything I'd ever done before. "I love this idea!"

Then, getting overly excited, I said, "Well, if the performance is going to be three acts of twenty minutes each, why don't we do two acts with my music people know and could I go away and write twenty minutes of new music and you could choreograph that?" She said, "Would you do that?" I said absolutely— it would be a challenge and get me into something completely different, which is what I'm always looking for.

I called Gordon up and said, "Help! I don't know whether I've done the right thing here, but I just suggested to the director of Cincinnati Ballet that we write twenty minutes of brand-new music for us to play live and them to dance to. What do you think?" He said, without missing a beat, "Let's do it!" We wrote all the music in my new condo in Nashville, and that was way before I had any furniture. We only had one small card-type table to put my computer and my two NHT M00 speakers on, and an antique stool that I had brought with me from Cincy, which we had to take turns sitting on. That was it, just the one stool for one person to sit.

Gordon is sensitive to cat dander and I have two cats. So as well as having to stand a lot, he was constantly sneezing—but safely, into his elbow. When neither of us was sitting, maybe listening to a playback, both cats jumped on the stool and wouldn't budge.

We recorded most of the basic tracks on my MacBook Pro with a UAudio Apollo interface and Nuendo music-recording program. We were laying down a template, but with master tracks of guitars and bass for the drummer to play to later.

When we had everything recorded that we could possibly do in my home, we moved to my new studio in Berry Hill. Wow. The sound in my empty living room, with just the card table, stool, and cats, had one of the most pleasing ambient sounds I've ever heard. Since it was furnished, it still sounds good, more controllable, but whatever instrument you play in the room it will sound the best it will ever sound. My profile on Twitter does say ". . . in search of the perfect sound." Well, my living room comes awfully close, but of course, there *is* no perfect sound—that's why I'll always be searching.

We took the title, *Hummingbird in a Box*, from a childhood memory of mine. When I was very little, probably about four years old, we would go to see my grandparents on Sundays for some cheese and cucumber sandwiches and tea. They were called Bandad and Nanna; Bandad was named by the extremely young yours truly, because obviously at first I couldn't say my "g" or "r" sounds. (When my brother, Clive, was born, we kept with Bandad, because why put him through the hassle of having to say "gr" when he was eighteen months old?)

One day, my grandfather—I mean, Bandad—went out of the room and came back with this beautiful inlaid wooden box. It looked like something from the Orient. He served in both World Wars and traveled all over the world in the Royal Navy as a submariner, so I'm thinking he must've picked up this box on a leave of duty.

He put the box on the table in front of me and said, "Do you think you can open it for me?" Well, it's a beautiful inlaid wooden box, but it appears there's just no way to open it. I'm looking at it and I said, "Bandad, I can't, can you help me?" So he said, "Okay, I'll show you."

It was a puzzle; the entryway was hidden, but then he slid a little piece of veneer up and another piece of wood pops out of the bottom, and he pulled that out and then all of a sudden, this thing starts to open up like a flower. And in the bottom, now I can see there's a little drawer. He says, "Pull the drawer out." And as I pulled out the drawer I could see a very colorful tiny bird. He tells me it's a hummingbird, a dead, stuffed hummingbird. Gorgeous, but dead. I said, "Oh, look at that!" And he said, "Now I'll close it up and you can learn how to open it."

So then, every weekend, "When are we going to Bandad's?" I *had* to open the box. (In hindsight, I wonder if this was the first time my parents saw an addictive personality in the making.) He gave me my earliest life lesson—I didn't get it then, but later on I saw that in life, if you make the right moves, good things will happen. And that's the story we told with the song "Hummingbird in a Box."

As I grew older, he gave me the box and I had it for a while, and then I gave it to my brother. The hummingbird was lost, probably by me, or it could've flown away. But my brother still has the box and sent me some beautiful pictures of it.

My band, Gordon, and I played this new music in Cincinnati for three shows in 2013; two one night and one the next, all sold out. It was great to be the pit band, but in view at the back of the stage. And then at the very end, the dancers all sat down on the stage and watched us play "Do You Feel." It was a great experience, something I would never have expected to do, and I totally enjoyed being completely out of my comfort zone.

There were parts in the songs that were more free-form; there would be a solo and I would play it differently than the recording that the dancers had rehearsed with. They would say, "You didn't play this solo like that." And I said, "I'm sorry, I can't ever play the same solo, and I can't remember what I played on the track!" You can't change too much, understandably, because they're used to it the way it was while rehearsing—but for me, you play in the studio and then when you go play live, it's a whole other thing. I wouldn't want to play the same exact solo, note for note, each night. Can't do it, wouldn't be prudent!

At one point, I had to walk to the front of the stage with the dancers moving all around me. That took me a while to get, because doing anything while you're playing is very difficult for me. You've really got to concentrate. I had to think about walking at a specific moment, and then maybe if I was early, I've got to step it up or they're going to crash into me. But all the dancers were so good and always gave me a wide berth. They loved dancing to the live music; it was loud, and they loved that—they could feel the music as well as hear it. We saw amazing performances by the dancers and I have so much respect for them; we got just an inkling of what it takes to become *that* good.

The next year, Cincinnati Ballet got to do the show in New York, but this time, because of logistics, we weren't able to play live behind them, so they used the studio recordings. The dancers had a great show and we loved it, but they said afterward they missed the *oomph* of us playing.

While I was still in the Herd, we went on a promotional trip to do an Italian TV show and the venue was a small, beautiful, ancient coliseum. The director wanted us to play live for the first two songs, to warm up the crowd, then after that lip-sync to the new single and they'd tape that for the show. I thought it was going to be very strange playing live for a pretty large crowd then turning off the amps and miming to the record coming through the PA.

Well, as I thought, when we played the first two songs live, there was an instant connection between the band and the audience. We got a great reaction and were enjoying playing. So for our third song, we turned off our amps and Andrew Steele, our drummer, put up the rubber cymbals. Time to mime. As the single started to play and we started playing/faking it, all of a sudden it was as if a curtain had dropped down between the band and the audience. I felt completely disconnected as soon as we started "playing."

It was the most bizarre feeling; I could feel us losing the audience. I don't remember which song it was, but I could tell it was time to buy the T-shirt or the beer or both. I learned a huge lesson right there—live music is so very powerful, it's a unique moment, and tonight it's for this one time and one time only. The next show will be completely different and, yes, another unique moment. You can't fake live, you know?

Nowadays it's a little harder to do certain things because of the weakening of the muscles in my fingers, so I'm playing slightly differently. People have said that what I'm playing is better, and I think my playing is coming more from inside; I finally know what I don't want to play.

Doing "Georgia on My Mind," it's fairly simplistic playing, but it takes a more mature player to know that it's not always necessary to go "squiddley-widdley" right there. I've found that I really enjoy playing fewer notes; when I'm recording, I listen back and I hear the feeling, I want to hear the soul. It makes me who I am, makes me play the way I play, and gives me the wisdom of knowing what works for me and what doesn't.

Doing the *Acoustic Classics* record was another suggestion of Ken's. He had done one with the great Richard Thompson, who he also manages and who I've known from England from many years ago. Richard came and joined us on the second Guitar Circus tour. Such a phenomenal artist.

I didn't know how I was going to do an acoustic version of "Do You Feel," so I did all the others and kept leaving that one till later. I thought maybe we could just fade bits of the intro in and out between tracks, but then I thought that might be cruel. So I went into the studio and recorded the intro on acoustic, and then put the harmony guitar part on, which is normally the piano part. I listened to it and I went, "Wow, that sounds pretty cool." I did play an acoustic bass part on it, to help give it some movement. It's the only one that has any bass or anything other than guitar, but it worked great and I was surprisingly very happy with it.

Just about everything starts off on acoustic. Even with "Do You Feel," I wrote the chorus the night before we put the whole thing together at rehearsals. It's right there, it's easy, you don't have to plug in, and you can use different tunings or whatever. So everything starts on either acoustic guitar or piano, very rarely on electric.

In the '80s drum machines and computer drums and all that stuff started coming out, where you've got a drum loop and then you play to that, and it locks you in straightaway. Now I don't turn on any machines until I've got the idea, because some songs are not supposed to have a click track. They're supposed to speed up and slow down. *Alcuni accelerando e alcuni rallentando!*

Humble Pie used to pull a song back and speed up, and it was for effect. It was orchestral. We did it on purpose, for the excitement level of the song. The bottom line is that if a song doesn't sound good with just a voice and an acoustic or keyboard, then no amount of highly programmed drum machines will turn it into a great one.

Doing the acoustic record was like going back to when I wrote the songs, all the way back to the drawing board. It was harder than I thought it would be. I first went in and recorded "All I Want to Be," but when I listened back, I thought, "No, that's not what I want." I was doing the songs the way that I do them now on stage, but when the microscope was on them, they weren't working for me. I got despondent, went home, took a few days to rethink, and then came back in and started to record again.

I soon realized that it was all down to the performance, that one take when it all clicks. I ended up going in each day and doing different takes of songs I had already put down, then comparing the different versions done on different days. I've been playing these songs for many years now, so choosing my definitive acoustic version of each one was not the easiest, but I was able to find the take of each one that made me smile.

Two years go by and I thought I'd lost the guitar forever. But then the son of the current "owner" came back to Donald's place again. He asked him, "So how much are you going to pay me for this guitar? I want to buy another one." Donald asked, "What do you want for it?" And the boy said $5,000—which was pretty close to the price of a nice new Gibson Custom Shop Les Paul. He said, "Give me your number and I'll contact Mr. Frampton."

Donald called Lisa Jenkins to let us know that he had made contact with the boy again, and he now wanted to sell the guitar. Lisa immediately started talking with Donald to facilitate the return of my old Black Beauty. Lisa suggested that we all meet in Nashville at the hotel where I always stayed when I drove in from Cincinnati. But we think Donald was worried that we were going to have whoever brought the guitar back arrested in Miami by the FBI, because it was still technically stolen merchandise. I had no such intent—all I ever wanted was to have my lost treasure back in my hands, and that it wasn't going to cost me an arm and a leg. This goes on and on; he's scared to bring it, and then he said that he couldn't pay for the guitar himself, anyway.

Donald went to Curaçao's Minister of Tourism and explained the situation. He said, "Look, it will be great if Peter Frampton gets his guitar back after so many years, and the island's Minister of Tourism gets to be the savior!" I guess he loved the idea, because in the end, both Donald and the Minister of Tourism flew up from Curaçao, bringing the guitar with them. Before they got on a plane, though, they were still worried that I was going to have them arrested. Lisa told them to call the hotel in Nashville we had booked for them, and once the hotel confirmed that they did have reservations, the trip was on. I could then, and only then, begin to see a light at the end of a thirty-two-year-long tunnel.

We had three cameras set up in the suite waiting. My tour manager, Donnie Lewis, had a friend stationed there who does personal security. We had no idea how this was going to play out.

The two very excited travelers came in and everyone was introduced. The thing I noticed first was the case that was covering the guitar. When I got my very first guitar, the case was just a plastic cover and a zip; it kept the dust off, but it wasn't protective. Well, that's what the Gibson was in, I swear.

Donald had read everything anyone had ever said about this guitar. He handed it to me, and it's a very light Les Paul, so before I even took the cover off I could feel the weight of it. He said, "It's light, isn't it?" Without even looking, I could just feel it was mine. I finally got the cover off and it was just like putting on an old pair of extremely comfy shoes. "Yes, it's mine." And there she was! Back home!

Once the expletives, cheers, and thank yous had all died down a bit, I was left in this wonderful kind of shock with a shit-eating grin. During the drive over to the Gibson Custom Shop, I couldn't help feeling I was having a weird dream and I would wake up any minute. We had some fine guitar aficionados waiting to see and check this baby out. All my friends at Gibson—Rick Gembar, SR VP/GM; Mike McGuire, head of the Custom Shop; and George Gruhn and Walter Carter—were there studying it, taking this plate off and that knob off. They finally all agreed that it was a 1954/55 Black Beauty (the serial number had been sanded off before Marc Mariana gave it to me) and retrofitted with three humbucking pickups.

In the end, I gave Donald a healthy finder's fee/reward. Things like this just don't happen—well, they sure don't happen very often. I started calling my guitar the "Phenix" because this thing literally rose from the ashes. (I didn't want to use the conventional spelling, like the city, so the dictionary gave me the French spelling—I just wanted it to be different.)

I got the guitar back for the last couple days of rehearsal before the second half of the Frampton Comes Alive! 35 tour, but the band didn't know I had it yet. I had my back to them as I put it on. We never run through "Do You Feel" or any of the older songs we play every night, so I casually said, "Let's run through the beginning of 'Do You Feel,' just so I can check my sound." I counted it in, we started to play the intro, and I turned around— and I could see the band had a look of surprise in their eyes, which were now huge, "Hey what is that? It's THE sound. That's the sound of the record! That's your guitar!" They realized what it was just from listening to me play the intro; the difference in sound is that noticeable. And then we played through just about everything off Frampton Comes Alive! that afternoon. Now we all had shit-eating grins! That was a rehearsal I will never forget. Thank you, Curaçao!

I had to leave the guitar at Gibson so they could bring her up to speed. I wanted all the scars left as is, but anything that didn't work properly, like the tuners or any bad electronics, had to be replaced. I can't thank all my friends who donated the original pieces for the model, like "patent applied for" pickups and '50s capacitors and volume and tone knobs, some still in their new old boxes. We call those beautiful old parts new old stock—NOS.

There are still burn marks, dents, and tons of other scratches, but that's the way she will stay. I only wish we could sit down together, have a nice cuppa tea, and find out what, when, how, and where she's been for the last thirty years!

It was finally ready by the time we played the Beacon in New York. Anthony Mason had already done an interview with me for CBS about the return of the guitar, so he was there that night, filming me on the bus before the show. He asked how I felt about playing it on stage, and I said, "I'm scared shitless that I'll make a mistake!"

Right before "Do You Feel," which is always the last number of the set, I walked off and the stage went dark. My tech brought out the guitar, placed it in the middle of the stage on a stand, pitch dark, and then all the spotlights hit it at once—bam! The crowd went nuts; she was the star of the show, they could see what she was. I picked her up and we started to play "Do You Feel"—and I did make a slight mistake in the intro, but they edited it out of the *CBS Sunday Morning* piece. The Phenix wasn't nervous, but I was. Thank you, Anthony.

Years after we had returned from South America in 1980, Barbara and I stayed over the weekend in New York, and on Monday morning, before we checked out, I had *Good Morning America* on and I heard my name. I sat up and it was the *Lifestyles of the Rich and Famous* guy, Robin Leach. He said, "News has finally reached me. I now have the true story about Peter Frampton escaping from Panama and Noriega's troops." What? "Back in 1980, a well-placed call was made to the White House, as Frampton had connections there"—yeah, because I'd been to the White House once!

He said that a military jet with troops had been sent down to Panama, that there was a rescue mission and Frampton, his band, and crew had all been rescued by the CIA and brought back to Andrews Air Force Base. We were in hysterics! We had gotten out of there all on our own. The American consulate wasn't a lot of help, if I remember. I just couldn't believe my ears hearing him spew all this bullshit. It was pretty exciting stuff, but it was totally untrue.

It's wonderful to have my old Les Paul back because for so many years after the crash, fans would ask me, "Is that the one you played on *Frampton Comes Alive!*?" and I'd have to say no. When I moved to Nashville in the '90s, Gibson's Mike McGuire suggested we work on a replacement. I was thrilled! He and I and many great people at Gibson worked for about a year on building one that was as close to the original as I could remember. I played it for years, but when the Phenix arrived back and I compared the old and the new, it was no contest. They both sounded great, but the Phenix just sounds and plays like the Phenix! When I announced her at the Beacon Theatre show, I could see this was her night in the limelight.

Chapter **Sixteen**

Sometime during the 2013 summer tour, the band and I were playing Frisbee backstage, and I was finding it really hard to run. I just couldn't get there in time and I kept on falling to my knees. What the hell was wrong with my legs? I thought, "Well, I'm just getting old."

Then July 18, 2015, we were playing in Walker, MN, at the Moondance Jam Festival and a big beach ball bounced on stage; weighs nothing. I went to kick it and I lost my balance. My left leg gave way and I fell, landed on my back with my guitar on top of me; Donnie Lewis, my tour manager, and Aidan Mullen, my tech at the time, picked me up. After the show we all laughed—"He's fallen and he can't get up," like that TV commercial. I was embarrassed, but thankfully they got me up quickly, and I wasn't hurt physically.

Our fearless leader, Donnie, printed out a really early homemade meme. It was a silhouette of someone falling, and at the top it said, The Frampton Falls Tour: Sioux Falls, Niagara Falls, Glens Falls, Fergus Falls, Idaho Falls, and Little Falls with Falls Church as the closer. Every city with the name Falls. It was very funny—even after falling, I can still always laugh at myself.

Two or three weeks went by, and it happened again. I still use a guitar cable, because I can't stand the sound of wireless. I bent down and then tried to stand back up while standing on my cable but I was caught, couldn't stand up; I went straight back down, again. That's when it wasn't funny anymore. That's when I thought, something's terribly wrong here. There's more to this than just me getting old.

On our next break I went straight to see my doctor in Nashville, Dr. Allen, and he wanted me to see a neurologist. I had seen Dr. Allen for a checkup recently and he was worried that I had lost ten pounds in a relatively short period. I went to see a neurologist, Dr. Kaminski, with my girlfriend, Robin Rains, and the first thing he did was a finger flexor test. Normally, if you don't have any muscle issues, the finger muscles will be very strong. I tested Robin's, and I couldn't budge her fingers; she held them in an open fist. But with me, as hard as I tried to keep the doctor from moving them, he had no trouble at all; he just pulled my fingers straight back. I told him that I was having trouble with my arms and legs feeling weaker, and that putting my computer bag or anything in the overhead compartment of a plane was becoming more and more difficult.

The last thing he had me do was go out into the hallway and jump ten times on my right foot and then ten times on my left foot. Well, I could've jumped fifty times on my right foot, but I couldn't make it to six with my left. That was the clue for him; it being asymmetrical meant that whatever I had was not affecting both sides equally. He said, "I'm so glad that we did that, because now I know what you have. I'm pretty certain you have IBM—Inclusion Body Myositis—but you don't have ALS, which was the other disease I needed to consider."

IBM can be hard to diagnose, and it's not life-threatening, but it is life-changing. It's a progressive muscle disorder characterized by muscle inflammation; it causes atrophy of the affected muscles. I now have weakness in my legs, arms, hands, and fingers. IBM usually starts to develop after age fifty, and there are no known causes, but it likely involves genetic, immune-related, and environmental factors. But it's not something I inherited from my family tree, either.

I asked him who I should see for an official diagnosis, and he said that the best place in the country is the Myositis Center at Johns Hopkins, and the director is Dr. Lisa Christopher-Stine. Dr. Allen called and set up a meeting for me, so off Robin and I went to Baltimore. Dr. Lisa examined me and we did a lot of different strength tests with her whole team—they have different machines to measure strength in all the affected muscles. One test is stair climbing, to see how fast you can go up and down. Then a six-minute walking test, to see how far you can go in that amount of time, and lots of dexterity tests too. Every test is repeated whenever I visit to compare the results with past and future biannual visits'.

Unfortunately, as of now, there is no drug that works for IBM. The only thing you can do to prolong the use of the affected muscles is to exercise. It was recommended that I see a physical therapist, and I met with Susan Underwood in Nashville, who is wonderful. I go to her for overall body tune-ups. (They say, "This guitar was in tune when I bought it!" Yes, but it'll go out of tune very quickly, just like our bodies will and do.)

Susan, in turn, recommended I call Colleen Bridges, a physical trainer who was already working with Parkinson's patients at my local gym in Nashville. We incorporate some of her "Rock Steady" program into my workout. I first became aware of Rock Steady watching *60 Minutes* with Leslie Stahl. Her husband unfortunately has Parkinson's and they had both learned about the program, and the episode showed him taking part in a session.

Colleen and I have been working out together since October 2015. I started off working out four days a week, but now I'm up to six. Can you say addiction? No, this time it's necessity—the more I exercise, the easier it is to move and the more confident I feel as I walk. The body does need one day of rest, but I do an hour every day now. So when I meet all the IBM people now, I ask, "What are you doing?" and hopefully they all say, "I'm exercising, like you said."

IBM is very different from Parkinson's in that it only attacks specific muscles: arms, wrists, fingers, quads, and the muscles that lift the feet. Both diseases are similar when it comes to walking and, unfortunately, falling. Therefore, fall prevention is one of the highest on our list of objectives. The other muscles that are sometimes affected are the ones you use to swallow. Yes, they have a test for that, too, with a vertically moving x-ray camera that follows the food from mouth to stomach. Being the gadget freak I am, this test I found to be the most interesting. Luckily, this test was negative for me, so that was a huge relief. It's one of the more dangerous symptoms due to possible choking and pulmonary aspiration, when food or saliva can go into your lungs.

During my first visit at Hopkins, Dr. Chung, one of my amazing team of doctors there, did the slightly-to-moderately painful EMG. Okay, it hurt like hell! It's an electronic test to find out if there are any neuromuscular abnormalities or, in my case, to locate the "inclusions," which he finally did. Later I could actually see the little blighters on my MRI.

I went back a couple weeks later for a muscle biopsy. They took a small amount of muscle from my left arm, near my shoulder. Even though it's not a huge deal, they put you out. As I was being wheeled into the operating room there was music playing, and I suddenly realized it was my favorite guitar player, Django Reinhardt! Someone had obviously read up on my musical tastes, because I always mention Django.

Okay, I know that right now you might be saying to yourself, "How come these people get treated so differently than me?" I understand, at times there are certain fringe benefits to fame, but apparently they always play music in the OR. I guess the difference is just that someone had done some research on me, for which I am extremely grateful; it was very calming. It was wild being told to count backward while Django was playing, fading into echo, and then by the time I got to "seven," I was out cold. They probably all waited until I was out and then put on some Iron Maiden. Seriously, it was very comforting knowing I was lucky enough to have the head of surgery at Johns Hopkins performing the biopsy.

After the lab had tested my muscle, the diagnosis came back positive for IBM. It was thought that my symptoms weren't strong enough for me to go into a drug trial at that point, because they thought they might not be able to measure the progression.

The Grammy tribute to the Beatles TV show in 2014 was probably one of my all-time favorite sit-ins. Ringo had asked if I could play guitar with him for a David Lynch Foundation for Transcendental Meditation benefit at a club in LA. Before I left for LA, though, I was also asked to play in the house band for the Grammy tribute. When I got to rehearsals, I saw it was Steve Lukather, Greg Phillinganes, Rami Jaffee, Kenny Aronoff, and Lenny Castro. Don Was was on bass and the bandleader, not a bad crew, oh, and me; plus an incredible brass section. We were playing with just about everybody—we were on the stage the whole night. At one point, there was John Legend on one piano and Alicia Keys on another playing together. So many incredible artists on one show.

I got to play with Stevie Wonder on "We Can Work It Out." He had the Hohner Clavinet and the distortion pedal, it was *the* sound, and it was so great to be standing right next to him playing my Motown guitar part. While we were taping the show, Stevie missed one note during the intro—but his performance was phenomenal.

At the end of the song, the crowd was rightfully going berserk, and as soon as the crowd died down Stevie said immediately, "Can I do it again?" And everybody, band and crowd, are yelling "Yes!" I'd hoped he would, and you can't say no to Stevie Wonder! Then the voice of the director, Ken Ehrlich, booms out a big "Yes." Of course, it was even better than the first time, which was only to be expected. It's Stevie Wonder. For me, it was another moment like playing next to George Harrison and overdubbing at Abbey Road; I don't think I could have smiled any bigger if I tried.

Katy Perry was going to do "Yesterday," and they asked Steve Lukather to play acoustic guitar for her and he said, "Okay, but Peter will play with me, too." That was so cool of him; he's a very generous man. Luke and I have been friends for many years since we met at Toto's first date of their very first tour, opening for me in Hawaii in 1978, and they blew us all away with how good they were. To say he's a great guitar player is an understatement; his playing is unbelievable. He knew he wanted to be a session guitar player very early on, and he studied to become one of the best-known and most highly respected guitar players in the world.

Keith Urban came and jammed with John Mayer. Dave Grohl was playing drums on some things, singing, playing guitar on something else. Joe Walsh played "Something" with Dhani Harrison and Jeff Lynne. Later in the show we played with Ringo for his set, which I always love doing, and then Paul McCartney and his amazing band played to cap off an incredible show.

Ringo always wants to be at the back, where drummers are, with the band wrapped around him. Well, of course when we walked in they'd set him up on a huge pedestal right in the middle and the band is nowhere near him; it was hard to even see us all off to the side. I looked at Jeff Chonis, his drum tech, and we just shook our heads—"Oh, that's not going to work." Ringo walks in and guess what? "I'm not having that there; move that. Why am I in the center on me own? I want to be with my band!"

At the David Lynch benefit show a couple of nights earlier, I had arrived at the club and was on my way to the dressing room. As I walked in, I almost bumped into someone and, looking up, I see it's Jim Carrey. As we both realize who we're bumping into, Jim starts saying, "Oh, wow, you're Peter Frampton," and I'm going, "Wow, and you're Jim Carrey!" Being a huge fan of his, this was a lovely surprise.

Two of my children, Julian and Mia, were at the show, and they're both megafans of his. When the show was over, I went out into the audience to find them, and Jim was hanging at the front, too. It was great to be able to introduce my children to him, I knew what that would mean to them. We're chatting away with Jim and this middle-aged, slightly sozzled lady is making her way through the crowd toward us. She gets within arm's reach of me and says something like "I love you Pet . . . er." On the "er," she lost her footing, fell right into me, and then fell to the floor at my feet. To which Jim quickly said, "So I guess it never ends, does it, Peter?"

I first met Steve Miller in London when I was nineteen, when I was in Humble Pie. We were recording with Glyn Johns, and Glyn called me up and asked, "Would you like to come up to Olympic? I'm doing some overdubs with Steve Miller." I had heard an earlier album of Steve's, and now they were working on his *Your Saving Grace* album. When I arrived, Steve was in the vocal booth stacking those incredible Steve Miller harmonies, and it was like, uh, yeah, he's good. He's *really* good.

Steve and I played shows together in the '70s quite a bit. We started in theatres and arenas and ended up playing football stadiums. He was already a huge artist when we first played together, and we were the support act. He would always come and watch us, and then one night after our show, he took me aside and told me how great he thought my band was. I'll never forget where I was standing when he said that to me on the side of the stage.

In the 2000s we did a couple of shows together again, and they went really well. He came to me and said we should do a whole tour. It took a while, but we ended up doing two years of summer tours together and it was phenomenal. I enjoyed every moment of it, and it ultimately gave me the idea to do the *All Blues* album.

Ahead of the first year's tour, Steve had asked if I would like to come up and play some blues with him during his set; we did anywhere from two to five songs every night.

When we decided to do another summer tour together, he asked if I wanted to sing one of the blues songs in addition to playing. Okay, so now I needed a blues number I could really get my teeth into. I was listening to an album by Freddie King and when "Same Old Blues" came on, I jumped up to see what it was. For a blues song, it has some extra chords in there, which I like a lot because it broadens the scope of where you can take it musically when ad-libbing a solo or doing guitar fills. It was the first one that I took to my band and rehearsed so that I would be ready to do it during Steve's show. We all listened to it before rehearsals, and when we all played it the first time it was phenomenal. I wish we had recorded it right then.

We had some solo dates before hooking up with Steve, so we played "Same Old Blues" in our set and it tore the place up. It was an unexpected number out of the blue, no announcement; we just started playing a slow blues, and I could hear people going, "Oooh!" It fit me like a glove, and I realized that maybe I should have done this before. I'd never thought I was good enough. But now I think I can't get enough of it.

The Peter Frampton Band is made up of not only incredible players, but also really wonderful human beings. Dan Wojciechowski is our drummer extraordinaire; he can play anything, always with a hugely deep pocket—which is "muso" talk for "Feels so good!" Not only does he play like Dan, but he also morphs into any other drummer who's ever played with me.

How nice is Dan? Well, we had a crew member for a while who would unfortunately imbibe a wee bit too much sometimes. One day he was slur-talking to one of the band members and out of the blue he said, "You know, there's something wrong with that Dan"—pause—"'cause nobody's *that* nice." Yep, that's Dan for you. But he really is that nice.

Adam Lester is my wingman on guitar, and again a super-cool friend who I call on for great musical ideas. He's very inventive and always comes up with great new parts for a song. If you give that man a slide, he'll paint a beautiful picture for you with his choice of notes and that great feel. It's a perfect fit of two completely different guitar styles, and he's as passionate about the music we play as I am.

Steve Mackey joined us on bass for the first six tracks we recorded for my next solo album. He is a great player with a really soulful feel and fit right in with us. So, I asked him if he could do the Finale Tour with us. When finding a new player for the band, we usually rent a tour bus and drive to Atlanta and back just to find out if they're "Bus-worthy." We took a vote and decided we could pass on that part with Steve. He's nuts like we are. So, he's perfect!

Rob Arthur is a phenomenal keyboard player, vocalist, and also my bandleader. He's a great musician and also a great painter. Nothing seems to faze him—well, on the outside, anyway. He wears a bunch of different hats, and on the Finale Tour, we decided that we wanted to do our own documentary, using the tour as the backdrop for a retrospective look at my career. Rob and I had already done a few promo videos for the tour and decided to start our own film company. What do we know? Nothing so far, but we know what we like! We're always learning, but Rob has woodshedded film class and because he has such a good eye (I believe it's the left one), he is now becoming a fantastic cinematographer and director. I believe we have great footage of the tour, as well as behind-the-scenes stuff already in the can ready for the documentary.

And finally, let's acknowledge that there are tour managers, and then there's Donnie Lewis! When Donnie first started with me, I had no idea how lucky I was to have him lead my team. In retrospect, I probably have to thank Garth Brooks and Trisha

Yearwood for getting married. Sounds funny, but Donnie was working with Trisha until she decided to take some time off the road due to her new relationship with Garth.

I remember the first time I met Donnie, we were checking into to the same hotel in New York. He walked up to the front desk and, quick as a flash, he had Trisha's key and *whoosh*, up to the room. I, on the other hand, had to wait and wait for a room. I think Trisha came down, having already unpacked and showered, and I was still waiting for my room. Well, guess what? I don't have to wait anymore because of the great Donnie Lewis. When you say, "I'll take care of the details," you don't understand that in the Donnie Lewis dictionary, it means something completely different.

Everyone in and around this band is here because they love what we do together. I've always maintained that if you were to put four musicians together purely because they were phenomenal players, it's not always going to work out as you might have hoped. I will never think of myself as being the best at anything. There's always someone better than you, and I always know that I still have so much to learn. I'll never stop learning. The different personalities in a team either work together or they don't. One bad apple in a road crew or band will infect the whole tour.

I had been aware that my IBM was progressing a little faster, but it wasn't time to tell anybody yet, because it wasn't affecting my playing. No one knew—the crew didn't know, the band didn't know, no one. But eventually I had to let the band in on it because I needed their help, to lend a hand if they could see I was falling. Then finally I had to tell the crew, which was devastating for everybody because it's been such a long-time, big Frampton road family. It's been the same core of people for donkey's years. So there were some tears, and it was very difficult, but everyone said they would be here for me till I couldn't do it anymore. I love my road family!

I don't think there are many bands or artists who regard the people around them quite as I do. I have a great deal of respect for my band and crew because they're all professional and know exactly what they're doing. One time I was meeting with a prospective new crew member at our rehearsal room and I welcomed him in at the door, and in the time it took to walk from the door to the stage, I knew this person was absolutely wrong for me and our team. It's just body language, the way they talk, or a lack of respect for others. Everyone in my band and crew are all at the top of their game and are just the best people.

I don't know how an artist could disrespect the crew or treat them badly. Hey, I've gotten mad, I've called people on the carpet when something's gone wrong, but usually it's because I don't want that person to have to leave. It's something that's happened, a spur of the moment mistake, an accident— whatever, it happens. You correct it and you move on. I'm a perfectionist, but the people who work for me are all perfectionists in what they do, too, every one of them.

In 2018, I had a wonderful week away with my daughter Mia in Maui. We had the best time together—sun, pool time, spa—and it was so great because I go on holiday . . . er, actually I can't remember the last one. About every four to five years, maybe? "Hey, Pete, take a break, would ya!"

Anyway, the last day I had chartered a two-hour cruise for Mia and me on a lovely sailboat. It was a beautiful day and the two crew members were great, and it was all sun and sea with no noise except the flapping of the sails and the swishing of the water against the hull.

As we docked, we all wanted a group photo, so we got up on the raised roof part of the front cabin and took photos and then everyone jumped down onto the deck—except me, who fell because my left leg gave way as I came down on the deck, and my back hit the metal wire that goes through the stanchions all around the boat, which is there to protect the crew from falling overboard. Well, it did stop me falling overboard, but I had broken two small bones in my back. Poor Mia was very upset and I felt terrible for her. We had to cancel going to dinner because I was in a wee bit of pain and then I fell again trying to get into the rental car to go to the restaurant.

We were walking back to the room feeling sad that we wouldn't be able to go to the great restaurant we'd been saving till the last night, and Mia got on the phone and called the restaurant and says, "We can't come, but can I come and pick dinner up?" Big hugs for Mia; what a great idea. Off she went, took the car and drove all the way there and back with the best meal of the trip. She saved the day and we had a great last meal on Maui together.

After that trip, I flew to New York with Ken Levitan; we were actually going to see publishers about this book. I told Ken that my IBM was starting to affect my hands, and my legs were getting weaker. I thought we ought to be really careful about what we were going to schedule from now on.

I knew that when I felt I couldn't play as well as I used to, then it would be time to stop. I will always play for my own enjoyment at home until, unfortunately, that too isn't possible anymore. I don't ever want to put myself in a situation where

I would play a show and have people in the audience say, "Oh, yeah, but he isn't as good as he used to be."

We had started booking dates for my first real co-headline tour with Alice Cooper, who is a dear, dear friend. But Ken said that if I was feeling this way, we ought to make this my farewell tour instead. So I called Alice up nervously and told him what was going on and said I was so sorry, but I wouldn't be able to do our tour. He said, "Never mind the tour. How are you?" I should have expected that from him, and I'll never forget it. Alice and his wife, Sheryl, are two of the nicest people I know, and they continue to call and text to check on me.

When I went public with my condition, I'd had years to think about it. I knew it was going to come, but I just didn't know when. But I did know who I wanted to talk to; I really wanted to ask Anthony Mason at CBS. I'd already done the piece with him for *CBS Sunday Morning* about the return of my long lost guitar, and that was a great experience. I felt very comfortable talking with Anthony.

So the decision was basically made in the back of a cab in New York, on the way to another book publisher. And then it was figuring out when do we announce, what do we do? This was a completely different situation for me; I'm normally talking about a new release or a tour.

I had already learned so much about the disease and what it does to the muscles. I knew I could speak with confidence; I knew what I was talking about. I knew there were a lot of people out there who had it, but I also knew that the number of diagnosed people was smaller than originally thought—maybe twenty-five thousand people in the US—but because its MO is so slow-moving that a lot of people don't get diagnosed. It normally affects people later in life so, like me, most people probably think, "Oh, I'm just getting older!"

After I made the announcement, a lot of people with IBM tweeted or sent messages to me. On the Finale Tour, I did the usual VIP meet-and-greets after each show. Donnie Lewis would let me know when there were any IBM visitors and we would have them wait until last so that I could spend a little extra time with them.

One couple in the queue to meet me came up. I welcomed them both and we were just about to take photos and the wife said, "You diagnosed my husband." I said, "Excuse me, what do you mean?" Then he started talking, and told me, "I'd been to many doctors and nobody could tell me what I have. And then I turn on *CBS This Morning* and there you are talking about what you have, and I'm checking off every symptom you're mentioning. I said, 'Hon, I think I've got what Frampton has.'" As soon as he could, he went to a neurologist, and he was right; he was diagnosed with IBM. That's why I know there must be many more people out there who have this condition, but they don't have a clue what it is.

IBM is known to progress at varying speeds, but for me so far it's been very slow, and I'm so very lucky I'm in that category. No, there isn't a cure right now for this kind of myositis. There are meds that help other kinds of myositis—"myo" is muscle, "itis" is inflammation—but so far we don't have anything for Inclusion Body Myositis.

When we were planning the tour, in some ways I felt like I was caught, that I had to announce what I had, so that everyone would know why it was a farewell tour. But from then on, every time I did an interview, I felt gun-shy from the old days—like, "Oh, no, there's the same story again. Aren't people sick to death of it?" I'm not looking for attention, I'm looking to help others.

I had no idea what to expect of the Finale Tour. And it exceeded all my expectations. I lost it at the end of every show. Because I could see the emotion on their faces. One night we played two and a half hours, and the crowd just didn't want us to go. It left me speechless at the end of each night, because the crowds were so full of encouragement and love. It was the same vibe and reaction every night; it was just a different city. I felt it, I felt so much love. It was unbelievable. Thank you to everyone who came out, much love to you, too.

There were a lot of people who saw me in '76 who also came to the Finale shows, but they hadn't seen me in between. I think they were the most shocked at where we were at musically and how much the show had developed over the years. I obviously turned a lot of people off, around the release of *I'm In You* and, well, maybe a few other things—the arc was pretty steep! People were commenting on how good my guitar and my voice were and that I was as good, if not better, than ever, which was very nice to hear. And maybe those people are saying, "Why didn't I come see him over the years?" It's definitely woken a few people up—I won't say better late than never, but I just did.

Eric Clapton emailed me and asked me to play at his Crossroads Guitar Festival in 2019, which was in Dallas this time around, so we kept space in the schedule for that. I was home on a break from the tour and I was actually steaming some clothes in my bedroom closet. No ironing now; I have one of the tall steamers that you can hang your clothes on while you're steaming. I needed to move it out of the way so I could get to my suitcases and somehow, I got my left foot caught underneath it. I twisted around and lost my balance and down I went, with my foot still stuck under the steamer. It hurt as I pulled my foot from underneath, but I thought I'd just stubbed my toes—but then they all turned black. Oh, dear.

I said, "Oh, well, it's not that bad." I was hobbling, but we played Crossroads and did eight more shows before I had two days off to get the doctor. I didn't want to know; I knew it was worse than I originally thought. Yep, the doctor said I had four broken toes. So I ended up playing fifteen shows with four broken toes and nobody knew, except the band.

Eric's in a similar place as me right now, because he has nerve issues. He doesn't give it a name, but what's happening to my muscles is happening to his nervous system. When I saw him walk out in Dallas, I thought, oh, that looks like me. He was walking cautiously.

The festival was held at a huge arena, the American Airlines Center, twenty-thousand seats sold out for two nights. After the sound check, I needed to speak to Eric about the song we were planning to play together. We had already agreed we would jam on "While My Guitar Gently Weeps"—the only song by the Beatles that an "outside" guitar player played on—and I wanted to know if he wanted to do his solo. I want to defer to him, obviously. But his dressing room was like a mile that way and mine was a mile this way. I've got four broken toes—I don't know that yet, but it's painful to walk, so how do I speak to Eric?

Donnie took his phone and walked to Eric's dressing room and Eric FaceTimed with me—but we're in the same building!

Once we could see and hear each other, I explained how we usually do "Weeps" when a guest is sitting in; I usually do the middle solo, but you can take it if you want, and then we can trade licks and jam at the end together. He said, "Okay, good, you do the middle solo, but what about if I do the fills in the verses?" I said, "Yes, that would be great." I have iPhone pics Donnie took of Eric talking to me while we were laughing. We're both of the "analog age" but now we're meeting in the digital one! It was hilarious.

Sheryl Crow was wearing a T-shirt with me on it, the same one she wore to the very first concert she ever went to, which was apparently mine. Sheryl and Bill Murray introduced me; it was fantastic. I think Bill was trying to auction off Sheryl's T-shirt.

We came out and played our instrumental version of "Georgia on My Mind." I looked up at the end and everyone stood up, it was unbelievable. And then we played "Do You Feel," and at the end I said, "We've known each other for fifty years, but we've never played together, so I'd like to bring on the reason we're all here, our dear friend, Eric Clapton." And he walked on, the place went nuts again—but he didn't stand out front with me; he stood back with the band. It's jam etiquette when sitting in with another artist, and I do the same. But I walked over to him at the end and we traded licks.

I made one goof on the lyrics. I was nervous! I'm never nervous doing that song, but I'm playing with Eric—he played on the record! At the very end, I went up to the mic and said, "You've just seen a dream come true." Everyone said that of the two days, we stole the show, with a lot of help from Eric. I was the only person Eric sat in with that night, and it was such an honor. It was, yet again, another one of those moments where no words can express what you're feeling inside. A day and a night the band and I will never forget.

Before every show, I usually stay in my dressing room and hang with my band. I still get nervous every night and meditate, then I warm up on guitar and change clothes. By the time I walk to the stage, I'm primed and ready for lift off! In the past, I've had people say the weirdest things to me on my walk to the stage and it can throw me off my game. But this night, it was a wonderful feeling backstage. My dressing room was closest to the stage, so everyone was hanging out, excited to see one another—Gary Clark Jr., Bonnie Raitt, Sheryl Crow, Sonny Landreth, Jimmie Vaughan, Alan Darby, just to name a few; an awesome bunch of incredibly talented people. John Siomos's original green drum kit from *Comes Alive!* was sitting on a dolly there, and Bill Murray was bowing down to it. "You're kidding me! This is the one?"

Last note about this show: as you now know, I was dealing with broken toes on top of the IBM, which causes the weakness in my legs. Having fallen on stage a couple of times due to the effects of the disease, the last place I wanted to go down was at Crossroads. After Eric and I had finished trading licks, I was backing up slowly in front of Eric's amp and in front of that was a microphone on a small stand. It's not usually there, so I'm backing up and I sense there's now something in my way and I start to lose my balance. In a flash, I was resigned to the fact I was going to fall, but at that exact moment between me being upright or on my back, my incredible guitar tech, Darren Hurst, like an angel, ran more than halfway across the stage to put his hands on my shoulders just in the nick of time to keep me upright. OMG! What a save! I can't wait to see the video of the show so I can see what actually happened. He literally "had my back!" Thank you, Darren, again and again!

Playing Madison Square Garden for the first time since the late '70s gave me an incredible feeling of resolve. It had been a long road back to MSG, but here we were again—I'm back playing the Garden and it's sold out! When we first came out and started playing, you could feel it was going to be a great show. The audience was right there with us every moment; you could hear a pin drop when I told the stories. My brother, Clive, and his wife, Tracy, and their children, Theo and Lorelei, all flew over from England for a long weekend. Clive had been at the Garden for the '70s shows, so it was very important to me that he and his whole family was there.

Usually for the encore, we start with Humble Pie's version of "Four Day Creep" and go straight into "I Don't Need No Doctor," but that night I said to the audience, "I've got to stop us here, because I need to tell you about how this song came about." I was one big goose bump while I explained that right here on this stage was where Humble Pie's version of the song was arranged at the sound check and played live that night—the track that put Humble Pie on the US charts.

The day finally arrived and we flew into San Francisco for what would be the very last show of the US Finale Tour. It was very much a family affair that day: my girlfriend, Robin Rains; three former wives, Mary, Barbara, and Tina; my children, Jade, Julian, Mia, and stepdaughter, Tif, were all there.

Julian had toured with me on the RAW: And Acoustic Tour and then the Julian Frampton Band opened for us on all of the West Coast dates on my US Finale Tour. It was so special to have him play my last show and I am so proud of him. He has matured into a great artist, always profusely writing great new songs and building his audience.

Jade has been working in fashion behind the camera, beginning at *Elle* magazine after college. When she first started there, she was a fashion assistant, but when she left *Elle*, she was Executive Market Editor and now Jade is the Editorial Director at ShopBAZAAR, the online shopping website for *Harper's Bazaar*.

Mia has been acting since she was twelve and had a really great part in the movie *Bridesmaids*. The little girl who gets Kristen Wiig fired after they argue in the jewelry store? Yep, that's my baby girl Mia. (I believe they call that a "pivotal" scene.) She is still acting and working on her license for industrial real estate.

Tif lives in Cincinnati with her husband, Adam, and their son, Wolfgang. She works at Procter & Gamble in research and development. We all miss each other a lot right now. It's the same for the whole world right now with COVID-19, not being able to travel and be with loved ones in different cities and countries.

Many friends were also there that night, including Jeff Ayeroff and Jordan Harris, who had both been with A&M and then went on to be presidents of other record labels. We talked about choosing the album cover photo for *Frampton Comes Alive!*

At the end of the show I said to the audience, "The reason that I've had this long career is because once upon a time I recorded this very successful live album, and I recorded it here in the Bay Area at the old Winterland Ballroom in San Francisco. I want to thank all of you—we were all there together at the beginning, and I wanted the last show to be here again, with you, where it all started."

At the end of every tour, I always thank my crew, and the audience would thank them, too. But that last night, I got everybody out on stage. I did my little speech, and then I hugged every person individually and thanked them. There were a lot of tears on that stage. The shoulders of my shirt were soaked when I came off.

But I truly wanted the audience to know that it's not just me, it's not just the band, but all these people are so crucial in making the shows possible, and every single person in my crew is the best at what they do. "Thank you" doesn't come close to how I feel about them. They all give me great confidence, knowing that when I walk out on that stage they all have my back.

I was the last one left standing on the stage and I just waved and said, "I'm not going to say goodbye." It was bittersweet, but it was such an amazing show. It was a celebration of my entire career of touring. Fifty-two years from the Herd to the Peter Frampton Finale Tour, and a tip of the hat to my beloved San Francisco and the Bay Area.

And as a postscript: a road family who tours together, Zooms together. I just had my seventieth birthday and we celebrated with a Frampton Road Family Zoom call, in the midst of the first wave of COVID-19. I had planned a UK/EU leg of the Finale Tour that was due to start at the end of May 2020, but it's been canceled for obvious reasons. So it was a happy birthday under the circumstances, but looking at all our faces in those little Zoom boxes on-screen, I could see the sadness we all share, thinking that maybe there really won't be any more touring if my IBM progresses too quickly.

My theory is that sometimes you're creative and sometimes you aren't. They say you should write every day, so I try to—even on my phone, in my notes, I do my little bits of writing every day, even if it's just a paragraph. I used to store all my music bits, my little tiny riffs and whatever, on cassettes. Then when digital recorders were available and iTunes came out, you could store everything on there. So I've got stuff that goes back to 2004. I better live till I'm 104, because I've got enough stuff to work on.

I'm finishing an album of instrumental covers—Roxy Music's "Avalon," "Dreamland" by Jaco Pastorius, "Isn't It a Pity" by George Harrison, Lenny Kravitz's "Are You Gonna Go My Way?" We also did the Radiohead song "Reckoner," which was so cool to do. Love, love Radiohead. Actually, the songs were all very interesting, because with a song, you usually have two or three verses, choruses, and a bridge. The way songs keep your interest is they have lyrics; the story moves on from verse to verse. So how do you build an instrumental that everyone already knows as a song? I really enjoy doing that. Remember, that's how I started playing—Hank Marvin to the rescue. I always go back and listen to the Shadows because they're so tasteful when doing an instrumental version of a known song.

Before we even started rehearsing for the Finale Tour, between September 2018 and April 2019, the band and I recorded three and a half albums together with our fearless leader and co-producer/engineer Chuck Ainlay. The first to come out was the *All Blues* album, which had started life after those tours with Steve Miller. During the Finale Tour we would play three songs from the album every night and it was so great to be playing some blues in the show again. We kept recording as many blues tracks as we could, and we finally had enough tracks for two blues albums.

I got into an argument on Twitter recently. I know I shouldn't have bothered, but this guy said, "I don't think I can actually bring myself to listen to Peter Frampton singing a B. B. King song." So okay, all right, I said maybe he should listen to it before he makes a statement like that. And, oh my God, the fans just reamed him! One guy said, "You're thinking of Peter Frampton in 1977, '78. Don't think that. Go listen, go see, you're basing your criticism on a preconceived notion that you have that's forty years old." That was the best one, so I retweeted it. I knew that some blues purists were going to have a go at me at some point, but the fact is that *All Blues* was number one on the *Billboard* Blues Albums Charts for seventeen weeks. *Say what?!* Yep, that's what we said, too!

The reason I wanted to record so much so quickly was because of my internal, ticking IBM clock. It's the unknown for me that is the hardest part. Will I be able to play as well tomorrow as I did yesterday? So we launched straight into recording the instrumental covers album—with the working title *Frampton Forgets the Words!*

Now we had finished three albums and so far, they were all covers of other people's music. My reasoning for this was that I needed to record as much as I could, not knowing how long I would be able to play the way I'm used to playing. To write music and lyrics for three albums would have taken a long, long time. My muscles most likely wouldn't have been able to wait that long!

I got so inspired by all the recording we were doing, though, that I started to write new "me" songs. So before we had to stop recording to begin rehearsing and touring, we recorded six completely new PF songs for my next solo album. I've got some serious writing left to do, because I really like what we've done so far. I'm definitely going to stretch out and change it up a bit. If it's going to be new material, a new solo record, then it's got to be great—I've got to step it up to the next level somehow.

So I'm writing all the time, but then I can get stuck in a rut. You come up against a creative brick wall and it's a little bit too high and you can't get over it. And then when you least expect it, you get a new idea, and all of a sudden you're on the other side of the wall, and sometimes that becomes the song or the musical piece that sets a new standard for the whole record. That's what I'm always looking for, that feeling of "Wow—even I think this is pretty good!" It's got to turn me on first.

In late 2018, Matt Cameron, of Pearl Jam and Soundgarden, called me up and asked if I wanted to play on this huge show honoring Chris Cornell after we lost Chris. I said, "Absolutely, who would I be playing with?" He said, "Well, Soundgarden—it'd be us and you doing 'Black Hole Sun,' with Brandi Carlile singing." It was the very last song of the night and the crowd went berserk—it came at the end of what must've been a five-, six-hour concert.

It was great to be there playing a small a part with the whole Seattle contingent, celebrating the life one of the most unique artists ever. I became a huge fan of Soundgarden as soon as I heard "Black Hole Sun," but then I heard Chris's solo album with "Can't Change Me." Oh, boy—I really needed to analyze what he was doing in that song. The way he composed it is so clever and, again, quite unique.

Just rehearsing with Matt Cameron, Ben Shepherd, and Kim Thayil, along with Brandi Carlile singing, was mind-blowing for me. It seemed like all the artists there wanted to see my Phenix guitar. Dave Grohl came rushing in, Jerry Cantrell, everybody—"Where is it? Where is it?" Oh, and great to see you, too!

I'd actually sat in with Chris Cornell. After the Grammy award for *Fingerprints*, I got a call asking if I would like to come and play "Black Hole Sun" with him live. I said, "Oh, my God, yes, of course!" We had to do the sound check without him. His plane had been delayed, so we arranged it the way he wanted it. Pete Thorn played the intro, the slide-y part, and then I played the first verse and chorus *a la* my instrumental version, and then Chris began to sing. That's a treasured moment right there. Then we did one more song together and he (inevitably) asked me to use the talk box, which I did.

We stayed in touch by email and we'd planned on hanging out at the studio at his house, but you know how things are; he's on tour, I'm home, and then vice versa, so unfortunately we never got to spend any more time together. But my son did get to meet Chris at a show, which was great for Julian.

I also played a tribute show for Jerry Garcia. I did a Junior Walker number that he had done, but in my style. Jerry's wife gave me one of his wooden picks. I also did a Lynyrd Skynyrd tribute. I love doing that stuff, but now when people ask me to play on this, play on that, I'm finding it harder and harder to say yes because I'm worried about my playing, my fingers.

I was recently asked if I wanted to be a part of one of these tribute shows honoring me and I turned it down. A lot of things I don't think I deserve, and I feel there are so many others who should be honored before me. I don't see myself on that level.

It's like the line in "Wind of Change" about "faking my way through." I just don't feel as if I'm due those kinds of accolades. It's not a form of modesty—I'm just not big on being honored.

It's wonderful and I really appreciate the ones I've received, but to have a concert honoring me just doesn't feel right. I can't explain it.

Right at the very beginning, when I started out, I got into all these bands because I was a good player and very young, and I was lauded for that. But the looks thing started immediately with the Herd, and I was dismissed as just a pretty face. And it really hurt, because I'd proven myself as a guitar player, even in the unknown bands before the Herd. I was a good player at a very young age, it's a fact.

People who have longevity in music are usually the ones who never think they're that special, so they keep on pushing the envelope, listening, learning more. I'll never be as good as I want to be, because the goal posts are always moving. If a player ever starts to think they're hot shit and stops trying to improve themselves, it's curtains, or stagnation at the very least. But my friend and yours, B. B. King, was the most humble man, till the day he died.

I started watching the TV show *Madam Secretary* when it first aired. One night I was watching a new episode and my eyes almost popped out of my head. Tèa Leoni was wearing one of my T-shirts as she and Tim Daly were having a late-night chat in their bedroom before lights out. My social media blew up with my loyal followers loving what they saw.

I immediately sent a tweet to Tèa thanking her for wearing me to bed. And, if she needed anymore, I had loads of vintage and new T-shirts stashed away. I got a lovely reply, and she said to send them along. Tim, on the other hand, sent me a tweet joking that I might want to take a cold shower. This, then, became a thing for her character to wear old rock T's to bed. Quite often she'd wear another one of mine on the show.

One day, I got a call and Tèa asked if I would appear on the show. Her character Elizabeth's favorite song is "Baby, I Love Your Way" and they needed a surprise artist to perform at the party after Elizabeth and Henry renew their vows. Having watched the series from the beginning, I felt I knew all the characters before I actually met them on set. Actors would come up to me to introduce themselves, and I could tell them, "I know who you are. I haven't missed a show yet!"

The last episode of the series covered the wedding of Elizabeth and Henry's oldest daughter, Stevie, to Dimitri. Unbelievably, I got another call from Tèa, and this time they needed a wedding singer! I have to thank her, the whole cast, and the crew for two of the most enjoyable days on the set of my favorite TV show.

Since the outbreak of COVID-19, people are out of work, in desperate need of food and so much more. Tèa's grandmother cofounded UNICEF USA in 1947 and ran it for twenty-five years. It must run in the family, as Tèa's father became president of the organization later. Tèa has been a UNICEF Ambassador since 2001 and asked me to be a part of an online UNICEF fundraiser to help children and their families all over the world who are in dire need.

Tim, Tèa, and I are waiting for the "all clear" so I can travel to New York for dinner. And afterward, jam with Tim, who has a lovely Gibson CS-336 I have to play.

We set up the Peter Frampton Myositis Research Fund at Johns Hopkins, and on the Finale Tour, a dollar from every ticket sold went to the fund. Live Nation was very generous, and we've raised a quarter of a million dollars so far. That's not a huge number like for cancer or Parkinson's, but it's a huge number as far as I'm concerned. It's a relatively unknown disease, so my job now is to bring awareness and raise more money for research.

I'm always in touch with Johns Hopkins and what they're using the money for. I do know that we need to concentrate on more drug trials. We really need the perfect drug for all us IBM-ers. Tenacity and money is what is needed to find a cure. The caregivers who are working on these drug trials are the most passionate people. (I recently started a new drug trial at Hopkins, but we're presently on hold, as travel for a seventy-year-old is not advised while we're in the middle of the COVID-19 virus pandemic.)

I want to go to the IBM conferences. I haven't been to one yet, but I'd like to speak—telling my story, from how I first discovered something was wrong to getting an official diagnosis, is something I think will be helpful for everyone. Whatever they ask me to do, I'm going to do. I've got a lot of new friends now in England and the US who have myositis, and I'm in a position to get things done, so people are counting on me to be loud and raise the money to find our cure.

My doctor has categorically stated that it doesn't matter whether you have a history of alcohol or drug abuse, or never had a sip or a puff, and they don't think it's genetic, either. Right now it seems there's no rhyme or reason for it, nothing they can put their finger on. Even when we get the drug that does the trick, you can only arrest this disease; you can't get it to reverse, because what it does to the good muscle is turn it into fat—when you x-ray my legs, you can see dark muscle, which is the good muscle, and then you can see all this white area, and that's the affected tissue.

I think most of the time it's more upsetting to everybody else than it is for me. My family was obviously devastated, and it was incredibly hard telling my children. The reason I'm still here doing what I do after problems with drugs and alcohol, the music industry, past managers, business managers—the reason that I keep coming back is the same reason that I don't really think this is that devastating to me. Not that I'm religious, I'm not, but I think everything happens for a reason. I think this is meant to slow me down and to change my trajectory. I realize I'm helping a lot of people, and that's what I need to do from now on.

I was thinking the other night about the strength of character that all parents during the Second World War must have had. Everyone was scared, like we all are now fighting this pandemic. My mother was working every day for the war effort in London during the Blitz, and she got through it. My dad fought in just about every major battle in Europe and Africa, and he got through it, amazingly so. It's a miracle, basically. But their strong characters had to have something to do with it, plus maybe a little luck. I know I got my perseverance from both of them.

At different times, life throws us all sorts of curve balls. This period of the COVID-19 pandemic is something I knew could happen one day, but never actually thought it would. Robin and I had gone to Naples, Florida, for a last-chance getaway in March, before the EU/UK tour prep was supposed to start. On the plane back to Nashville, I saw someone in front of us wearing a mask. I knew the virus had arrived in the US, but seeing this gave me a chill and I wondered if I had missed the memo. After we got home, all hell started to break loose and we were, all of a sudden, in the throes of the pandemic.

Nine months earlier, though, I had received the best news; my daughter Jade and her husband, Sam, were going to have a baby. Jade was due April 12—the day of the expected peak of infection in New York City, where they live. I said, with all my "I've been through this a few times already" wisdom, "The baby will definitely be a few days to a week late; it's your first!"

Well, well, Elle Frampton Homburger was born a week early, on the 6th of April at 9:23 p.m., and both baby and mom did just beautifully. Initially, it didn't look like Sam would be allowed in the room while Jade gave birth, but luckily, just in time, Governor Cuomo changed the rule so husbands and partners could be the coaches they had rehearsed to be. Jade spent the whole next day alone in the hospital, no Sam allowed, but was able to leave the following day. I gave a huge sigh of relief when I heard they were back safely in their bubble, happy and relieved in the middle of all this craziness, and now FaceTime and Zoom rule!

As I write this, it's been one month and I still haven't seen little Elle in person. But I've already been given my grandpa name—it's "Frampa!"

The end of touring doesn't mean I'll never set foot on a stage again. But I don't like playing without my band, so to do a pop-up with somebody is not my favorite thing. When you have these tribute shows, there's ten acts, twenty-seven songs. They're always great musicians, but it's not like having your own players. So it's hard for me, especially knowing how comfortable it is with my band, to go and play my music with other people.

I want to play guitar, and I do play every day, but sometimes I look at it and I go, "What's the point?" It's a diminishing return. I want to pick it up to prove that I'm still okay, and get better, but I'm scared stiff of picking the damn thing up and being disappointed. I shouldn't think that way, and I don't all the time, but I have my moments when it all comes crashing down for a second or two.

I'm taking it as it comes, basically. When I pick up the guitar, I'm usually not thinking about my fingers at all. I'm going, "Ooh, this is good, this bit here." Then if I have to use a different finger to do that particular thing, I work that in. So it's evolving, or devolving, whichever way you want to look at it.

I just have to think of the positive side. What will I be able to do? Well, I can always sing. But I live to play guitar; I'm definitely not what I would call a stand-alone great singer. That's not me; never has been. Hey, there's always slide! I've even thought about that. I could go and hang with the great Sonny Landreth for a while, maybe have Bonnie Raitt come over, too, for a couple of days and all three of us can share licks. I'm sure I'm always going to have at least one finger that works! I know it sounds glib, but I have to think that way, right?

I think you start off, when you're younger, with this angst. I knew I wanted to get good at something really quickly and do it really well. It's like you're driving a fast car with no fear. You have yet to find wisdom; you're just going for it. This can lead to tasteless playing, and I've been guilty of that. But as you go through life, your taste becomes more defined, and mine shows up in the choice of notes over a lovely bed of changing chords.

Les Paul himself said it best, I think: "I learned a long time ago that one note can go a long way if it's the right one, and it will probably whip the guy with twenty notes."

What's most important, and kind of unbelievable to me, is how these songs continue to mean so much to people. In 2020, for his sixtieth birthday, Bono made a list of the "60 Songs That Saved My Life," which spanned from the Beatles to Beyoncé. I was stunned that he included "Show Me the Way" on the list. He wrote that U2 played it when they first started out, and that he "used to turn it into a prayer." He recalled meeting me in Cincinnati, saying I was "a proper person who wanted no fuss." I was humbled by such high praise from a magnificent artist.

I don't want to know what's around the corner and I don't want to think about what might be coming. I don't even think ahead about eating—I forget to eat lunch and I'll get hungry about 4:30 and go, "I'm hungry!" I've always got so much else on my mind, so I never plan. And that's my MO; I never plan on stage, I never plan off stage. I get an idea and work on it, whether it's something I have to do or something to write. But I'll still get hungry about 4:30, one way or another.

Who else has had the career arc, the crazy ups and downs, that I've had? I've been to the moon and back without a rocket. But I've always managed to stay optimistic. I mean, just think about the Phenix. The whole thing sounds like a fairy story. I was given the guitar; I lost it for thirty-two years, then I found it again. If you wrote that up in a script, everyone would say it's too good to be true—it would never really happen that way.

But it did. There's always reason to hold out hope. At least, that's what I think. How do you feel?

Acknowledgments

Rodney Eckerman: Your ingenuity and loyalty saved me numerous times.

Gordon Kennedy: For all the years and so many great songs.

Mary Lovett: For reminding me of what really happened.

John Regan: For our lifelong friendship and stirring the memories.

Jerry Shirley: My dear mate and brother.

Mark Snyder: For our great friendship and my unbelievable guitar sound.

Ringo Starr: It's been peace and love since our first recording session.

Bill Wyman: For recognizing my potential before anyone else, including me.

Robin Rains: For your precious love, caring, and understanding. You are my heart and soul mate.

Alan Light: For the many hours and being my partner in crime on this enlightening journey.

Brant Rumble: For your impeccable direction, and to all at Hachette who helped me through this.

Ken Levitan: For your great guidance, friendship, and incredible team at Vector Management.

Lisa Jenkins: What would I do without you? Well, for one thing I would never have finished this book. You are the very best right hand anyone could have.

Brad Goodman: It's been a long road back to where I never thought I would be again.

Carla Sacks and Cami Opere: The best publicists one could ever hope for.

Rick Fisher, Ron Nash, and David Zeisler: For always having my back.

Bruce Resnikoff, Sujata Murthy, Vartan Kurjian, Barry Korkin, and all of the A&M/UMe family: For all of the wonderful years together.

Jerry Moss and Herb Alpert: For discovering a diamond in the rough, Humble Pie, and believing in me.

Gary Haber: For saving me from myself.

Andrew Oldham: For your direction, nurturing Humble Pie, and our friendship.

Gary Gilbert at Manatt, Phelps & Phillips.

Lance Freed, Linda Chelgren, Suzanne Moss, Tom Rowland, and all at Almo Irving/Universal Music Publishing.

Dawn DeBisschop and Howard Schomer at Hi Fidelity Entertainment.

Thanks to all of my incredible bands and crews over the years. Especially Rob Arthur, Adam Lester, Dan Wojciechowski, Steve Mackey, Donnie Lewis, Matt Fitzgerald, Eric Gormley, Cody Bailey, Darren Hurst, Lisa McLaughlin, Genevieve Neace, Jim Yakabuski, and Jared Rarick.

Apogee, Epiphone, Eventide Audio, Robin Geary, Gibson, Simon Husbands, Elliot Kendall, Marshall Amplification, Martin Guitars, Eric Stuart, and Universal Audio.